THE TRANSATLANTIC DIVIDE

EUROPE IN CHANGE

SERIES EDITORS: THOMAS CHRISTIANSEN AND EMIL KIRCHNER

The formation of Croatian national identity
ALEX J. BELLAMY

Committee governance in the European Union
THOMAS CHRISTIANSEN AND EMIL KIRCHNER (EDS)

Theory and reform in the European Union, 2nd edition
DIMITRIS N. CHRYSSOCHOOU, MICHAEL J. TSINISIZELIS,
STELIOS STAVRIDIS AND KOSTAS IFANTIS

German policy-making and eastern enlargement of the EU during the Kohl era
STEPHEN D. COLLINS

Germany, pacifism and peace enforcement
ANJA DALGAARD-NIELSEN

The European Union and the Cyprus conflict
THOMAS DIEZ

The changing European Commission
DIONYSSIS DIMITRAKOPOULOS (ED.)

Supranational citizenship
LYNN DOBSON

Reshaping Economic and Monetary Union
SHAWN DONNELLY

The time of European governance
MAGNUS EKENGREN

An introduction to post-Communist Bulgaria
EMIL GIATZIDIS

Mothering the Union
ROBERTA GUERRINA

The new Germany and migration in Europe
BARBARA MARSHALL

Turkey: facing a new millennium
AMIKAM NACHMANI

The changing face of federalism
SERGIO ORTINO, MITJA ŽAGAR AND VOJTECH MASTNY (EDS)

The road to the European Union
    Volume 1 The Czech and Slovak Republics   JACQUES RUPNIK AND JAN ZIELONKA (EDS)
    Volume 2 Estonia, Latvia and Lithuania   VELLO PETTAI AND JAN ZIELONKA (EDS)

Democratising capitalism?
The political economy of post-Communist transformation in Romania, 1989–2001
LILIANA POP

Europe and civil society
Movement coalitions and European governance
CARLO RUZZA

Constructing the path to eatern enlargement
ULRICH SEDELMEIER

Two tiers or two speeds?
The European security order and the enlargement
of the European Union and NATO
JAMES SPERLING (ED.)

Recasting the European order
JAMES SPERLING AND EMIL KIRCHNER

Political symbolism and European integration
TOBIAS THEILER

Rethinking European Union foreign policy
BEN TONRA AND THOMAS CHRISTIANSEN (EDS)

The European Union in the wake of Eastern enlargement
AMY VERDUN AND OSVALDO CROCI (EDS)

Democratic citizenship and the European Union
ALBERT WEALE

The emerging Euro-Mediterranean system
DIMITRIS K. XENAKIS AND DIMITRIS N. CHRYSSOCHOOU

OSVALDO CROCI & AMY VERDUN
EDITORS

THE TRANSATLANTIC DIVIDE

Foreign and security policies
in the Atlantic Alliance from Kosovo to Iraq

MANCHESTER UNIVERSITY PRESS
Manchester and New York

distributed exclusively in the USA by Palgrave

Copyright © Manchester University Press 2006

While copyright in the volume as a whole is vested in Manchester University Press, copyright in individual chapters belongs to their respective authors, and no chapter may be reproduced wholly or in part without the express permission in writing of both author and publisher.

Published by Manchester University Press
Oxford Road, Manchester M13 9NR, UK
and Room 400, 175 Fifth Avenue, New York, NY 10010, USA
www.manchesteruniversitypress.co.uk

Distributed in the United States exclusively by
Palgrave Macmillan, 175 Fifth Avenue,
New York, NY 10010, USA

Distributed in Canada exclusively by
UBC Press, University of British Columbia, 2029 West Mall,
Vancouver, BC, Canada V6T 1Z2

British Library Cataloguing-in-Publication Data is available

Library of Congress Cataloging-in-Publication Data is available

ISBN 978 0 7190 6507 1 paperback

First published by Manchester University Press in hardback 2006

This paperback edition first published 2013

The publisher has no responsibility for the persistence or accuracy of URLs for any external or third-party internet websites referred to in this book, and does not guarantee that any content on such websites is, or will remain, accurate or appropriate.

Printed by Lightning Source

Contents

List of tables		*page* vii
List of contributors		ix
Acknowledgments		xi
List of abbreviations		xiii
Introduction *Osvaldo Croci and Amy Verdun*		1

Part I   The international context

1. Transatlantic security relations from Kosovo to Iraq *Stanley R. Sloan* 9
2. NATO after Atlanticism *David Long* 19
3. Which Venus? A normative reading of the transatlantic divide *Sonia Lucarelli* 36
4. From out of adversity: Kosovo, Iraq and ESDP *Anand Menon* 49
5. Kosovo, Iraq and the evolution of the theory and practice of humanitarian intervention *Francis K. Abiew* 64
6. Managing multilateralism? EU–US relations and the challenges of regime building in South-eastern Europe *Lenard J. Cohen* 77
7. Kosovo and Iraq: two test cases for the partnership between post-Soviet Russia and the West *Isabelle Facon* 92

Part II   The domestic contexts

8. From compellence to pre-emption: Kosovo and Iraq as US responses to contested hegemony *Michael Wallack* 109
9. Competing for leadership in West European defence: France, Great Britain and the wars in Kosovo and Iraq *Alex Macleod* 126
10. Between Kosovo and Iraq: changing paradigms of German foreign and security policy? *Udo Diedrichs* 142

11 A tale of two coalitions: Italy faces Kosovo and Iraq *Osvaldo Croci*	159
12 The neutral states and the challenge of ESDP: Kosovo, Iraq and the transatlantic divide *Nicholas Rees*	173
13 A change of road: Canadian foreign policy from Kosovo to Iraq *Bill McGrath*	190
Conclusion *Osvaldo Croci and Amy Verdun*	206
Bibliography	211
Index	229

TABLES

12.1 Support for CFSP and ESDP in EU member states 177
12.2 Participation of neutral states in peacekeeping operations (2004) 179
12.3 Military expenditure as a percentage of GDP in the neutral states 180
12.4 Military commitments of neutral states to the Headline Goals, 2003 180

Contributors

Francis K. Abiew is Assistant Professor in the Department of Political Science at Kwantlen University College, Surrey, Canada.

Lenard J. Cohen is Professor in the Department of Political Science at Simon Fraser University, Burnaby, Canada.

Osvaldo Croci is Associate Professor in the Department of Political Science at Memorial University, St John's, Canada.

Udo Diedrichs is Senior Research Fellow and Lecturer in the Department of Political Science at the University of Cologne, Germany.

Isabelle Facon is a Research Fellow at the Fondation pour la Recherche Stratégique, Paris, France.

David Long is Professor of International Affairs in the Norman Paterson School of International Affairs at Carleton University, Ottawa, Canada.

Sonia Lucarelli is a Lecturer in International Relations at the University of Bologna-Forlì, Italy.

Bill McGrath is Associate Professor in the Department of Political Science at Memorial University, St John's, Canada.

Alex Macleod is Professor of Political Science and Director of the Centre d'études des politiques étrangères et de sécurité at the Université du Québec, Montréal, Canada.

Anand Menon is Professor of European Politics and Director of the European Research Institute at the University of Birmingham, UK.

Nicholas Rees holds a Jean Monnet Professorship in European Institutions and International Relations at the University of Limerick, Ireland.

Stanley R. Sloan is Director of the 'Atlantic Community Initiative' and a Visiting Scholar at Middlebury College, USA.

Amy Verdun is Professor of Political Science and Jean Monnet Chair at the University of Victoria, Canada.

Michael Wallack is Associate Professor in the Department of Political Science at Memorial University, St John's, Canada.

Acknowledgements

The idea for this book on transatlantic security relations was conceived at a panel entitled 'The EU and Kosovo' which was part of the European Community Studies Association – Canada (ECSA-C) biennial conference (European Odyssey: the European Union in the new millennium) held in Quebec City on 30 July–1 August 2000. The rapid pace at which events unfolded thereafter – the 9/11 terrorist attacks, the war in Afghanistan, the gathering storm over Iraq and, as a consequence, over the Atlantic, obliged us to keep redirecting the original focus of the project. The revised and expanded version of some of the papers presented in Quebec City, plus a number of new commissioned ones, were presented at a conference entitled 'A transatlantic divide on security policy: Canada, the European Union and the new Bush doctrine', held at the University of Victoria on 11–13 June 2004 and organised to celebrate the European Union Centre award to the University of Victoria by the European Commission. The two conferences and this publication were generously supported by ECSA-C, the European Commission, the Social Sciences and Humanities Research Council of Canada (SSHRC) (grant number 646-2003-1148 held by Amy Verdun), the Department of Foreign Affairs and International Trade (DFAIT), the North Atlantic Treaty Organisation (NATO), the University of Victoria, and Memorial University. Additional funding was provided by the Dutch Consulate in Vancouver, the Italian Cultural Institute in Vancouver, and the Irish Government. The final product includes what we think are high quality chapters that cover the breadth of the issues at stake.

Besides institutional and financial support, this book would not have been possible without the support of many individuals. We wish to thank Stefanie Fishel, Sandra Lohmann, Natalie Payne and Peggy-Ann Coles for their research and editorial assistance at different stages of this book. Our gratitude extends also to Emil Kirchner and Tony Mason for their continuous support of this project. Though we cannot list here all those who have commented on parts of the book, we do wish to acknowledge Ben Tonra for his comments on the papers presented at the Conference at the University of Victoria and Thomas Christiansen for his insightful suggestions on the entire manuscript.

Osvaldo Croci and Amy Verdun
St John's and Victoria

Abbreviations

AFSOUTH	Allied Joint Force Command Naples
AWACS	Airborne Warning and Control System
CARDS	Community Assistance for Reconstruction, Development, and Stabilisation (EU)
CDU	Christlich-Demokratische Union (Christian Democratic Union) (Germany)
CFSP	Common Foreign and Security Policy (EU)
CIS	Commonwealth of Independent States
CJTF	Combined Joint Task Force (NATO)
COPS	Political and Security Committee (EU)
DPC	Defence Planning Committee (NATO)
DS	Democratici di Sinistra (Left Democrats) (Italy)
ECR	Electronic Combat Reconnaissance (Tornados)
EPC	European Political Cooperation
ESDI	European Security and Defence Identity (within NATO)
ESDP	European Security and Defence Policy (within EU)
ESDU	European Security and Defence Union (a mainly French idea)
EUAM	European Union Administration of Mostar
EUFOR	European Union Force (Bosnia)
EUMS	European Union Military Staff
EUPM	European Union Police Mission (Bosnia)
ERRF	European Rapid Reaction Force (EU)
FDP	Freie Demokratische Partei (Free Democratic Party) (Germany)
FYROM	Former Yugoslav Republic of Macedonia
G-8	Group of Eight countries (US, UK, France, Germany, Italy, Canada, Russia, Japan)
GAO	General Accounting Office (US)
HARM	High-speed Anti Radiation Missiles
ICC	International Criminal Court
IGC	Inter-Governmental Conference (EU)
IGO	International governmental organisation
IFOR	Implementation Force (Bosnia)
ICTY	International Criminal Tribunal for the former Yugoslavia
IPTF	International Police Task Force (UN in Bosnia)
ISAF	International Security Assistance Force (Afghanistan)

JCS	Joint Chiefs of Staff (US)
KFOR	Kosovo Force (NATO)
KLA	Kosovo Liberation Army
NACC	North Atlantic Cooperation Council
NAFTA	North-American Free Trade Agreement
NATO	North Atlantic Treaty Organisation
NGO	Nongovernmental Organisations
NORAD	North American Aerospace Defence Command
NORDCAPS	Nordic Coordinated Arrangement for Military Peace Support
NRF	NATO Response Force
NSA	National Security Advisor (US)
NSC	National Security Council (US)
OAS	Organization of American States
OSCE	Organization for Security and Cooperation in Europe
PdCI	Partito dei Comunisti Italiani (Party of Italian Communists) (Italy)
PDD	Presidential Decision Directive (US)
PDS	Party of Democratic Socialism (former Communist party, Germany)
PfP	Partnership for Peace
RC	Rifondazione Comunista (Communist Refoundation)(Italy)
RMA	revolution in military affairs (USA)
RRF	Rapid Reaction Force (EU)
SAA	Stabilisation and Association Agreements (EU)
SAP	Stabilisation and Association Process (EU)
SDI	Socialisti Democratici Italiani (Italian Social Democrats) (Italy)
SFOR	Stabilisation Force (Bosnia)
SHAPE	Supreme Headquarters Allied Powers Europe (NATO)
SPD	Sozialdemokratische Partei Deutschlands (Social-Democratic Party of Germany) (Germany)
SPSEE	Stability Pact for South-eastern Europe
TRIPS	Trade related aspects of intellectual property rights
UAV	Unmanned Aerial Vehicle
UDEUR	Gruppo Unione Democratici per l'Europa (Union of Democrats for Europe) (Italy)
UNDP	United Nations Development Programme
UNMIK	United Nations Interim Administration Mission in Kosovo
UNPROFOR	United Nations Protection Force (in Bosnia)
UNSC	United Nations Security Council
WEU	Western European Union
WMD	weapons of mass destruction
WTO	World Trade Organisation

OSVALDO CROCI AND AMY VERDUN

Introduction

The period between the military intervention against Serbia by the North Atlantic Treaty Organisation (NATO) in March 1999 and that by the United States (US) and a so-called 'coalition of the willing' in Iraq in March 2003 was a turbulent one for the Atlantic Alliance. Fissures in the Alliance had of course appeared during the first fifty years of its existence but they had been papered over by the belief that US and Western European security depended on it. Things changed with the end of the Cold War. Western Europe was at the centre of the Cold War confrontation, but is no longer central in any sense of the word with respect to the new threats that have emerged since then, particularly that of Islamic terrorism. Consequently, Europe has become less important in US security calculations. The reverse is also true, although perhaps to a lesser extent given Europe's limited military capabilities. Not surprisingly, it was precisely at the end of the Cold War, as Yugoslavia embarked on its violent process of disintegration, that European allies - or at least those who were also members of the European Union (EU) - decided to strengthen their informal and intergovernmental mechanism of foreign policy consultation known as 'European Political Cooperation' (EPC). The Maastricht treaty renamed EPC 'Common Foreign and Security Policy' (CFSP), and brought it under a common roof with the European Community (EC) by making it the 'second pillar' of the newly-established EU. It also expanded its scope which from then on would also comprise 'all questions related to the security of the Union, including the eventual framing of a common defence policy which might in time lead to a common defence'. The 1997 Amsterdam treaty in turn expanded the security and defence aspects of CFSP by introducing the so-called Petersberg tasks i.e. giving the EU competence for 'humanitarian and rescue tasks, peacekeeping tasks, and tasks of combat forces in crisis management, including peace-making'.

Notwithstanding these developments, the effectiveness of CFSP throughout the 1990s remained rather limited, as the failure of the EU to act as peace-maker in the long Yugoslav crisis demonstrated. The EU had to rely on a reluctant US, and NATO, to bring the situation at its south-eastern border under control. The recognition of this weakness, especially in military terms, led EU member states to launch a new ambitious project aimed at giving the

EU 'the capacity for autonomous action, backed up by credible military forces, the means to decide to use them and a readiness to do so, in order to respond to international crises'.[1] First, at the 1998 French–British summit meeting in Saint-Malo, the United Kingdom (UK) dropped its erstwhile reservation about the EU acquiring competences in security and defence matters, as long as such competences would be exercised in conformity with NATO obligation. Then, at the June 1999 meeting in Cologne, while NATO was dropping bombs on Serbia, the European Council launched the European Security and Defence Policy (ESDP).

NATO's military intervention in Kosovo, albeit successful in terms of bringing the situation under control, caused some strains within the Alliance, because of disagreements between its European members and the US concerning both the overall strategy to be adopted (i.e. ground invasion vs air-strikes) as well as the conduct of operations (e.g. the selection of bombing targets). Overall, the intervention underlined European continued military dependence on the US. The Kosovo experience played a role in the decision taken at the Helsinki meeting of the European Council in December 1999 to set up a sizeable European Rapid Reaction Force (RRF) with air and naval components, deployable in sixty days, and capable of sustaining at least a year of operations in the field. Ironically perhaps, given that the US had for decades encouraged its European allies to improve their military capabilities, the launching of ESDP created a number of misgivings in Washington about its significance for the future of NATO (Sloan 2000). This is not surprising given the fact that the relationship between ESDP and NATO was and remains fuzzy, and that at least France occasionally seems to look at ESDP with Gaullist eyes, that is as a potential alternative to NATO (Hulsman 2003).

In the wake of the terrorist attacks of 11 September 2001 (henceforth 9/11) the Alliance seemed to have reached a degree of solidarity and cohesiveness rarely observed in the past. This all ended, however, as soon as the time came to devise a strategy to deal with the problem of Islamic terrorism. The Americans outlined a complex and multidimensional plan of which the first and most visible aspect was to go after the Taliban regime in Afghanistan, which had a symbiotic relationship with the terrorists responsible for 9/11. The Europeans thought that it was more important to address the root causes of terrorism than to deal with its symptoms, and accepted only reluctantly that part of the strategy would have to be military. These differences of view caused heated exchanges across the Atlantic throughout the first half of 2002 and became particularly harsh once the US administration manifested its intention to confront Saddam Hussein's protracted defiance of the disarmament terms imposed on him by the United Nations Security Council (UNSC) at the end of the 1991 Gulf War. The US case for intervention rested primarily on the need to prevent a rogue state with weapons of mass destruction (WMD) from supplying them to terrorist groups. The US decision to intervene militarily in Iraq caused a serious rift in transatlantic relations. There were two major reasons for this rift. The first was that the US justified the intervention primarily in terms of 'preventive self-defence' - an extension of the well-established doctrine of 'anticipatory' or 'pre-emptive self-defence' which authorises states to take action to repel an 'imminent' attack. In the case of rogue states likely to use WMD, or supply them to ruthless international terrorist groups – so the argument went - the adjective 'imminent' has to be understood in a less restrictive way than has traditionally been the case, and states are justified in taking action before the threat has materialised.² The second was that once it had resolved to act the US government was not too willing to pay attention to the position of some of its European allies or to put up with the constraints and slow pace of multilateral institutions. The US, in other words, seemed to act under the assumption that in a unipolar system it has special responsibilities for maintaining order in the system as well as for choosing the means and the time of action. The intervention in Iraq also caused an intra-European split, both within NATO and the EU. France, Germany and some other European countries took a position against the timing of the intervention, denounced 'American unilateralism', and some of them even mentioned the desirability of moving towards a multipolar world as if system polarity was simply a matter of preference. The UK, Italy and Spain, as well as the quasi-totality of the new NATO and EU members, supported the US position. The rift was so severe as to lead some observers to worry about the very future of the Alliance (Kupchan 2002; Pond 2004).

This book examines the Atlantic Alliance from NATO's intervention in Kosovo to the US intervention in Iraq. It is divided into two parts. The first part focuses on the 'international context'. Stanley Sloan offers a brief historical survey of the main issues that have characterised transatlantic security relations from Kosovo to Iraq as well as a prognostication of the future of the Alliance. David Long examines different theories purporting to explain the Alliance's current difficulties and argues that the recent divisions among the allies are a result of the decline in 'Atlanticism' understood as transatlantic solidarity based on a community of values. Sonia Lucarelli builds on this insight and argues that transatlantic problems arise primarily out of the different interpretation that the US and European members of the Alliance give to shared political values and by the different modes of translation of such values into political action. Anand Menon focuses on the development of the ESPD. He argues that the failure of the EU to play as significant a role as it would have liked in the Kosovo and Iraqi crises reinforced the determination of member states to strengthen EU defence policy capabilities to the point where the latter can now deploy limited military forces in support of broader security operations. Although to a different degree, both Kosovo and Iraq represent examples of the emerging practice of international military interventions in defence of human rights. Francis Abiew explores the emergence of the theory and practice of humanitarian intervention by offering a review of the debate among legal scholars. He also examines the attitudes towards this emerging practice in general and the Kosovo and Iraqi cases in particular by a number of states – including of course those in the Atlantic Alliance – as well as international governmental and non-governmental organisations. Lenard Cohen's chapter focuses on one area in which transatlantic cooperation has been relatively successful: South-eastern Europe. Here, the US, the EU and NATO have worked in different ways first to dampen internal conflicts, then stabilise the region, and promote regime building. Finally, the chapter by Isabelle Facon focuses on Russia, an actor which played a central role in transatlantic relations during the Cold War but which has receded into the background since the end of bipolarity. Facon examines Russia's position on the Kosovo and Iraqi issues against the background of the country's difficult adjustment to its diminished status in the international system and the evolution of its ties with Europe and the US after the Cold War.

The second part of the book focuses on the domestic contexts. Its six chapters examine the evolution of foreign policies of key members of the Alliance as well as those of the so-called 'neutrals' since the end of the Cold War. They focus not only on the role played by each country in the Kosovo and Iraq crises but also on their views of the Alliance and their stance on some of the issues that the two interventions brought to centre stage in international politics. Thus each author examines the attitude of their respective countries vis-à-vis the issues of humanitarian intervention, the question of how to provide order and stability in a unipolar system, the emergence of a defence vocation within the EU and the relationship between ESDP and NATO. Each chapter focuses also on some foreign policy aspects which are specific to the country in question. Thus Michael Wallack explains the reasons that have led the George W. Bush administration to adopt a new strategy on the international scene. Alex Macleod reviews the different way in which France and the UK conceptualise European security notwithstanding their common effort to develop ESPD. Udo Diedrichs explains the dynamism German foreign policy has manifested since reunification, and what made the German position on Iraq different from the French one. Osvaldo Croci shows that Italy, notwithstanding accusations made by political opponents, has not made a Euro-sceptic turn under the Berlusconi government and that there is a remarkable continuity in Italian foreign policy. Nicholas Rees examines how the concept of 'neutralism' in the so-called European 'neutrals' (Austria, Ireland, Finland and Sweden) is changing as a result of the end of the Cold War. Bill McGrath illustrates the reasons that pushed the Canadian government to promote the concept of 'human security' as well as the difficulties the government faces when, as in the case of Iraq, it is unwilling to lend a helping hand to its southern neighbour. The concluding chapter brings together the insights offered by each chapter to give a snapshot of the predicament the Alliance currently faces.

As is usually the case, in an edited book, not all angles can be equally covered while, at the same time, some degree of overlapping is inevitable unless one is willing – and able – to act as a stern general with the contributors. We hope that our effort will not only provide a convenient survey of developments in the Atlantic Alliance between Kosovo and Iraq but will also make a worthy contribution to the debate on the future of the Alliance.

Notes

1 'Joint declaration issued at the British–French Summit, Saint-Malo, France, 3–4 December 1998: www.atlanterhavskomiteen.no/publikasjoner/andre/dokumenter/malo.htm.
2 For a political and philosophical discussion of 'preventive self-defence' see Luban (2004).

PART I

The international context

STANLEY R. SLOAN

1
Transatlantic security relations from Kosovo to Iraq

Intervention against Serbia in Kosovo: NATO on its own

In April 1999, the North Atlantic Treaty Organisation (NATO) allies met at a summit in Washington with the original intent of celebrating NATO's 50th anniversary and approving guidance to carry the Alliance into the twenty-first century. However, before the allies could issue the revised Strategic Concept on which they had been working for some two years, they were forced by developments in the Balkans to move from debates on principles to decisions in practice. This chapter provides an overview of the events that occurred between Kosovo and Iraq and concludes with some reflections on their impact on the Atlantic Alliance in general and NATO in particular.

The disintegration of the former Yugoslavia had unleashed several power struggles among ethnic and religious groups whose animosities toward one another had been suppressed for decades. By 1999, Bosnia had been pacified by NATO and had begun the long path toward stability and democracy. The Balkan focus fell next on Kosovo, a region in southern Serbia (more formally known, together with Montenegro, as the Federal Republic of Yugoslavia) populated mainly by ethnic Albanians. In 1989, Serb leader Slobodan Milošević had removed the region's former autonomy. Kosovo became an explosion waiting to happen. During 1998, open conflict between Serb security forces and ethnic Albanian forces in Kosovo resulted in the death of over 1500 ethnic Albanians, about an equal number of Serbs, and the displacement of some 400,000 residents from their homes. In October 1998, NATO decided to begin a phased air campaign against Yugoslavia if the Milošević regime did not withdraw part of its forces from Kosovo, cooperate in bringing an end to the violence there, and facilitate the return of refugees to their homes. United Nations Security Council (UNSC) resolution 1199 of 23 September 1998 called for these and other measures.

With Milošević clearly playing for time in late 1998, the deteriorating situation in Kosovo led the international Contact Group, formed by the US, the UK, France, Germany, Italy and Russia, to produce a draft peace plan on 29 January 1999 which they then proposed to the Serb authorities and representatives of the Kosovo ethnic Albanian population. On 30 January, the North Atlantic Council agreed to authorise NATO Secretary General Javier Solana to initiate air attacks against Serb targets if Milošević did not accept the terms of the plan. The Kosovo Albanian authorities accepted the plan on 18 March but the Serbs rejected it. NATO initiated air strikes against Serbian targets in both Serbia and Kosovo on 24 March. In response, Serb forces began driving Kosovo ethnic Albanians from their homes in Kosovo.

Summit accomplishments

At the time of the summit, it was unclear whether or not the Kosovo air campaign, 'Operation Allied Force', would ultimately have the desired result of driving Serb forces out of the province. The Clinton administration decided the main goal of the summit should be to demonstrate allied unity. Most other allied leaders apparently agreed. British Prime Minister Tony Blair had hoped to convince allied leaders to bring ground forces to bear in Kosovo. But the desire for at least a facade of unity won out. Compromise formulations were fashioned to paper over allied differences about the relationship of NATO to the UN and the limits of the application of NATO's crisis management operations.

By late 1998, France and most other allies had accepted that Kosovo could constitute the kind of exception that they still objected making into a new rule. Nevertheless, French and US differences over how to treat the mandate issue in the new Strategic Concept persisted, requiring carefully crafted compromises in the document issued by allied leaders in Washington. The European allies all accepted that the new threats identified by the US were serious and merited their attention. But most were reluctant to make cooperation in any given peace enforcement or counter-proliferation operation more or less automatic. They saw their willingness to act against Serbia without a UN mandate as an exception. Future decisions were left to be made on a case-by-case basis, with Kosovo seen neither as a new rule nor as the last time NATO might act without a UN mandate.

In spite of claims by some US officials that the 1999 Strategic Concept would guide NATO for a decade or longer,[1] the summit produced what was largely an incremental step down the road toward twenty-first century security requirements. This was not necessarily a failure of allied governments, but rather a reflection of the extent to which the Kosovo experience could affect the future development of the Alliance and the more traditional fact that no one meeting in NATO's history has ever resolved all outstanding issues.

The impact of Kosovo: prelude to the march on Kabul

The Kosovo operation left two important marks on the Alliance that would have a profound effect on its future evolution. The political and command issues raised by European involvement in the decision-making process convinced many Americans that NATO command had largely handicapped the military operation while not producing significant and helpful resources. The operation's almost complete reliance on high-tech US air capabilities convinced many Europeans that their future influence over military operations would require more useful capabilities.

The NATO air campaign that drove Milošević's forces out of Kosovo accomplished its objectives, but the victory was not without a price.[2] Even during the operation, critics complained that the air campaign had provoked the final and most brutal phase of Serbia's ethnic cleansing operation. As the operation dragged on with no sign of a Milošević concession, differences arose among allies and in domestic political debates about an air campaign that was conducted under rules intended to minimise the risks to allied forces and which denied strategically-important targets to NATO forces. Some argued strongly that ground forces would have to go in to drive Yugoslav forces out.

The ultimate success of NATO strategy surprised the vast majority of military experts and pundits. Most of them had blamed President Clinton, his advisors, and Supreme Allied Commander US General Wesley Clark for concocting an air-only campaign designed to avoid NATO casualties but, in their judgment, unlikely to bring Milošević to heel. In retirement, General Clark argued that constraints imposed on his operations by Washington and interference from other NATO allies, particularly France, in targeting decisions had delayed a successful end to the campaign (Clark 2001a).

Meanwhile, a US General Accounting Office (GAO) report released in July 2001 added to the critique. The report found that the need to maintain Alliance cohesion during the conflict led to important departures from standard US military doctrine and resulted in a limited mission with unclear objectives. The GAO reported that many US military officers and civilian officials who participated in the campaign felt that these departures resulted in a longer conflict, more extensive damage to Yugoslavia, and significant risks to Alliance forces (US General Accounting Office 2001: 2). From the US side, the 'lesson learned' for many was that it was best not to manage such military campaigns through NATO decision-making structure. This was the lesson carried into the post-9/11 period by key decision-makers in the George W. Bush administration.

NATO's theology holds that it is almost always best to make the compromises necessary to maintain a unified alliance. However, the Kosovo experience suggested it would not be a surprise if, in some future non-collective defence military contingency, *ad hoc* approaches were to appear more attractive to NATO main military players (the US, the UK and France). The US obviously chose this course when planning its campaign against Taliban and al Qaeda forces in Afghanistan, partly as a result of the 'lessons learned' from allied management of the Kosovo conflict.

As for the 'lessons learned' on the European side, some critics of the Kosovo air campaign portrayed it as another example of the US imposing its hegemonic solutions on a hapless Europe. This extreme interpretation ignored the fact that European politics as much as American unwillingness to risk casualties had determined Alliance strategy. Nevertheless, the heavy European reliance on US military capabilities, once again, added urgency to the initiatives of British Prime Minister Tony Blair and other EU leaders to develop military capabilities more in keeping with Europe's economic and financial resources. There was good cause for Europeans to be concerned about their military capabilities, because a healthy US–European security relationship requires that both burdens and responsibilities be shared equitably.

The question left over from the Kosovo campaign, with its full mix of positive and negative features, was whether or not the Alliance would in the future use the experience to improve its military preparedness and command arrangements for such conflicts. The fact that the US and Europe apparently learned different lessons made it difficult to translate the experience into constructive changes for the Alliance. The US learned that it did not like to run military operations largely with its own forces but with allied political interference; the Europeans learned that they would prefer to have more influence on the course of a conflict whose outcome directly affected their interests.

9/11 and a unilateral US path to Kabul

The new US administration led by President George W. Bush that came to office in January 2001 had no clearly formed agenda for transatlantic relations. In fact, it appeared that the traditional relationship with the NATO allies was far less important to the new administration than it had been for any other US administration in NATO's history. When the administration pursued items of high importance on its international agenda, the approaches often clashed with the interests and perceptions of the European allies, for example on developing anti-missile defences, voiding the Anti-Ballistic Missile Treaty, not joining in the Kyoto Protocol to diminish global warming, and establishing an International Criminal Court.

In the midst of uncertainty about how the US would use its growing hegemony, the 9/11 terrorist attacks on New York and Washington profoundly changed the strategic environment for transatlantic relations. The allies acted almost immediately to invoke NATO's Article 5, calling on all NATO members to view the attack on the US as an attack on all of them and to act accordingly. NATO and individual Alliance members made offers of assistance as the US began preparing to go after al Qaeda and the Taliban regime in Afghanistan that hosted the terrorist organisation. At least initially, the US seemed to say 'thanks but no thanks' to these offers. Some assistance was eventually accepted, but the administration did not use the opportunity to expand the NATO consensus on the relevance of Alliance military cooperation to the new security challenges emanating far from NATO borders. The administration's assertion that 'the mission should determine the coalition' raised questions about whether the administration was preparing to downgrade NATO as an instrument for US–European military cooperation.

Preparing for and conducting combat operations in Afghanistan, the US administration sought help from the allies mainly through bilateral channels, not through NATO. In the weeks following the attacks, some Pentagon officials privately dismissed NATO's formal invocation of the Alliance's mutual defence provision and complained that the Alliance was not relevant to the new challenges posed by the counter-terror campaign. Meanwhile, some NATO allies were led to believe that the US did not value or want contributions that they might make in the battle against terrorism.

In spite of the Bush administration's initial reluctance to involve NATO in the war on terrorism, many allies ultimately contributed forces to post-conflict peacekeeping duties in Afghanistan. In 2003, NATO itself took command of the peacekeeping part of military operations there. NATO command of the International Security Assistance Force (ISAF), a UN-mandated force responsible for providing security in and around Kabul, became NATO's first mission beyond the Euro-Atlantic area.

The *ad hoc* coalition road to Baghdad

Immediately following 9/11, if not before, some key officials in the Bush administration began to act on the assumption that Saddam Hussein was part of the terrorist problem that should, and could, be eliminated. By early 2002, it seemed clear that the US was intent on bringing about regime change in Iraq. Europeans generally agreed that Saddam Hussein was a problem and that his regime was in clear violation of international law. Furthermore, they shared some of the US frustration that international sanctions had done much to hurt the Iraqi people but little to undermine Saddam's rule. However, most Europeans and many European governments reacted strongly to the Bush administration's determination to go to war against Iraq no matter what other countries thought, irrespective of how unilateral action might affect the future of international cooperation, and with little regard for the impact on international law.

Although the unilateral US approach to Iraq was the instigating event for the crisis in US–European relations, French President Jacques Chirac and German Chancellor Gerhard Schröder helped make it a full-blown crisis that produced deep divisions among Europeans as well as between many Europeans and the US. Given German public opinion in the summer of 2002, Chancellor Schröder undoubtedly needed to take a stand against attacking Iraq in order to be returned as Chancellor in the autumn elections. Schröder, however, disappointed many Americans, and surely President Bush, by failing to soften his opposition after the election.

Many Americans expected France to side with the US when the time came to use force, to ensure that France would have a say in the important post-conflict period in Iraq. Damage to the transatlantic Alliance and to European solidarity, already serious, was aggravated when France not only remained opposed but happily took on the role of leader of the opposition. France's attitude, supported by French and broader European public opinion, nonetheless was highly divisive in the European framework, particularly when President Chirac 'derided those Central and East European countries that [had] signed letters expressing their support for the US as "childish", "dangerous", and missing "an opportunity to shut up"'(*New York Times* 19 February 2003).

For its part, the Bush administration further fanned the flames of European concern when, in September 2002, the White House released a policy statement entitled the National Security Strategy of the United States of America. The paper focused on 'those terrorist organisations of global reach and any terrorist or state sponsor of terrorism which attempt to gain or use weapons of mass destruction (WMD) or their precursors'. With regard to such threats, the document laid out an unambiguous strategy of pre-emption, stating that 'as a matter of common sense and self-defense, America will act against such emerging threats before they are fully formed'. It then added that 'while the United States will constantly strive to enlist the support of the international community we will not hesitate to act alone, if necessary, to exercise our right of self-defense by acting preemptively against such terrorists' (White House 2002). Even though much of what the document said reflected realities of the contemporary security environment, it was interpreted widely as a unilateral assertion of rights beyond the accepted norms of international law, which could be misused by the US or copied by other countries with destabilising results.

An enlightened detour through Prague

Just as Kosovo had been the uninvited guest at the 1999 Washington summit, Iraq was the new dark cloud shadowing Alliance leaders when they met in Prague in November 2002. The Prague meeting fortuitously fell at a time when the US, the UK, France and Germany were still trying to develop a common approach to Iraq through the UN. This lull in the controversy over Iraq helped produce a better environment for the Prague meeting. One also suspects that the Bush administration and the European allies wanted to show that their differences over how to deal with Iraq would not prevent them from making the Prague summit a success. Not only did the allies invite seven new members (Bulgaria, Estonia, Latvia, Lithuania, Romania, Slovakia and Slovenia) to join the Alliance but they also took giant strides toward making NATO an important player in security well beyond Europe.

In anticipation of the summit, Czech Republic President Vaclav Havel wrote that 'for the Alliance to define clearly the role it wants to play in the global campaign against terrorism, the Prague Summit will have to ... set in motion a still more radical transformation of the Alliance in order for NATO to reaffirm its position as a key pillar of international security' (Havel 2002: 3). Havel's goals were largely met. The leaders confirmed the decision to create a 'NATO Response Force' (NRF) intended to be capable of taking on virtually any military mission anywhere in the world. They approved reform of NATO command structure to move away from its old geographic focus into a new functional approach organised around a command for 'operations' and another for 'transformation'.

As a result of decisions taken at Prague and after, NATO was given a mandate and some of the instruments required to play a meaningful role in dealing with twenty-first century security challenges. It has already begun using these new tools with the International Stability Assistance Force in Afghanistan as well as in Iraq.

NATO's crisis over aid to Turkey

Even with the successful Prague meeting, the Iraq issue continued to plague the Alliance. Early in 2003, the issue exploded of whether to begin planning defensive assistance to Turkey should it be attacked by Iraq during a presumptive US-led coalition attack on Saddam Hussein's regime. The controversy threatened the very underpinnings of the Alliance. On 15 January, US Deputy Secretary of Defense Paul Wolfowitz formally asked NATO members to consider what supporting roles NATO might play in a US-led war on Iraq. Six areas of assistance were discussed, including: sending Patriot missiles and AWACS surveillance planes to defend Turkey, the only NATO member that borders Iraq; sending naval forces to help protect ships in the eastern Mediterranean; providing personnel to help protect US military bases in Europe; giving access to airspace, ports, bases, and refueling facilities in Europe; backfilling US forces sent to the Gulf; and deploying NATO troops to Iraq after a possible war to help rebuild and govern the country.

After considerable discussion within the North Atlantic Council, Belgium, France and Germany publicly announced their opposition to

NATO starting to plan to provide military assistance to Turkey. The three recalcitrant allies said they were not opposed to aiding Istanbul but believed that planning for such action was premature while UN arms inspectors were still seeking to disarm Iraq peacefully. The initiative was seen as an attempt by the US to get pre-emptive NATO support for a military action that was not sanctioned by the UNSC. Once before, in the conflict over Kosovo, NATO had acted without a UNSC mandate. In that case, however, all the allies agreed that Russia and China should not be allowed to block a military action in Europe deemed necessary by NATO allies. In this case, the three allies wanted to make it clear that a NATO mandate would not be sufficient to justify military action against Iraq. The choices of the US to put the issue before the Alliance and of the three allies to block the requested planning brought existing political differences over Iraq into NATO in a form that put the Alliance's mutual defence commitment on the line. To break the stalemate, NATO Secretary General Lord Robertson and some member states suggested bringing the issue before the Defence Planning Committee (DPC), in which France has not participated since 1996. Agreement was finally reached in the DPC when Belgium and Germany dropped their opposition to beginning planning possible military aid to Turkey.

The scenario illustrated to what extent the Iraq issue had frayed political bonds among the allies. It also demonstrated that NATO remains an alliance of sovereign states, and that it works only when serious efforts have been made to build a political consensus behind a course of action, particularly when that action requires the use of military force.

Travelling beyond Iraq

Where do the Euro-Atlantic allies go now, having suffered through a period of deep political divisions while at the same time bringing about dramatic changes in NATO's mission and structure and successfully working out NATO/EU cooperative arrangements?

As at any time since the Alliance was formed in 1949, it is impossible to predict which path the transatlantic Alliance will follow in the years ahead. History suggests that the Alliance has incredible staying power. It has survived crises over the development of Soviet strategic nuclear weapons (1950s), the advent of détente (1960s), France's departure from the NATO integrated military command (1967), the Soviet invasion of Afghanistan (1979), the deployment of intermediate range nuclear missiles in Europe (1980s), the end of the Cold War, the Warsaw pact and the Soviet Union (1989–91), and the recent differences over Iraq. Against this backdrop, it seems safe to suggest that the Alliance will survive its recent crisis and persist as a viable Euro-Atlantic organisation for the foreseeable future.[3]

However, each crisis has left the Alliance somewhat different than it was before. Today, the sceptics say the end of the Cold War removed the glue that had held the Alliance together, and that the Iraqi dispute is the most recent case in point. If the Alliance continues, they argue, it will be an empty shell. More optimistic observers note that while the US and European member governments were fighting over what to do about Iraq, they were agreeing to dramatic changes in NATO's missions and capabilities, perhaps giving the Alliance key roles in the global struggle against terrorism, conflict and instability.

The most important characteristic of the new international system remains the emergence of the US as the only true global power – not omnipotent, but more powerful than any other nation or organised group of nations on this earth. Being subjected to a brutal terrorist attack on innocent civilians at this critical point in its national history left the US a more intense and less predictable international actor. How the US decides to use its power and influence will have a major impact on the future of the Alliance that it still leads. Will it continue to act with a degree of unilateralism and paranoia that irritates and alienates even its best allies, or will it find a way to be a confident and effective benign hegemon? The bottom line is that, for the transatlantic Alliance to recover from its recent crisis, the US will have to find ways to balance the advantages of multilateral cooperation and burden sharing against the temptations and attractions of unilateralism.

How the hegemon's allies react to US leadership is also important. Most European nations appear prepared to follow a benign US hegemon on most major issues. Will the incredible power and capabilities of the US convince the allies to follow, even when the US leads with a clumsy hand? Or will the allies revolt, periodically, individually or as a group, in response to heavy-handed US unilateralism? In terms of capabilities, will the allies respond to US leadership by creating the capabilities required to make serious military contributions to global military operations? Will they decide to take the 'easy road' of concentrating on their soft-power resources and allow the US to take most responsibility for military capabilities? Or will they build up significant European military capabilities intended to give Europe more leverage over US decisions? If the European Security and Defence Policy (ESDP) is to be taken seriously in Washington, the EU members will have to demonstrate that the new aspect of the unification process adds capabilities to the transatlantic inventory of security tools, not just institutions and acronyms.

At the national level, for Europe to play its part in reconstructing a positive transatlantic dynamic, Germany will be required to find a new balance in its policies that serves two old masters – Europeanism and Atlanticism – while responding to its re-discovered, re-defined and re-energised sense of national interests. France will have to give more weight to the transatlantic dimension of its interests. Great Britain will be required to be a 'good European' while remaining Washington's trusted partner.

The attitudes and capabilities the US and Europe bring to the NATO table in the years immediately ahead will determine whether the Alliance will become part of the answer to problems of global stability. If NATO – meaning, of course, the NATO nations – successfully manages the stabilisation effort in Afghanistan, it will establish its credentials as a serious and constructive device for multilateral security cooperation for the international community. The same is true for any possible direct NATO role in Iraq. Of course, failure in any mission the members assign to the Alliance could have disastrous consequences for NATO's credibility and future utility.

At the end of the day, there are two basic requirements for NATO to be perceived as important enough for the member states to ensure its survival. Put most simply, the US must be convinced that political and military cooperation with the European allies makes an important net contribution to US interests. By contrast, the Europeans must believe that contributing to international security efforts alongside the US will produce influence for Europe over US decisions that affect their security. These are the fundamental terms for continuation of a vital, productive transatlantic bargain.

Will the NATO members continue to find NATO cooperation to their advantage? Only time will tell. However, history suggests that, in spite of their differences, the US and Europe will try to keep their act together. And today, NATO remains an important part of the script for that routine.

Notes

1. This claim was made in off-the-record administration briefings to the Senate NATO Observer Group in which the author participated.
2. A 'dispassionate assessment' of NATO's operations in the Kosovo conflict is provided in Peters et al. (2001).
3. The author has argued elsewhere that NATO is a 'necessary but not sufficient' condition for the future of transatlantic relations and that a new 'Atlantic Community Treaty Organisation' should be established to solidify US-European soft power cooperation (Sloan 2005).

DAVID LONG[1]

2

NATO after Atlanticism

Introduction

Though commonly regarded as the most successful military alliance in history, NATO has persistently been portrayed as being in crisis. In the last couple of years, moreover, the differences among its members seem to have become more acute and the wounds deeper than heretofore. NATO has survived continuous rumours of its imminent demise. Is there any reason to be more concerned today than in the past? Are today's difficulties of some qualitatively different order or are they no more than current symptoms of a recurrent problem that has been overcome in the past and will be again in the near future?

This chapter addresses what I have elsewhere described as bipolar disorder in transatlantic relations (Long 2003). The first section offers a brief account of NATO after the Cold War. It underlines the persistence and relative success of NATO as it reorients its activities and expands its membership in spite of the decline of the threat that called it into existence. It also points out the growing differences that should have made commentators less surprised about the Iraq debacle than they were. The second section examines the causes of the divisions in the Atlantic Alliance through a consideration of theories purporting to explain what has brought it and kept it together for over half a century. As NATO is both a military alliance and an international organisation, this chapter considers theories of alliance formation as well as the creation and maintenance of international organisations to see whether they explain NATO's continued role in the post-Cold War era. While explanations based on interest (realism) or utility (institutionalism) provide some insight into current turbulence in transatlantic relations, the key issue in the divisions among the allies has been the decline in Atlanticism. Understanding Atlanticism means understanding the transatlantic relationship not as one of identity, as constructivists argue – there is no Atlantic identity – but rather as a solidarity based on (a community of) values. Atlanticism – that is, the notion of a shared fate and common values of the peoples of the countries bordering the North Atlantic – precedes the creation of NATO. The most important feature of Atlanticism is that it is an idea that neatly summarised and bounded that international solidarity between Europe and North America. Though often dismissed – yet, at the same time, occasionally absurdly overblown – as a factor in the creation of NATO, Atlanticism not only influenced the origins of the Alliance but has shaped the ideas of what the Alliance is for, which states should be members, and how it is organised. Atlanticism was not simply a rhetorical flourish at the origins of NATO; nor was it merely a reason for this military alliance's rather odd name.

Today, for a variety of reasons, Atlanticism is in decline both in Europe and in North America. This chapter argues that this decline has less to do with internal strife among allies and the wider global strategic and economic context, than with divergent American and European reactions to these challenges. It also argues that even if there are shared or compatible interests or if there is a utility to NATO – the realist and institutionalist arguments respectively – that we should not expect the coherence that we have come to expect in the past. While the divisions in NATO were most obvious during the recent debacle over the war in Iraq, they are much more long term and more fundamental. This argument might seem redolent of Robert Kagan's (2003) conclusions. However, where Kagan resorts to an astronomical analogy as a veil for realist premises, this chapter starts from a concern with the ethics of international responsibility – the norms and values states advance in their international relations – and the framing of that responsibility along the coast of the Atlantic. This chapter does not focus on the operational aspects of NATO nor directly on the Iraq debacle, but on the mental maps with which we organise our views of the world and specifically here, the curious view that transforms a large, unforgiving, cold, dark expanse of water into a link between peoples with a normative value. Though curious perhaps, and it is notable there is no analogue in the Pacific, there are reasons to mourn the decline of the idea, a point on which this chapter closes.

NATO in the post-Cold War period

The end of the Cold War seemed to have removed NATO's military *raison d'être*, namely to contain the Soviet Union and the Warsaw Pact. Since the early 1990s, facing a transformed geopolitical reality in Europe and globally, NATO has first of all evolved politically and organisationally, taking on new tasks and new members while modifying its structures. In addition, the Alliance has responded to crises in Europe, specifically the Balkans, and more recently beyond Europe. These military operations have been a significant move away from the ready but essentially passive posture of the Alliance during the Cold War. Finally, NATO has also accommodated changes in European international relations, particularly the European Union's encroachment into matters of international security including its military dimension (Yost 1998).

During the Cold War, the many differences that existed in the Alliance were for the most part put aside for the sake of NATO unity.[2] The post-Cold War period can be considered in two phases: one from 1990 to 2001, and the other after the 9/11 attacks. While the 1990s were not without conflict within NATO, 9/11 heralded a new phase since it changed not only American strategic analysis but also the nature and extent of threat perception within NATO more generally. Alliance members were thus forced to re-evaluate both their interests and the strategies to deal with new threats (Toje 2003). The threat posed by trans-national terrorist organisations not only had a different location (the Middle East), it involved non-state actors operating according to a different code than that shared by the two superpowers during the Cold War standoff. However, 9/11 did not so much transform NATO as provide a significant impetus to changes that were already under way, exacerbate some differences, render others moot, and resolve some disputes for the most part in favour of the American preferences.

Institutional Change

With the Soviet Union gone, NATO members had begun to devise a new Strategic Concept that would reflect the changing security situation in Europe. Unveiled at the Rome summit in November 1991, it acknowledged the fact that NATO should reduce its dependence on nuclear weapons and would no longer need to maintain large conventional forces in Europe. A new definition of security 'based on dialogue, cooperation and the maintenance of a collective defence capability' was put forth, as was the goal of fostering greater rapprochement with the new democracies in Central and Eastern Europe. To facilitate the latter goal, NATO established a North Atlantic Cooperation Council (NACC – later to be restyled the Euro-Atlantic Partnership Council) to include Central and Eastern European states as well as the remnants of the former Soviet Union. At the political level, NATO's eastward expansion was the dominant issue of the 1990s. In 1994, at the behest of US President Bill Clinton, NATO began a new Partnership for Peace (PfP) programme that sought to increase the Alliance's security cooperation with the Central European states until they themselves could be admitted into NATO. The latter had always been a delicate topic as Russia was sensitive to any eastward expansion.

While containing the Soviet Union, NATO's original military objective, seemed outdated after the Cold War, countries like Hungary, Poland and the Czech Republic, with forty years of totalitarianism still vivid in their memories, sought the security that NATO membership would bring. At the 1997 Madrid summit, the Czech Republic, Hungary and Poland were formally invited by the Allied governments to begin accession talks with NATO, and were admitted two years later (Asmus 2002). The signs of differences over this round of NATO expansion were clearest in the sponsorship of the case for Romanian membership, primarily by France. The limited enlargement in 1999 set the stage, however, for a further enlargement as NATO kept ahead of its institutional rival the EU in organisational engagement with the countries of Central and Eastern Europe. Seven states – Bulgaria, Estonia, Latvia, Lithuania, Romania, Slovakia and Slovenia – were invited to join the Alliance at the Prague summit, formally becoming members in March 2004, raising NATO's membership to 26.

NATO also instigated moves to reassure the Russians that this was not encirclement. The NATO–Russia Council in May 2002, making Russia a partner of NATO arguably more important indeed than a number of its own member states, was symptomatic of the changing global security context. NATO Secretary General Lord Robertson later acknowledged that 9/11 had made Russia key partner in the war on terror. The Prague summit helped to shape how the Alliance would participate in the fight against terrorism. Among the measures agreed upon by the allies was the creation of a NATO Response Force (NRF). Officially launched on 15 October 2004, and scheduled to be operational by 2006, the NRF will include 21,000 soldiers ready to deploy anywhere in the world within five days. Most observers have chosen to interpret such new and changed institutions, new members, and new and cooperative relations with former enemies, as positive successes for NATO. The conditions for, and the nature of, these changes also suggest, however, a different story: namely an increasingly desperate search for a role in European and global security.

Military operations
Clearly, the biggest military challenges facing NATO during the 1990s were the wars in Bosnia and Kosovo. In Bosnia, NATO enforced UN mandated no-fly zones and the UN embargo; used its air superiority to strike Serb positions that were in violation of the UN's designated 'Safe Areas' and that were besieging Sarajevo; enforced a maritime embargo at sea; and provided air cover and tactical air support for the UN Protection Force (UNPROFOR). Indeed, the use of force in the form of air-strikes played a role in bringing the Serbs to the negotiating table and helped lead to the Dayton Accords and the 1995 Bosnian Peace Agreement. NATO was then given authority to implement the military aspects of the Agreement, and did so through the Implementation Force (IFOR), later Stabilisation Force (SFOR). Not all was smooth sailing in Bosnia, of course, with differences among members over the American suggestion for 'lift and strike', especially the notion of using US airpower while various members had soldiers on the ground in peacekeeping roles.[3] In addition, the role of the UN and the extremely problematic 'dual key' approach, wherein both NATO and the UN were to agree to the deploy-

ment of air-strikes, led to rifts within the Alliance. Differences among the allies were serious because the issues themselves were extremely serious, most of them having to do with the requirements of peace-enforcement as opposed to traditional peacekeeping.

NATO's intervention in Bosnia set a precedent. In 1998, with escalating violence in Kosovo between Kosovo Albanians and Serb forces, fears of another humanitarian disaster prompted NATO to draw up contingency plans for military action against Serbia. NATO's attacks against Serbia, Operation Allied Force, began in March 1999. It would take over two months for the Serbs to agree to withdraw their military forces from Kosovo. Once again, the veneer of consensus hid some hard negotiations among Alliance members and in particular a difference of opinion among the usually like-minded British and Americans about the deployment of ground forces. In addition, it is evident that Tony Blair's sense of the manifest inadequacy of the European response was a key factor in the revival of a set of initiatives on European security and defence within the EU.

The events of 9/11 were a watershed for NATO's military activism. For the first time in its history, the allies invoked Article 5, proclaiming that an attack against the US was an attack against them all. However, as it became clear that al Qaeda was behind 9/11, the Alliance was presented with a dilemma. NATO's mandate included Europe and the North Atlantic; never before had NATO forces been deployed beyond the European continent. Thus, 9/11 resolved a long-running dispute in NATO between the US and European positions on the geographic range for the Alliance in favour of the American position for a global scope and activist role. NATO's deployment in Afghanistan under the auspices of the International Security Assistance Force (ISAF) in August 2003 was another first. Never before had NATO taken control of a mission outside of Europe; now NATO forces were being asked to restore stability and democracy, facilitate reconstruction, and act as peace-keepers in Afghanistan. While the Europeans were firmly behind the US as it launched attacks against the Taliban and al Qaeda in the autumn of 2001, the military campaign confirmed how far behind the Americans they were, technologically and in terms of force projection capability. This provided ammunition for those in the US who argued that NATO had ceased to be an effective military alliance and that unilateral action was to be preferred to multilateral cooperation in dealing with global issues of import to American interests.

In spite of the subsequent strife within NATO over intervention in Iraq, important steps have been taken to help promote stability after the end of the war. In the Alliance's second deployment outside of Europe (agreed to on 22 September 2004) NATO forces as part of the Training Implementation Mission are helping train the new Iraqi security forces as well as providing technical assistance and logical support in equipping the troops. However, both these initiatives need to be seen in the context of increasing American reluctance to use NATO as anything more than a source of bases and a force multiplier.

Relations with the EU

The third dimension of the changing character of NATO since the early 1990s has been adaptation in response to the emergence of the EU as a security organisation and lately a military actor. Formally begun with the Maastricht and Nice treaties respectively, the EU Common Foreign and Security Policy (CFSP) is still being refined and the European Security and Defence Policy (ESDP) is very much in its nascent stages. Indeed, what is emerging does not readily fit within the usual categories of military forces, since as a number of commentators have observed the D in ESDP is still largely silent. Howorth (2003a: 45) suggests that for the UK, there was a realisation that 'unless Europe got its act together, NATO was dead in the water'. He also maintains that a European security capacity, far from being prejudicial to the Alliance, is 'now being openly touted as the very salvation of the alliance'. The Europeans have finally tackled the issue of burden sharing seriously. There are those, however, and among them the French, who perceive the ESDP as the basis of an autonomous European defence capacity.[4] Among the various concerns about capacities and effectiveness, the motivation behind ESDP is at the heart of a serious schism in the transatlantic relationship. Does ESDP help NATO manage crises and thus fix the weakening transatlantic link or is it a European solution to a European problem, that is, the inadequacy of European security and defence capacity? Despite the apparently contrary goals, for the Europeans it is a bit of both.

The developing EU capacity and innovations in security institutions and mechanisms has paralleled the moves to reorganise NATO forces in light of post-Cold War challenges. Thus, the Combined Joint Task Force (CJTF) idea and the mechanisms that now come under the rubric of 'Berlin Plus'[5] both reflected a sense that NATO needed more flexible and faster reacting forces and the desire of Europeans to have a separable if not separate configuration of forces that could be deployed with or without American participation or direction (Howorth and Keeler 2003). ESDP means that past attempts to create some sort of European mechanism within NATO have now been superseded by a direct EU–NATO relationship.[6] The difficulties at the heart of the relationship remain the same, though: the US wants burden sharing without power sharing whereas Europe wants more responsibility while free-riding (Boniface 2003). This is not simply a matter of military capacity, although the enormous differences in this regard exacerbate the problem (Sperling 2004). It is rather a dispute over responsibility in the Alliance. This issues in differences of opinion over the geographic range of the Alliance, its military control and direction, definitions as to its core mandate (territorial defence), defence spending and procurement issues. In this sense, Iraq is simply the latest manifestation of a problem of managing European developments within a European–American relationship.

The 'troubled partnership': explaining the decline of 'Atlanticism'

International relations theory offers a number of hypotheses to explain the problems that have emerged in the Alliance and that have been highlighted with the Iraq War.[7] For the realist school, for instance, a military alliance is the product of shared interests responding to a common threat. If the threat disappears, so will the alliance. Hence, according to realists, NATO is likely to disintegrate in the absence of its *raison d'être*, the Soviet threat (Mearsheimer 1990; Sens, 2003) unless it is reinvigorated by new threats such as fundamentalist Islamic terrorism (Stevenson 2003) or China (Kaplan 2005). Realist analysis, of course, rests on the assumption that NATO is a military alliance and little, if anything, more in terms of its shared interests. Competing explanations suggest that NATO continues to exist precisely because NATO is more than what the realists see: besides a military alliance formed to respond to a common threat to territorial integrity, NATO is also a highly institutionalised international organisation with a number of additional roles and functions. Institutional theorists (Keohane and Martin 1995; Wallander 2000) argue that NATO performs many functions for its member states and in the wider international system, including being a forum for multilateral discussion across the Euro-Atlantic area, a collective security system for its own members, a mechanism for transition to democratic rule in former communist countries, and a system for military-to-military cooperation. Hence, institutional theory predicts that NATO will continue to exist long after the disappearance of the Soviet threat. In developing its Partnership for Peace programme, through being a vehicle for international interventions such as in Kosovo and peacekeeping missions such as Afghanistan, by modifying its membership and opening a structured relationship to its erstwhile enemy, NATO has evolved into something much more than a single purpose defensive alliance. It was never simply this, of course, but the post-Cold War period has seen a remarkable inventiveness with respect to what previously appeared to be secondary aspects of the organisation. It should also be pointed out, as William Wallace (2001: 28) does, that the Alliance is 'embedded in a dense network of multilateral links'. The US and Europe, in other words, cooperate on a wide range of issues. The vast majority of these issues are technical and complicated and hence these aspects of the relationship do not get much media attention. By contrast, disputes and failures by officials to manage transatlantic differences make good copy for the press, thus creating the impression of a very fractious relationship. Although NATO's 'secondary' functions are undoubtedly useful, they hardly make NATO indispensable. Thus, institutional theory suggests NATO may persist but it cannot reassure those who are concerned that the organisation may decline and become a marginal player in world politics.

If one acknowledges that NATO was not simply founded on interest or utility, one enters a different theoretical terrain, one of ideas and identities. From this 'constructivist' point of view, NATO is more than a pragmatic response to threat or a useful device; rather, the organised territorial defence of Western Europe appears to have been poured into the already extant mould of an Atlantic identity during the dire emergency of disintegrating post-war East–West relations. Such an identity is 'Atlanticism', developing first from the links across the Atlantic established by successive waves of immigration and trade and transferred then to the strategic imperative of Canada and then the US in supporting the efforts of the allies against Germany's challenge to world order, and along the way becoming associated with the notion of Western civilisation, a world of peace, liberty, democracy, and the rule of law.[8] Constructivists (e.g. Risse-Kappen 1996) basically argue that 'Atlanticism' is the basis for cohesion in NATO. While having the merit of pointing out the importance of norms and ideas, constructivist readings stretch and idealise the existence of a common Atlantic identity since they highlight the centrality of common values and self-identification, underplay differences and miss the unequal relationship that has been the reality of transatlantic relations: the US has provided security for Europe and not – not even after 9/11 – the other way around. Constructivists also tend to conflate identity and solidarity, which is a sense of commitment to another rather than identification with self, and implies an ethical discourse of responsibility. 'Atlanticism' from such a perspective is not based on ideas and identity but is the framing of international responsibility and commitment between North Americans and Europeans (Strausz-Hupé, Dougherty and Kintner 1963; Hodge 2004; Sloan 2005). The transatlantic partnership is troubled because the bond that has cemented the Alliance has loosened and this has occurred not because such a bond was based on mutual security, compatible utility, or common identity, but because of declining solidarity. There is nothing intrinsic about the Atlantic framing Euro-American solidarity; it has to be constantly rebuilt and rehearsed. Such solidarity is historical (shared memories, common history and so on) but cannot only be historical. But today NATO is perceived as useful rather than necessary: the centrality of European security has been transcended by 9/11 which has set a new agenda, while, at the same time, the (near) completion of the project of enlargement has completed the shift of the Atlantic view away from the original close cooperation of a few friendly nations.

The recent difficulties among Alliance partners are commonly associated with the differences over the war on Iraq. These differences were real and substantial, yet concentration on this axis of difference does a disservice to a clear understanding of the problems currently facing NATO. The fundamental issues are not about this specific case. They concern questions of world order, the role of the US and Europe in it, and differences in threat assessment and strategic approach. On Iraq, the 'European' position, exemplified by the stance taken by France, Germany and Russia, clearly contrasts with that of the US, but there were clear differences within North America, where Canada (and Mexico) decided not to join the war, as well as in Europe, where the UK joined together with many of the EU traditionally more 'Atlanticist' members and those countries in Central and Eastern Europe which had only recently joined the EU – 'new Europe' in the lingo of US Secretary of Defence Donald Rumsfeld. The difficulties caused by the Iraq debacle have been serious because of the underlying decline in 'Atlanticism' brought about by a series of developments on each side of the Atlantic. On the American side, while engagement with Europe is less strategically central than it once was, there are also growing ideational, ideological, and identity-based distinctions that make the association with transatlantic cooperation less of an automatic reflex. On the European side, there is an enlargement of both membership and functions for both NATO and the EU, which is a mixed blessing at best. Maintaining transatlantic solidarity, a difficult business in any event, is made all the harder because it is being undercut by another trans-national collective identity project, the EU.

The US as a global power
Because of its stature, the US is not simply concerned strategically with the fate of Europe or Europe for itself. In this context, the importance of 9/11 is impossible to overstate. American strategic interests are global and Europe, while still an important ally, is no longer the most important strategic region for the US. As realists argue, differences in threat perception and in strategic interests are real and do matter. However, these differences relate to American identity. To begin with, the Pentagon's shift of emphasis from the Cold War concept of large regular forces to a more mobile and rapid reaction capability as the centre of American military operations raises an important issue in NATO in terms of organisational culture and outlook as well as relationship to other departments of government. In contrast to most other NATO members where defence ministries tend to be more favourable to NATO than foreign ministries, the Pentagon has always been more sceptical of NATO than the State Department. Of late, American policy has become more prone to use force in international relations. This has elevated the Pentagon relative to the State Department, as evidenced in the case of Iraq, thus accentuating the unilateral element in US foreign policy. As the US was invading Afghanistan, Defence Secretary Donald Rumsfeld was reported to want 'a unified command' and was adamant that the Pentagon and US Central Command (CENTCOM) control the operation and 'not the UN, not NATO' (Woodward 2002: 306). After 9/11, US Deputy Defence Secretary Paul Wolfowitz thanked NATO allies for their offer of help but suggested that the US would not need it in this case (*Financial Times*, 1 July 2004).

An underlying theme of the Bush administration since 9/11 has been prevention. In international affairs this has translated into the Bush doctrine of 'preventive war' as a pillar of the strategy against terrorism. Its proponents construe it as a reasonable reaction to a genuine and compelling threat. It can also be interpreted as the doctrine of a supremely dominant power, especially when seen against the increasingly prevalent American belief that the US is an exceptional nation. This exception extends to international morality; there should indeed be one set of rules for the US and one for the rest of the world (Luban 2004). Belief in 'exceptionalism', especially when coupled with 'unilateralism', constructs difference between the US and others, including its allies across the Atlantic.

The Presidency of George W. Bush is a temporary factor in the transatlantic relationship; the basis of his election and re-election in the US is much less obviously so. While there was a good deal of attention to the (religious) values question in the immediate aftermath of the 2004 election, this religiosity versus the secular character of much of modern Europe is only a part of the increasing distance between the US and Europe. There has long been a controversy among scholars about the character of the US. One of the competing views sees the US as fundamentally a nation built from its connections to the immigration from Europe and the construction of significant populations in New England and along the Atlantic seaboard. An alternative view sees US identity constructed fundamentally as a frontier society, on the basis of the exploration, expansion and conquest of the American West (Taylor 1972). The growth in the population of the southern states as well as the 'values-based', Christian orientation of those populations is a significant counter to the views predominant along the north-east Atlantic seaboard. Ultimately with respect to Western or Southern orientations, explaining the causes is less important than understanding the effects, which include the marginalisation of views that default to common cause with Europeans, not so much when it suits Americans interests or values, but as a sharing of values and norms per se. Such views are not simply crude renderings of geopolitics but rather the product of historically developed social identities.

American views about Europe, the EU, and the transatlantic relationship can also be broken down into two broad-based schools of thought, a neo-conservative view and a liberal internationalist view, the latter being the more amenable to relations with Europeans on the basis of multilateralism, international law, and so on. It is the former, however, that is currently in the ascendant, not only in the White House but across the US media (newspapers, talk shows, and so on), especially among television pundits and in the op-ed or opinion pieces in publications such as *National Interest* and *National Review* as well as leading think tanks such as the American Enterprise Institute.

International security and defence issues are hardly the only matters on which Americans and Europeans differ. The Bush administration is often the ideological opposite of its counterpart in Brussels and elsewhere on the continent, whether regarding approaches to the Israeli–Palestinian conflict, Iran's nuclear pretensions, social issues (the death penalty, gay marriage, etc.) and even national fiscal and international monetary and trade policies. Of course, not all Americans share the view of the neo-conservatives in the Bush administration and in Congress about the Europeans and the EU. Democrats for the most part see the Europeans as essential allies and believe in greater consultation, though not surprisingly the discourse is usually about European responsibilities for 'cost sharing' and lessening the American burden.

Transatlantic differences would be less of a problem if the reorientation of American priorities and capabilities worked in tandem with European moves to increase the coherence of their own action, creating division of labour across the Atlantic. That is, the disarticulation of visions among the allies need not mean disengagement of interests. Nor need the division of labour be, per Kagan's rather snide description, the Americans doing the cooking and the Europeans doing the dishes. Rather, the Bush administration's policy of deciding to release US troops (primarily in Europe) to move elsewhere might diminish Washington's concerns over the EU plans to establish its own military capacity – even though this was a huge source of tension in 2003 – as this could be a European regional complement to global American policy. As we know, the EU has begun to take on larger military missions and is aiming to succeed NATO in Bosnia and Kosovo. But, 'the US remains frustrated at Europe's relatively meagre military resources, while many European governments are deeply uneasy about US policy without a clearer sign of engagement in the Middle East peace process' (*Financial Times*, 27 October 2004). Unfortunately for its proponents, this is not the only problem with the idea of a transatlantic division of labour. More serious is the lack of trust between Americans and Europeans that the other has their genuine interests at heart (Whitman 2004). Such a decline in belief in the reliability of the other is hitting those that are traditionally the strongest Atlanticists, that is, the British and the Canadians certainly, as can be seen in their concerns with American policy in the Balkans.

To sum up, developments in the US have increased the emotional distance across the Atlantic and it is this, and not the much vaunted divergence of interests, strategies and assessments, that has left the Atlantic Alliance mired in the fallout from the dispute over Iraq. While the differences of opinion were often serious during the Cold War, American commitment to European allies, though oft-times muttered about, was rarely questioned to the degree it is today.

A wider and deeper Europe
The difficulties across the Atlantic are hardly all American in origin. While EU diplomats were apparently 'outraged' by the 'divide and rule' tactics that the Bush administration played with the EU, i.e. pitting 'Old Europe' against

'New Europe' during the Iraq crisis, the furore over Europe's divisions hid an un-stated assumption, that Europe should be united on an issue like Iraq. Such an assumption of unity is historically unprecedented and produced both much of the acrimony in Europe that went above and beyond that occurring elsewhere in the Alliance while also providing grounds for the restoration of relations and the reinvigoration of the ESDP.

Highlighting the increased salience of European identity and its contradiction to Atlanticist solidarity, Timothy Garton Ash warned in the *Washington Post* (24 October 2004) that if Bush were re-elected, 'many Europeans will try to make the European Union a rival superpower to the United States. Led by French President Jacques Chirac, they will find the main justification for further European integration in counterbalancing what they see as irresponsible, unchecked American power. In the great European argument between Euro-Gaullists and Euro-Atlanticists, these Euro-Gaullists will be strengthened. The temptation for Europe to define itself as Not America will be increased'. He also pointed out, however, that 'the forces of Euro-Atlanticism are still much too strong, especially in an enlarged European Union of 25 member states'.

There are two major macro-political factors in Europe affecting transatlantic relations: the enlargements of NATO and the EU; and the growing importance of the EU as the hub of regional cooperation in Europe. In EU jargon, these trends are summarised as widening and deepening. While enlargement is in one sense an indicator of the attractiveness and success of an organisation, the dual enlargements of NATO and the EU have in their different ways undermined Atlanticism. With regard to NATO, it has occasionally been suggested that it is odd to the point of being preposterous to consider Vancouver Island the western border of an Atlantic Alliance. Whatever the merits of this observation, it bears mentioning that there are analogous geographic difficulties with the Baltic States and Slovenia as members of an Atlantic community. While it is important not to fetishise the idea of the Atlantic in NATO – it is at bottom only an idea joining the various members of the organisation, and specifically a commitment of North Americans to European security – stretching geography is just one more example of how far the Atlantic idea and 'Atlanticism' has come. For it is clear that, though it has a border on the Pacific, Canada can at least claim to be geographically an Atlantic nation. And historically, Canada was also an important player in the idea of an Atlantic community. Enlargement of NATO, however, has taken it geographically, historically, and in ideational terms outside the realm of the Atlantic (Asmus 2002). For some this means not a great deal and the functions of NATO mean more, but it is interesting that while NATO is going 'out of area' in its enlargement and its policies, the EU has strictly delimited the final extent of its borders albeit in terms of a fuzzy definition of Europe.

Aside from the geography of Atlanticism, realist and institutionalist arguments point to deleterious effects of enlargement. For institutionalists, the latest and largest enlargement will mean that there is less overall coherence in both organisations; a larger and more diverse NATO will require greater efforts to create consensus or resort more often to lowest common denominator agreements. We should expect more horse trading and disputes, and not only because the superficial *raison d'être* for NATO has disappeared. NATO enlargement does not simply add strength of numbers and capacities; rather, to the extent that there is diversion from original focus and dilution of common purpose, widening may mean weakening.

Dilution of purpose and policies has preoccupied the EU for decades; a factor pointed to by realists, the hegemony of the US, has allowed NATO to be more cavalier. But for realists, NATO expansion, indeed its transformation more generally, has been a product of the changed geopolitical environment that began with the end of the Cold War and was accentuated after 9/11. And precisely as NATO has been able to reconcile with former adversaries because of the changed geopolitical context so NATO has been rendered less relevant. The problem at the heart of European security has been transcended; the real security issues are now elsewhere. With regard to these other issues NATO is one institution/arrangement among a number, though certainly an important one.

More specifically, a realist view of enlargements highlights the fact that it means that the European component of transatlantic relations is growing in size and to some extent in cohesion. Realists and institutionalists thus see the potential difficulties resulting from enlargement differently. Realists see a Central and Eastern Europe transformed through NATO and EU membership, admitting former Soviet republics that even as recently as a few years ago would have been dubious propositions for membership. Given the turnaround in cooperation between the US and Russia, the opportunity to expand into the Baltic states turned out to be considerably less troublesome than pundits and academics alike had predicted. The ease of this enlargement suggests the transformation of these new members and the creation of a 'heavier' European bloc. In effect, American realists worry that this might be the basis for an increase in bipolarity and divisions within the Alliance. By contrast, it is the relative failure to transform the new members and the heterogeneity introduced into the organisation that worries institutionalists.

Enlargement also redirects policy with the addition of new members' concerns. Relations with Russia, while always significant, take another twist with the inclusion of the Baltic states alongside the already added concerns of the Poles. Aside from specific regional concerns, there is the question of differing worldviews. Differences over Iraq, and the role played by 'new Europe', in part reflected the new NATO members' association of US power with their liberation. The Atlanticist orientation of the new and prospective EU and NATO members was based on a clear calculation of present and past interest, and a more general historical sense of geopolitics of which these new members of the Alliance are acutely aware. However, there may be reasons for doubting whether this Atlanticist orientation will last. Enlargement is Europeanisation not only in terms of the numbers but in terms of the norms of membership, and this is particularly the case for the new members of EU.

EU enlargement brings all of the concerns just mentioned in the context of NATO enlargement, plus two others. First, it has been argued that synchronisation of NATO and EU enlargements and the common border it would create would be a good thing. For example, the case for division of labour between the organisations is easier to make when memberships are all but identical. However, synchronisation does raise the spectre of a new dividing line in Europe, leaving those on the other side of the line in limbo, as Ukrainians well understand.

Second and more fundamentally, this chapter has suggested that Atlanticism is not a discourse of identity. However, Atlanticism does have to compete and cope with an identity project in the form of the EU. The challenge to Atlanticism is in the EU's appropriation of Europe and its discursive deployment. While the forces of regionalisation are evident on both sides of the Atlantic, including the Canada–US Free Trade Agreement, the North-American Free Trade Agreement (NAFTA), and discussions toward a Free Trade Area for the Americas, North American discourses of regionalisation are rarely connected to those concerning identity as they are in Europe. Transatlantic solidarity has had to compete with an emerging European identity which has both intentionally and inadvertently resulted in exclusionary practices on the part of the Europeans.

What is 'Europe' in this discourse and how does it relate to Atlantic solidarity? There is a conflation and confusion of different meanings of Europe which allows certain claims about transatlantic relations to be advanced and others to be rejected. At the most banal level, Europe is a geographic place and this is the meaning deployed when it is claimed that Canada is not a European country. However, such a literal sense is not what is usually meant by the word Europe. Europe is also an aspiration, a goal, even a pretence associated with European values and culture. Interestingly, Europeans share many such values with Canadians and Americans (Welsh 2004; see also Lucarelli in this book). This is also the meaning at work when Central and Eastern European leaders have sought to return to Europe, and it is also the idea underlying a good deal of the enlargement process, especially in the EU, and notions of a Europe whole and free (Neumann 1998; Sjursen 2002). In the notion of the transatlantic relationship, however, Europe has neither of these connotations; rather Europe is an entity and more specifically it is a partner. This attribution of 'thing-ness', or reification as social scientists call it, is an important shorthand, integral to our understanding of our social world, from the notion of a local business to the idea of the United Nations. But in this case, the use of the word Europe is not only descriptive but prescriptive and conveys rather too much unity, deliberately indeed for the ideologues of European unity and particularly in the rhetoric calling for a European Constitution. In fact, Europe is probably better thought of as a collective noun.

The deployment of Europe in its various guises nevertheless frames the increasingly tight caucusing among European states or more particularly EU states. The members of the EU are caucusing more seriously and on more issues (defence, immigration, money), more cohesively, and more consistently within the EU rather than in a smorgasbord of European regional organisations; and as a result of enlargement, with more members. Caucusing as a process is not a manifestation of success in getting consensus; indeed it is commonly most in evidence during periods and over issues where there is dissent and disagreement, representing efforts by the Europeans to create a more unified policy, patch up differences or simply hide them behind high-minded European rhetoric and vague future commitments. Caucusing is important because it polarises transatlantic relations, transforming the transatlantic partnership from a largely multilateral relationship (politically, at any rate) to a bilateral one. Such a transformation might be welcomed by many in Europe and in the US as a reflection of strategic reality or a harbinger of greater simplicity. By contrast, the impact of caucusing on new EU members suggests that though their historical connection to the US will not go away in a hurry, the more practical involvement in EU business, trade and investment flows and the need to work in the EU context will reorient (a.k.a. Europeanise) their policies (Olaf 2004). The increase in the size of the EU and its greater coherence and cohesion is the basis of a stronger sense of identity as well as a tendency for the policy of its member states to oppose the US rather than each other.

Conclusion

NATO can survive without Atlanticism, as Kaplan has argued and as seems evident from the experiences of the last several years. The Alliance can work perfectly well as a coordinating mechanism for its members in response to a variety of defence and security issues while retaining the remnants of its character as a collective defence organisation. Indeed, this is precisely what has occurred with NATO's missions in Bosnia, Kosovo and Afghanistan. The new NATO is now essentially a variation on a collective security system rather than simply a territorial defence organisation, involving primarily coordinated efforts at building a community among security and defence establishments within NATO and concerted efforts to deal with a variety of security problems, such as leading a 'Stabilisation Force' in neighbouring conflict zones, dealing with terrorism and with nuclear technology, material and missile proliferation. NATO has, in short, gone out of area rather than going out of business. What we should not expect is that NATO will be the central player that it was during the Cold War or the decade and a half interregnum since then and before 9/11. For the American and European allies, NATO is now one instrument among many.

While troubling, the factors pointed to by realism (power/interests), institutionalism (utilities/preferences) and constructivism (ideas/identities) do not point to the end of NATO, though they do in their various ways explain and interpret its reorientation. However, the importance of the Atlantic idea as the collective solidarity suggests that NATO's basis is more fragile today. The unusual merging of a defensive collective alliance and an international organisation within a frame of Euro-American solidarity has become disarticulated: superficially, the organisation thrives, diversifies and expands; but the sense of shared commitment has declined and future differences must be expected to engender more concern and more rancour than they have heretofore.

While transatlantic cooperation will continue, it will be less certain and more *ad hoc*. We should expect more coalitions of the willing and flexible arrangements in response to crises. On the one hand the original military bargain of NATO, that the US provide the high tech, high end, and high flying support for Europe, and the Europeans provide the forces on the ground and the long term political and diplomatic investments, continues with the current division of labour. On the other hand, we should expect more disputes about military and security matters, more differences of opinion generally, as has occurred for instance over the EU's insistence in moving forward with its Galileo satellite system in the face of US objections that it rivals rather than complements the American Global Positioning System (GPS); over the wars in the Balkans and in Iraq; and divergent strategies to counter Iran and North Korea's nuclear ambitions. Divisions such as those during the 1950s over Korea, though serious, did not jeopardise NATO's relevance; the differences over Iraq and the war on terror do. The halcyon days of transatlantic multilateralism and mutual influence so nicely portrayed by Risse-Kappen (1996) now only exist in the wishful thinking of Atlanticists themselves.

Notes

1. The author wishes to thank David Zadak for excellent research assistance, including his report on the recent history of NATO and American perspectives on the transatlantic relationship on which this chapter draws extensively.
2. This is not to diminish the numerous spats such as the Soviet gas pipeline dispute, Cocom restrictions, Ostpolitik, etc. (Kaplan, 2004).
3. The idea of 'lift and strike' was to lift the arms embargo on the parties in order that opposition to the Serbs would be given what advocates saw as a more level playing field, while striking the Serbs in order to rebalance the conflict as well as deter the violent ethnic cleansing ascribed largely to the Serb community in Bosnia.
4. In the wake of the US invasion of Iraq, for instance, France with the support of Germany, proposed a plan for closer European security and defence cooperation involving the creation of an independent military headquarters in Tervuren, Belgium

and 'structured cooperation' among the key EU countries to improve the EU's military capabilities (*Financial Times*, 16 October 2003).
5 'Berlin Plus' refers to a package of agreements between NATO and the EU which ensure access to NATO assets and planning capabilities for EU-led crisis management operations (CMO).
6 On the relationship between NATO and the EU, see Kupchan (2000), Cornish and Edwards (2001), Lindley-French (2002a), Cameron vs. Moravcsik (2004), Cimbalo (2004) and Lantis (2004).
7 For a discussion of international relations theories as they apply to the persistence of NATO after the Cold War, see McCalla (1996).
8 The pinnacle of 'Atlanticist' thinking appears in the years shortly before and after the Second World War in face of the challenge of fascism and communism, and in response to the need for the restoration of world order after the war (e.g. Streit 1939). For discussions of the origins of the Alliance from an 'Atlanticist' perspective, see among others Healey (1957) and Baylis (1993).

SONIA LUCARELLI

3

Which Venus? A normative reading of the transatlantic divide

Introduction

Current debates on transatlantic relations tend to point at deep political differences on the two sides of the Atlantic ultimately grounded on different basic political values. Europe criticises the US for its unilateral and short-sighted foreign policy, while the US criticises Europe – in particular the EU – for its military weakness and utopian view of world politics. Robert Kagan's representation of Europe as Venus and the US as Mars received a great deal of attention because it captured, though perhaps in a simplistic way, the idea of a basic difference in the worldviews of the two. According to Kagan (2003), on one side of the Atlantic, Europe has undertaken a process of profound internal transformation that has led it to the mistaken conclusion that the entire world can work in a Kantian way. On the other side, the incomparable power and responsibilities of the US and its historical experiences are such that the Americans cannot believe in what sounds to them like a fairy tale of cooperation in a post-Hobbesian world. Conflict and war continue to be features of international politics and the construction of security still requires the ability to deter and compel, even by force if necessary.

Such a representation of the transatlantic divide is unfair to both Europe and the US. A transatlantic normative divide exists but is considerably more complex than Kagan's representation of it. Europe and the US, after all, still form a security community in which shared norms and values constitute the political glue of their reciprocal security guarantee (see Deutsch et al. 1957; Adler and Barnett 1998). For instance, the security-through-democracy formula is by no means a novelty introduced by American neo-conservatives. A Wilsonian tradition in American foreign policy has always co-existed with other radically different or compatible traditions of foreign policy. Such a tradition is based on a liberal understanding of foreign policy that combines the Kantian recipe for 'perpetual peace' – domestic democracy, international *foedus* of democratic countries, development of cosmopolitan law (Kant [1795] 1991) – with a messianic mood that allows the use of forceful means for the purposes of exporting the values believed to preserve peace.[1] This tradition found its personification in US President Bill Clinton who stressed its Kantian components. More recently, it has regained prominence with the George W. Bush administration which has combined the Wilsonian understanding of foreign policy with a Jacksonian one, which aims at pursuing military and economic security by any means, and possibly a Hamiltonian one, which considers a strong alliance between the federal government and big business to be fundamental (Mead 2001). However, the George W. Bush administration's reading of the Wilsonian tradition seems to emphasise its messianic component to the detriment of its Kantian character. Difference in the interpretation of common values therefore counts more than the values themselves. Kagan's failure to investigate more thoroughly the difference in values interpretation, therefore, leads him to misleading conclusions about the normative basis of the transatlantic rift.

On the European side, a large literature has already emerged regarding the peculiarities of the EU/Europe as an international actor. Most of this literature points to a distinct European way of being in the international system. The EU has been described with terms such as 'civilian power' (Duchêne 1973), 'normative power' (Manners 2001; 2002), or as an actor having 'structural power' (Telò 2001; Keukeleire 2002). *Eurobarometer* opinion surveys show that Europeans perceive the EU as an international actor that plays a different and better role in the world than the US (European Commission 2003a: 78–9). What is most interesting, however, is that this image corresponds to the self-representation of the EU/Europe. Key actors in European foreign policy frequently refer to values, worldviews and principles that characterise Europe – if not the EU – and should provide the basis for Europe's role in world politics. Article I-3 of the EU Constitutional treaty (whose future is in doubt after the French and the Dutch failed to ratify it) reads:

> 1. The Union's aim is to promote peace, its values, and the well-being of its peoples. [...]
> 4. In its relations with the wider world, the Union shall uphold and promote its values and interests. It shall contribute to peace, security, the sustainable development of the Earth, solidarity and mutual respect among peoples, free and fair trade, eradication of poverty and the protection of human rights, in particular the rights of the child, as well as to the strict observance and the development of international law, including respect for the principles of the United Nations Charter.

The 'European security strategy' paper defines Europe's responsibilities and principled-aims as follows:

> The European Union is, like it or not, a global actor; it should be ready to share in the responsibility for global security. [...] The development of a stronger

international society, well functioning international institutions and a rule-based international order is our objective. [...] *The best protection for our security is a world of well-governed democratic states. Spreading good governance, supporting social and political reform, dealing with corruption and abuse of power, establishing the rule of law and protecting human rights are the best means of strengthening the international order.* [...] We need to be able to act before countries around us deteriorate, when signs of proliferation are detected, and before humanitarian emergencies arise. Preventive engagement can avoid more serious problems in the future. A European Union which takes *greater responsibility* and which is more active will be one which carries greater political weight. (European Council 2003, emphasis added)

This self-representation of the EU cannot be dismissed as simply rhetorical and hence politically irrelevant because rhetoric is a fundamental element in the construction of identities and interests of agents (Giddens 1979). It is a kind of performance which might respond to the actors' interests in a given structural context, but which eventually contributes to shape the collective understandings of that context and the identities of the actors involved. In the case of the EU then, this is even more relevant, since neither the political identity of the Europeans nor the international image of the EU (i.e. the perception others have of the Union) are consolidated. If we regard the European 'political identity [as] ... the set of social and political values and principles that we recognise as ours, or in the sharing of which we feel like *us*, like a political group or entity' and we acknowledge that 'recognition ... unfolds argumentatively ... as well as a-logically or symbolically' (Cerutti 2003: 27–8), we immediately understand the relevance of political discourse – rhetoric included – in the formation of a European political identity. Argumentation, however, must always come to terms with political practice. For this reason, equally important in the definition of a European political identity and EU international image are its concrete policies, or lack thereof. In the case of an actor like the EU, which builds its self-representation around the idea of a special way to deal with international problems, a special sense of responsibility, and a stabilising effect in world politics, foreign policy failures or lack of action imply stepping back from the proclaimed principles and values (e.g. Yugoslavia and Kosovo). Hence, they represent a bigger challenge to the formation of a European political identity and to the international credibility of the EU, than in the case of a traditional state.

For this reason, although political discourse is by no means irrelevant, political action cannot be disregarded. Does the analysis of EU foreign policy confirm the EU's, and academic, representation of the Union as a special power? To a certain extent it does. One can indeed point to specific foreign policy decisions in which the EU and its member states have actively challenged the principles adopted by other international actors, particularly the US. During the international negotiations on climate change, for instance, in Kyoto (1997), Bonn (2001) and later in Johannesburg (2002), the EU showed an attitude towards environmental protection and towards the possibility of turning to alternative sources of energy that was different from that of the US (Vig and Faure 2003). Differences with the US also emerged at the Doha summit of the World Trade Organisation (WTO) in November 2001 and in various other trade negotiations (Damro 2004; Van den Hoven forthcoming). The EU role in the creation of an International Criminal Court (ICC), including building the momentum that carried along its more reluctant governments, Britain and France, is a further example of activism and faith in the development of international norms and cosmopolitan institutions that seems to differentiate the EU from the US. The EU has also adopted a distinctive attitude on the issues of food protection and research on genetically modified organisms (Sicurelli 2004), development aid, democratisation and the respect of human rights as well as the fight against landmines (Manners 2002).

The analysis of EU foreign policy broadly defined also shows, however, the presence of a number of fundamental values most of which are shared with the US, or regarded as universal. The main claim of this chapter is that EU peculiarity as an international actor does not reside in specific guiding values, but in its interpretation of universal values and principles, which is different from that of the US. This different interpretation is the result of the integration process in Europe and, at the same time, feeds back into it. This focus on interpretation is not only completely absent in the literature on EU foreign policy and transatlantic relations, but also largely disregarded in the theoretical literature on international relations, which tends to be generically focused on norms, with no specific attention to values and principles nor to the interpretative dimension of them.[2] Interpretations of values and principles, however, are fundamental as they provide the transmission belt between abstract concepts on the one side, and concrete norms and acts on the other (Cerutti 2001). Values, understood as notions laden with an absolute (i.e. non-instrumental) positive significance for the overall order and meaning we try to give to our world, suggest concepts such as freedom, whether as a moral or a political concept, dignity, liberty, equality, solidarity, justice. These values, however, lead to different norms and action depending on the interpretation that is given to them and their actual translation into principles of conduct. The latter are normative propositions that translate values into general 'constitutional' norms. The mode of translation depends on how values are interpreted according to a particular worldview and the underlying cultural traditions. Freedom, for instance, can have different meanings depending on whether one adopts an individualistic-liberal or a communitarian-collectivistic view of the social world. A worldview is the picture one has, based on experience and cultural traditions, of the relationship between the physical world and the social.

In the normative analyses of the current transatlantic rift, attention tends to be limited to diverging worldviews (Kagan 2003) or vaguely recalls the existence of common transatlantic values, with no attempt to analyse where or how such common values eventually lead to the development of different domestic legal systems and actual foreign policies. This chapter contributes to filling this gap in the literature by dealing with major values, principles and worldviews that emerge in EU foreign policy, showing how they are peculiarly interpreted in the EU context. It then goes on to show the modes and limits of translation of abstract values and principles into EU foreign policy, and ends with some concluding remarks.

Interpreted values in EU foreign policy

The analysis of EU foreign policy broadly defined confirms the presence of a number of fundamental values. Some of them (e.g. peace) have been clearly mentioned in EU documents since the beginning of the integration process. Others (e.g. democracy, human dignity, justice, solidarity, liberty, equality) represent *de facto* founding values even if they have not been spelled out as values in the early days of integration. The analysis of EU policy shows that other values are also at play. They are less fundamental either because they are derived form the previous ones (embedded liberalism) or just because they have appeared more recently (harmony with nature). Most of these values (e.g. peace, democracy, equality, liberty, justice) are definitely not exclusive to the EU, while others are, or at least tend to be, specifically European in so far as they are ranked higher than elsewhere in the order of values (harmony with nature, embedded liberalism). Some interpretations of those values and their translation into guiding principles, however, tend to be specifically European.

There are two distinct classes of interpretation of values and principles in EU foreign policy. The first is the case of a universal value that is translated by the EU into a principle or policy and by other actors into different, even opposite, principles or policies. For instance, in the Charter of Fundamental Rights, 'dignity' is recognised as a value on the basis of which it is affirmed that 'everyone has the right to life' (Chapter 1, Article 2.1) and 'no one shall be condemned to the death penalty, or executed' (Chapter 1, Article 2.1). This implies that the 'right to life' (expression of the value of 'dignity') trumps any other value and should be read together with a certain interpretation of the value of 'justice', where 'justice' does not translate into directly proportional punishment for the offence. This is clearly not the case in the US, where many states as well as the federal authorities apply the death penalty. This has implications also for EU foreign policy and has already had consequences on cooperation in the fight against terrorism. Europeans are reluctant to release captured terrorists to the US where they might face the death penalty.

Particularly interesting are the different interpretations given on the two sides of the Atlantic to the value of 'liberty' in the context of freedom of speech. While in the US blasphemy and racist speech are treated in the same manner (there is a right to both on the basis of a right to free speech), in the EU blasphemy is legal because it is an attack on ideas, while racist speech is illegal because it is considered an attack on a person. As Guy Haarsher notes, 'this distinction between attacks on persons and on ideas distinguishes the European view... from the primary American view that blasphemy and racist speech both belong to the vague category of "hate speech". At issue, here, are two different interpretations of the concept of liberty based on two different historical experiences' (Haarscher 2001: 98–101).

Another interesting example of different interpretation of the same set of values on the two sides of the Atlantic is offered by the American-contested constitutional right to carry a weapon for personal self-defence, a right which is not explicitly recognised as fundamental in European constitutions or in the EU Charter of Fundamental Rights. It is apparent that two different conceptions of the role of the state in safeguarding individual security are at work here. Other examples of EU/European specific translations of values into principles include, as we shall see more in detail below, the translation of the values of 'solidarity' and 'harmony with nature' into the principles of 'prevention', 'precaution', 'responsibility towards future generations', and 'sustainable development'.

The second type of interpretation of values and principles in EU foreign policy concerns a specific interpretation of a certain value in the light of other values or principles, which then produces a new value. An example is that of the value of 'economic liberalism' which when conjugated with those of 'solidarity' and 'justice' becomes in Europe the value of 'embedded liberalism'. The creation of the Bretton Woods system after World War II, and its maintenance afterwards, were the result of a shared belief on the two sides of the Atlantic that free trade should become a pillar of a new and better world order. Europeans and the EU in particular have then given an interpretation of this value in connection with two other values and a principle of the European tradition: 'solidarity', 'justice', and the principle of the 'rule of law'. The result has been a peculiar understanding of liberalism and of which policies are acceptable to achieve it, which sees the logic of free trade embedded in and limited by the need to safeguard the other two values. This has meant embedding international trade in a regulative framework so as to avoid threats to the domestic welfare state. This enlarged form of 'embedded liberalism' which rests on the principle of 'responsibility' (Habermas 1998; Badie 1999) is by no means the rule, but a significant exception. If we take the case of WTO negotiations, we can point to cases in which the position taken by the EU can not be explained by the material benefits that the EU could derive from it, but can be more effectively explained by EU efforts to support/export its own distinct values. For example, in order to facilitate access to inexpensive medicines by developing countries, at the 2001 Doha WTO summit, the EU Commission fought hard for a declaration on TRIPS (Trade related aspects of intellectual property rights) and health emergencies, despite warnings from the EU pharmaceutical industry that this could injure European economic interests.[3] Clearly, values seem to matter as much as interests.

The WTO example is telling also because it helps us understand the faith of the EU in regulatory systems. The EU vision of the WTO system can be described as one that should regulate the global economy to ensure that economic gains from trade are redistributed (Van den Hoven forthcoming). The EU has confidence in the WTO because it conceives it as a regulatory system, which advances the EU values of 'justice' and 'embedded liberalism'. Europe sees the WTO as supported by the value of 'federalism', understood here not technically as a federal political system, but as the value that the EU attaches to systems in which there is a sharing and shaping of sovereignty for the purpose of producing solutions to collective problems in the public sphere. All of this reflects Europe's faith in regulation, support for multilateral institutions, and structured international cooperation both as guiding principles and as policies, and not only in the economic sphere. The value of 'federalism' and the historical practice of it in Europe since the 1950s, explain EU support for the creation of supranational institutions such as the ICC. The latter could not be supported exclusively by the value of 'justice', shared also by many other international actors.

The combination of 'justice', 'solidarity', and the new value labelled here as 'harmony with nature' has then produced the principle, widely used by the EU, of 'sustainable development'. The label 'harmony with nature' conveys the idea not only that nature has become a value to safeguard by avoiding practices that are not explicitly proven to be inoffensive (through the 'precautionary' and the 'preventative' principles), but also that human progress cannot be disconnected from its effects on the natural world of which mankind is part. Hence derives the centrality of the implementation of the principle of 'sustainable development' both within the Union and as part of its environmental and development cooperation policies (European Commission 2000a, 2000b; Baker and McCormick 2003). Within the context of the EU environmental policy, particularly as far as global warming is concerned, we find the specification of a further principle, derived from 'responsibility' and from 'sustainable development': 'responsibility towards future generations' (European Commission 2000c: 7).[4] Similar values and principles ('harmony with nature', 'precautionary principle', 'responsibility towards future generations') are at work in the case of the EU policy on genetically modified organisms. The latter case in particular seems to point in the direction of a constitutive difference in European and American conceptions of the relationship between science, technology and nature and, ultimately, of 'individual freedom', which is a shared value in the Western world and a cornerstone of modernity. In Europe, most voices call for a compromise between 'individual freedom' and the duty to protect present and future generations from the negative consequences of manipulations of the DNA of nature. The 'principle of responsibility' together with that of 'sustainable development' and the value of 'solidarity' are central to the EU developmental cooperation policy. Developmental cooperation is pictured in EU documents not just as an instrument for the pursuit of EU interests (security of its borders, for instance), but also as a direct application of the value of 'solidarity' and, as the Commission states, a 'global projection of European values of democracy, social justice and [the principle of] sustainable development' (European Commission 2000a: 10).

'Peace' is probably the most universally recognised value and it would seem impossible to see some EU peculiarity in it. However, the specific link that the EU has made between this and the other values mentioned here is a distinctive EU/European feature. The EU claims to pursue 'peace' by active respect of all the other values and their translation into the principles of 'conflict prevention', 'democracy promotion', 'international law promotion', 'sustainable development', etc. This imposes a demanding understanding of 'peace', which cannot be limited to the absence of war. However, such an understanding encounters a severe limit in its yet unresolved tension with the use of force.

The worldview underlined by the European interpretation of its values and translation into principles and then policies seems to be a transformative one, one that shows a clear faith in human progress and in the power of legal frameworks. It is an image based on a liberal understanding of foreign policy that combines the Kantian recipe for 'perpetual peace' – domestic democracy, international *foedus* of democratic countries, development of cosmopolitan law – with a Grotian faith in the positive effects of regulation and international law. According to this image, the margin of peaceful transformation and improvement of world politics is still large. Conflict prevention through 'structural foreign policy'[5] is understandable only within this worldview. In this context, the Thucydides *incipit* in the Draft Constitutional treaty ('Our Constitution ... is called a democracy because power is in the hands not of a minority but of the greatest number') was at best controversial since Thucydides can be considered the founding father of the 'Realist' tradition of thought whose faith in the transformative power of law and democratisation is very limited.

From values to foreign policy: modes and limits of translation in the EU case

Values, principles, and worldviews can be put into practice in several ways. If we look at EU foreign policy, we find several ways of translation and several limits to such translation. The broadest mode of translation is 'structural prevention': the analysis of EU foreign policy suggests that the EU addresses the causes rather than the symptoms of problems (such as environmental degradation and inter-group conflict). This attitude is well captured by the concept of 'structural foreign policy' (Keukeleire 2002). Telò argues that EU foreign policy is structural for a number of reasons. First, it aims to affect 'the economic and social structures of partners (states, regions, economic actors, international organisations, etc.). Second, it is implemented through pacific and original means (diplomatic relations, agreements, sanctions and so on). Finally, its scope is not conjunctural but middle and long range' (Telò 2001: 264; see also Padoa-Schioppa's concept of 'gentle power Europe' 2001). Within this general framework, there are several, more specific ways in which values, principles and worldviews manifest themselves in EU foreign policy.[6] The first is 'institutionalisation': the EU slowly institutionalises principles through policies, treaties and legal arrangements and, more recently, 'policy mainstreaming' (e.g. gender mainstreaming, conflict prevention mainstreaming since the 2001 Göteborg Council, environmental protection mainstreaming since the Maastricht treaty). This way of translation is common also in the US, where it tends however to be more pragmatic and shows a greater concern for possible constraints to state sovereignty. The issue of the creation of the ICC and the US refusal to sign its founding treaty is a case in point.

A second mode of translation of values and principles in foreign policy is 'regulation', in which the EU shows a strong faith. This leads the EU to regulate (some might say over-regulate) domestically as well as develop and support regulation internationally. The EU shows a particular faith in the virtues of international regulation, treaties, conventions (those concerning human rights are now part of the EU Charter of Fundamental Rights and were inserted in the text of the Constitutional treaty), and international regimes (that on climate change being a particularly good example of this attitude). Regulation is usually pursued within a multilateral framework.

The third mode of translation is 'multilateralism'. The relevance of multilateralism for the EU has been recalled by the 'European Security Strategy' (European Council 2003) and by the Commission's communication to the Council and the European Parliament 'The European Union and the United Nations: The choice of Multilateralism' (European Commission 2003b). 'Multilateralism' has eventually become part of the European political identity, as it had been the case for post-World War II Germany (Maull 1995–6). The US instead seems to regard it as merely one tool among many in the conduct of foreign policy.

The fourth mode is 'partnership'. The EU tends to work in partnership with other actors/states/institutions, in particular by emphasising political dialogue, constructive engagement, and positive conditionality. The EU seems generally opposed to the use of sanctions and negative conditionality (Youngs 2001), although it sometimes makes recourse to these methods.

The last mode of translation is 'solidarism'. Case studies suggest that the EU aims at solutions with a focus on individuals, rather than on pluralist claims of national/cultural exceptions. Thus, implementation is often bottom-up (focused on individual needs), rather than top-down (focused on governmental role). Such an approach usually entails working closely with civil society, NGOs, social movements, and social partners both within and outside the EU.

The translation of values and principles in foreign policy encounters, however, several limits, with important consequences both for the internal and international credibility of the EU and, consequently, the political identity of Europeans. These limits have been well explored in the literature. The limit mentioned most frequently is 'inconsistency'. The analysis of EU foreign policy suggest that there is a central tension between the need for consistency in the application of principles, and the need for pragmatism in dealing with different issues and actors. This tension manifests itself in a whole range of global relations where, on the one hand, horizontal coordination and consistency demands one type of approach, but where, on the other hand, constructive engagement and pragmatism demands a different type. Another complicating tension exists between the foreign policy of the EU and that of its member states. This produces further inconsistencies, not only over time but also over cases. The latter type of inconsistency is better referred to as 'double standards'. The problem of 'double standards', frequently recalled in the case of democracy and human rights promotion (Smith 1998; Youngs 2001), is relevant also in the case of the interpretation of relevance of international law. A regulative and normative system such as the EU, which aims at constructing its international identity around this distinctive quality, cannot assume its inconsistent support and respect of international law to be costless. Such inconsistency, frequently displayed in the case of debates on the use of force, undermines the credibility of EU foreign policy. For instance, the EU has adopted two different concepts in the evaluation of armed interventions in Kosovo and Iraq. In the first case, the intervention was *de facto* considered acceptable because it was 'legitimate' (i.e. pursued in order to stop severe violations of human rights), despite being 'illegal' (i.e. lacking UNSC authorisation). In the second case, intervention was considered non-acceptable because it was 'illegal' i.e. lacking UNSC authorisation. This is but an example of the most problematic aspect of a fully-fledged EU foreign policy: its relationship with the use of force. More and more frequently, there is a call for a clarification of the EU position on this point, namely how to combine the EU structural/normative foreign policy with the creation of an EU security and defence capacity. Two recent examples can be found in the 'European Security Strategy' document (European Council 2003), and Commission President Romano Prodi's call for limiting the use of force to humanitarian intervention (*Corriere della Sera*, 27 March 2004).[7] A final clarification has not yet been attained, and probably cannot be, because of the different positions on this point among member states and between them and EU institutions. The risk in these inconsistencies is that EU principled foreign policy may be seen as pure rhetoric, or ridiculed as that of an international actor from the comfortable and idealistic planet Venus (Kagan 2003).

A second limit is 'efficacy'. Measuring the success of EU foreign policy is a highly complicated task made even more difficult by the simple fact that a structural foreign policy encounters the same problems that the literature has identified in the case of conflict prevention: easy to see when if fails but difficult to evaluate when it works. A principled EU foreign policy has so far failed to show a significant difference in what it can achieve. The evaluation of any policy cannot rest exclusively on the good intentions of those who make and implement policy. It must rest also on its effectiveness. The EU Constitutional Treaty defines the Union's objectives as the promotion of its own values. These include human dignity, liberty, democracy, equality, the rule of law and respect for human rights (Art I-2); and the well-being of its peoples, the promotion of peace, security, sustainable development of the earth, solidarity, free and fair trade, eradication of poverty, protection of human rights, and strict observance and development of international law (Art I-3). Has EU foreign policy been able to attain these objectives? Has the EU been able to use its 'difference' to eradicate poverty, fight environmental degradation or prevent violent conflicts? The difficulties of the EU to show the 'relevance' of its difference is a limit of its foreign policy which has implications for its credibility, a relevant term in the current transatlantic debate.

A third limit is represented by the external and internal challenges to the practice of multilateralism and the value of solidarity. Multilateralism represented one of the pillars of the Cold War world order (Ikenberry 1996): multilateral institutions were created and developed, both in the political and economic realms: the UN system and the Bretton Woods system being the two most important examples. The end of bipolarity did not bring multilateralism to an end, but threatened two core elements that had contributed to its creation and maintenance: the US role of benevolent leader, and good transatlantic relations. The recent US unilateral momentum is threatening multilateralism and European cohesion in support of it. The crisis in transatlantic relations is proving to be divisive for both transatlantic and intra-European relations. This is not, moreover, the only challenge to multilateralism. The EU itself is undermining the credibility of a multilateral approach. The return of *directories* in EU foreign policy, and EU behaviour at the 2004 WTO Cancun meeting (when it agreed on a common stance with the US vis-à-vis third world agriculture producers but then decided against reducing Community farm subsidies) are good examples of an inconsistent behaviour that threatens its credibility. Furthermore, in the Cancun case, the EU drastically reduced the credibility of a foreign policy based on the value of 'solidarity' and the principle of 'responsibility' (frequently recalled in the self-representations of the Union and sometimes displayed also in actual foreign policy).

Finally, there are external and internal challenges to the main mode of translation of values into EU foreign policy, i.e. to 'structural prevention' through 'democracy promotion'. As we have recalled, US foreign policy has frequently adopted a similar formula, but the current US interpretation of it draws a dividing line between the EU and its members and the US, as far as their interpretation of the link between two core values (peace and democracy) is concerned. Should Waltz re-write his path-breaking *Man, the State and War* (1959), he could easily exemplify the two liberal-republican options – interventionist (à la Wilson and Mazzini) and non interventionist (à la Kant and Cobden) – by referring to the EU and the US under George W. Bush. This different understanding of the implementation of common values on the two sides of the Atlantic is a threat to the West's credibility and effectiveness. Furthermore, the limits of EU policy as regards democracy promotion, which is increasingly being recognised in the literature, undermine the credibility of such a promotion as an efficient and effective foreign policy tool. To make its policy credible, the EU should be concerned with stimulating and monitoring the respect for the liberal component of the democratic institutions it exports, a component that, particularly due to security concerns, is also currently being challenged in consolidated democracies.

Conclusions

This chapter has argued that EU foreign policy is based on a number of values that Europe shares with the US. However the EU interpretation of such values and their subsequent translation into principles and policies often differs from that of the US. This finding helps us better understand the characteristics of the EU as an international actor, and various aspects of the relationship between its foreign policy and the process of European integration. This chapter has also warned against an easy reading of the EU as an ethical power: incoherence, double standards, and ineffectiveness (or failure to show effectiveness), all threaten the EU foreign policy's credibility, with significant repercussions both on the EU international identity and on the political identity of the Europeans. As for transatlantic relations, this chapter has shown the existence of a different interpretation of the same values in the EU and the US. Such a difference explains part of the recent transatlantic rift which became politicised with the end of bipolarity and the arrival of the George W. Bush administration, but whose reasons have deeper roots in the political history of the EU and the US. Actors' identity, however, is not fixed, nor is the relationship between different international actors unchangeable. The EU will have opportunities to re-launch its integration process, notwithstanding the ratification problems encountered by its Constitutional treaty in the spring of 2005, and push its member states and citizens to think in more European terms. This will be possible only if some member states are able to avoid either getting trapped in 'neo-Atlanticism', that is privilege their bilateral relations with the US (as Italy, Spain, and the UK have done in the Iraqi case), or think of Europe as antagonistic to the US (as France and Germany seem to have done in the Iraqi case). Both options would have negative repercussions for the future of Europe and the transatlantic Alliance. Only an EU that becomes a self-confident partner aware of its peculiarities and limits can provide a response to the difficulties (also for the US) of a unipolar (and, too frequently, unilateral) world.

Notes

1. Kenneth Waltz (1959) refers to Wilson and Kant as representatives of an interventionist liberal approach and a non-interventionist one, respectively.
2. The largest part of the literature on norms and values deals with conditions for effective norms transfer and tends to include in the broad category of norms various elements that should be kept separate such as values, principles, beliefs, etc. In my view, norms should be regarded as prescriptions regarding behaviour in certain given circumstances. Norms can be of various types (utilitarian/functional, ethical, etc.), but all, to different degrees, reflect a system of values, which do not have a prescriptive function until they become embedded in normative frameworks of a sociological or a juridical type. Principles serve to translate values into norms. The literature on norms is large and growing. Surveys include: Florini (1996), Finnemore and Sikkink (1998), and Shannon (2000). On norms transfer, see Checkel (2001), Lucarelli (2002a, 2002b) and Flockhart (2005).
3. The TRIPS Agreement, the most comprehensive multilateral agreement on intellectual property rights, came into effect on 1 January 1995. The most controversial aspect of the agreement was the copyright on medicaments on serious illnesses such as AIDS.
4. Reference to responsibility towards future generations is, however, vague both in the Charter of Fundamental Rights (limited to a sentence in the Preamble, with no specification of the rights of future generations) and in the Draft Constitutional treaty, the Preamble of which recalls individual 'responsibilities towards future generations and the Earth'.
5. A 'structural foreign policy', as opposed to a 'traditional foreign policy', is one aiming at influencing in an enduring and sustainable way the relatively permanent frameworks within which states relate to each other, relate to people, corporate enterprises, or other actors, through the influence of the choice of the game as well as the rules of the game (Keukeleire 2002).
6. I am grateful to Ian Manners for helping me shape this typology.
7. According to Prodi, war is illegitimate and immoral, and conflicts should be solved by political means. He recognises however that a legitimate use of force is possible. The use of force is legitimate when: (i) the use of force is 'indispensable' to protect people, bring peace and justice, but not to impose a regime change or solve an international dispute among states; (ii) it is approved by the international community – better if by the UN, but in case of a veto power used for other reasons, a less institutional 'approval by the international community' is to be considered sufficient (as in the case of Kosovo).

ANAND MENON

4

From out of adversity: Kosovo, Iraq and ESDP

Introduction

Twice over the course of the last decade, the EU found itself reduced to the role of a spectator as West European nations intervened in conflicts, first in the Balkans and then the Persian Gulf. On each occasion, recent developments within the Union spawned heightened expectations of it as a security actor. Hardly surprisingly, therefore, the immediate consequence of each conflict was a rash of critical comment, with analysts vying with each other to condemn the Union's security policy aspirations as doomed. This chapter argues that, such grim prognoses notwithstanding, it transpired that each crisis served, in its own way, to strengthen the determination of the member states to equip the Union to play a more effective role as a security actor. Certainly, the EU is still in no position – and is unlikely ever to be in a position – to carry out major military operations. In this sense, the criticisms of it for inactivity in major conflicts were misplaced. However, developments that occurred as a result of the perception of failure have strengthened its defence policy capabilities to the point where it can now deploy limited military forces in support of broader security operations.

The conflict in the Balkans and ESDP

The outbreak of conflict in the former Yugoslavia coincided with the negotiations that culminated in the Maastricht treaty. This, for the first, time, explicitly provided the Union with a role in security affairs. Perhaps unsurprisingly the signing of the treaty heightened expectations about the Union's ability to deal with security challenges. Thus Jacques Poos, Foreign Minister of Luxembourg, declared that the Union's somewhat lukewarm initial diplomatic intervention in Yugoslavia represented 'the hour of Europe, not the hour of the United States' (*Los Angeles Times*, 29 June 1991). Almost five years later, in early February 1996, it took sustained American involvement to engineer a peace settlement of sorts for the region.

The chasm between earlier expectations and actual performance inevitably spawned a plethora of negative comment. Richard Holbrooke, Assistant Secretary of State for European and Canadian Affairs, stated baldly that unless 'the United States is prepared to put its political and military muscle behind the quest for solutions to European instability, nothing really gets done' (*International Herald Tribune*, 8 February 1996). Philip Gordon, a respected American security specialist was equally caustic: 'if the Yugoslav crisis on Europe's periphery – combined with a US policy that was erratic, uncertain, and domineering at the same time – was not enough to motivate the EU genuinely to adopt common security policies and military integration, what will?' (Gordon 1997/98: 96). The answer was: the very fact of the Union's abject performance in the Balkans. Its palpable failure to play an active role in the resolution of the crisis on its borders persuaded France and the UK in particular that more needed to be done. Despite a limited rapprochement with NATO undertaken from around the end of 1995, the French had come to decide that the Americans were not serious about creating a meaningful European pillar within the Alliance, and that a European alternative was necessary (Menon 2000). More fundamentally, the British – traditional supporters of NATO and opponents of Paris-backed schemes for separate European defence structures – undertook a policy shift.

The reasons that prompted Prime Minster Tony Blair to reassess Britain's traditional position on the European defence debate were many and varied (Biscop 1999; Whitman 1999). Some were purely instrumental – it is no coincidence, for instance, that he chose to act at a time when Britain risked isolation because of its refusal to participate in EMU, when, consequently, its influence within the EU as a whole appeared threatened. Defence policy represented an obvious venue for the reassertion of a leading British role in the EU as it was the one area where progress without the British was unthinkable. More importantly, Britain had come to believe that the Europeans needed at least a limited ability to intervene militarily without the US. Partly, this attitude was the result of the close cooperation between British and French forces on the ground in Bosnia. Partly, too, it resulted from frustrations concerning American policies there. When, in November 1994, Congress forced President Clinton to cease implementation of the UN Bosnian arms embargo even some in the UK were led to question whether they could still rely on Washington. Following the Berlin NATO summit of June 1996, American actions served to alienate London still further. Washington's tendency to use the Contact Group as an arena within which to announce its latest unilateral initiative, Madeleine Albright's bullying tactics at Rambouillet, and US strategy during the Kosovo conflict – particularly

President Clinton's decision to declare in advance that ground intervention was out of the question – all served to make British policy-makers doubt the continued reliability of their erstwhile closest ally and partner. The final straw as far as many in London were concerned came with the confrontation between Generals Clarke and Jackson over the appropriate NATO response to the arrival of Russian troops at Pristina airport. A British establishment brought up to believe – almost as a matter of faith – in the efficacy and reliability of the NATO command structures found this faith challenged.

The fruit of this convergence between Paris and London was the Saint-Malo declaration of December 1998. Whilst undoubtedly the single major event behind the launching of plans to equip the Union with a defence capability, it is important to bear in mind that the document did not mark any real convergence between the British and French positions. However, disillusionment with American policies in the Balkans did have the effect of moving Britain close enough to the French position to enable the Saint-Malo summit to produce its declaration, and to initiate and sustain the process of creating defence structures within the EU – something previous British Governments had always opposed.

Between the wars: headline progress, backroom squabbles

Buoyed on both by the memories of failure in the Balkans and the fillip provided by the Anglo-French summit the so-called European Security and Defence Policy (ESDP) developed apace. By 2000, Jolyon Howorth was moved to remark that there 'has been more progress on CESDP in the 18 months since Saint-Malo than in the entire 50 years preceding that summit' (Howorth 2000a: 383). By the time of the Nice summit of December that year, the institutional structures necessary to implement ESDP were in place. Relations between the EU and NATO were strengthened and formalised, with regular meetings being initiated, from February 2001, between the North Atlantic Council and the Political and Security Committee (COPS), and, from June of the same year, between the NATO and EU Military committees (Howorth 2003b). By the end of 2002, after almost two years of wrangling involving first Ankara and then Athens, the EU and NATO signed a declaration on ESDP which provided the basis for formal partnership between the two organisations. At the Laeken European Council of December 2001, the Belgian presidency declared ESDP operational. The following May, the first EU crisis management exercise was held, as was the first formal meeting of the Council of Defence Ministers. At the June 2002 Seville European Council, the Union announced its willingness to take over from the NATO mission in Macedonia (Howorth 2003c).

Behind the scenes, however, tensions between the member states as to the appropriate scope of, and ambitions for, ESDP underscored such progress.

Divergences crystallised around three issues: the relationship between the EU and the US (which translated itself into debates about the EU–NATO relationship), the scope of ESDP, and the role within it of the three large member states.

The question of the appropriate relationship between the Union and the US was one that had remained live throughout the short history of ESDP. The Saint-Malo declaration had represented more a statement of, than reconciliation between, divergent Anglo-French perspectives on the issue. The fundamental tension separating the two sides was pithily summarised by a senior Foreign Office official: 'The distinction between the UK approach and that of some in Paris (or of some French rhetoric) is that we see it as a European project that needs to be built and run constructively with NATO, not as a project designed to compete with or relegate the Alliance' (Interview, London, March 2004). British thinking was mirrored in many of the accession states. Comments by Polish Foreign Minister Włodzimierz Cimoszewicz that NATO represented the only structure which could guarantee Poland's security (*Libération*, 21 March 2003), reflected a view shared by many in the region.

These different attitudes had very different practical implications. From a French perspective, the assumption characterising the genesis of ESDP was that 'at some stage in the future ... the EU will have developed sufficient advanced military capacity to be able to cope with, say, a Kosovo crisis without having recourse to either NATO or US assets' (Howorth 2000b: 55). For the British, given the complementary nature of ESDP and NATO, the Union simply did not need to develop capacities on this kind of scale. As UK Defence Secretary Geoffrey Hoon remarked in Washington in January 2000: 'For meaningful large-scale military operations, NATO remains and will remain, the only game in town. It will be the sole organisation for collective defence in Europe. It will be the organisation that we expect to turn to for significant crisis management operations' (Howorth 2000b: 60).

The first real test of these competing conceptions came over the proposed EU takeover of the NATO peacekeeping mission in the Former Yugoslav Republic of Macedonia (FYROM). While there had been much talk of this – particularly since the Seville summit of July 2002 – a final decision was delayed as a result of the failure to solve the so-called 'Berlin plus' dispute which led first Turkey, and then Greece, to block agreement between the Union and NATO. In the light of repeated delays, several member states, including France and Belgium, argued that, because the operation was relatively small (the NATO force numbered only some 800 troops) the EU mission should go ahead even in the absence of any EU–NATO accords. The British took a different stance, exemplified in a leaked Ministry of Defence paper of March 2002 which emphasised the dangers of a precipitate EU takeover. Britain, Spain and Germany blocked agreement on an early EU intervention, partly through concerns about the implications for the transatlantic Alliance, partly too because of concerns voiced by military commanders that, whilst the proposed mission itself was small, there was still the possibility of escalation, in which case the EU would need support from NATO. As the senior EU official in charge of the operation put it: 'We should never exclude even the worst-case scenario. If there would be a requirement to extract the force, then that would be done under NATO command and control with the assistance of NATO-led forces' (*BBC News online*, 28 March 2003). At the European Council meeting of 24–5 October 2002, the UK vetoed a decision on the deployment of a EU force. The following November, President Chirac tried to block the requested six month extension to the NATO force in FYROM in favour of a two month extension after which an EU force would replace it (*Daily Telegraph*, 20 November 2002). He was ultimately overruled, but the attempt bore eloquent testimony to the levels of bitterness beginning to characterise intra-EU disputes over the NATO link.

The second area of discord centred on the continued uncertainty about the appropriate scope of the Union's military ambitions, and in particular the relative weight that should be accorded to 'soft' and 'hard' elements of security policy. The fifteen have historically adopted very different attitudes towards the concept of defence, ranging from neutrality (Sweden fought its last war in 1813), to an acceptance of military engagement, often far from home, as an integral part of a nation's 'mission'. Differences of emphasis marked discussions over, for instance, whether a putative ESDP should be a tool to stabilise Europe's periphery or, rather, something used globally as a means of increasing Europe's political weight.

Consequently, the early years of the development of ESDP were characterised by a lack of consensus over whether priority should be placed on the 'soft' or 'hard' end of the Petersberg spectrum. On the one hand, Sweden insisted on greater priority being given to including a significant police element in any EU reaction force, while Finland refused to contemplate participation in peace-enforcement missions. On the other, Britain and France emphasised a military approach to EU security policy, involving the existence of armed forces capable of responding to military crises. One outcome of such continued uncertainty was the 'studied ambiguity' which surrounded the Helsinki Headline Goal (Howorth 2000b: 77). This ambiguity did little to foster progress in rendering ESDP effective.

The final tension that characterised the early phases in the development of ESDP was that between the three large member states – France, Germany and the UK – and the rest concerning the pretensions of the former group to play a leading role in policy formulation in this sector. Disagreements came to the surface at a meeting of the European Council in October 2001, when Tony Blair, Jacques Chirac and German Chancellor Gerhard Schröder held informal talks on Afghanistan an hour before the summit started – leading to angry reactions from both the EU Presidency and the Commission. More strikingly, tensions burst into the open on the occasion of a Downing Street dinner the following month when, initially uninvited, the Prime Ministers of Belgium (holder of the Council presidency), Italy, Spain, and the Netherlands, as well as High Representative Javier Solana, forced their way to the table (*Economist*, 10 November 2001).

The Laeken summit clearly underlined the degree of bitterness inherent in relations between 'bigs' and 'smalls'. Louis Michel, Belgium's Foreign Minister, proudly declared on that occasion that the Union had agreed to form a multinational peacekeeping force to be deployed in Afghanistan, describing it as a 'turning point in the history of the Union'. He was quickly contradicted, however, by diplomats and senior political leaders from the larger member states, angered by what they saw as his attempt to grab credit for an initiative undertaken by the larger member states under a UN mandate (Interviews, Brussels and London, January 2002). Thus, for all the undoubted speed with which ESDP developed following Saint-Malo, tensions lurked just beneath the surface. These were exacerbated by the crisis over Iraq which burst onto centre stage in early 2003 and which, just as had the Balkans, threatened to undermine the very idea of European security cooperation.

The Iraqi crisis and European divisions

The build-up to the war in Iraq revealed increasingly apparent and bitter divisions between the European states. At the heart of these disputes were opposing conceptions of the appropriate relationship that Europe should maintain with the US (Menon and Lipkin 2003). By mid April, the French President was confiding to the Latvian President that NATO was no longer relevant (*Financial Times*, 15 April 2003). Intra-European relations reached a nadir during the impassioned debate about the forthcoming war which took place in the British House of Commons on 18 March 2003. During the course of his crucial intervention, Tony Blair cited France's threatened veto of the second resolution as the factor that had rendered war inevitable. The coming war, apparently, was the responsibility of those who had opposed it rather than those about to wage it.[1]

By the end of April 2003, it appeared that the divisions within the EU were to be institutionalised, as Belgium, France, Germany and Luxembourg held a mini summit aimed at breathing new life into ESDP. Involving the four member states most openly hostile to the continuing military action, the meeting – inopportune in its timing if nothing else – provoked fears in London and elsewhere that the four were intending to use the forthcoming Inter-Governmental Conference (IGC) as a means of enabling the Union to compete with NATO and the US. Press comment certainly echoed such concerns (*Financial Times*, 29 April 2003; *Guardian*, 30 April 2003; *Le Monde*, 30 April 2003). Particular attention focused on one of the key proposals to emerge from the meeting: the creation of a permanent EU operational cell, to be established within a year at Tervuren, a suburb of Brussels. The summit provoked an angry reaction. State Department spokesman Richard Boucher contemptuously dismissed the four as 'chocolate makers' (*Le Monde*, 3 September 2003). At the end of August, London circulated a Ministry of Defence paper proposing the creation of an EU planning capability within Supreme Headquarters Allied Powers Europe (SHAPE), which would serve the dual function of providing the Union with its own planning capabilities, whilst ensuring that such a development was fully consistent with the continued primacy of NATO (*The Times*, 25 August 2003).

Intra-European divisions, apparent yet relatively contained before the Iraq conflict, had finally burst into the open. Confronted with the inaction of and splits within the Union, commentators, as they had during the conflict in the Balkans, united to condemn EU security policies. Following the cessation of hostilities in Iraq, and at the moment the treaty of enlargement was signed in the shadow of the Acropolis, two respected columnists wrote of a 'Europe gripped by self-doubt and traumatised by weeks of recriminations over the war in Iraq'. According to them 'the US-led invasion raised profound questions about whether the EU [could] develop its own foreign and defence policy and whether the disagreements that opened up during the crisis [would] solidify into permanent divisions' (*Financial Times*, 15 April 2003). Alexander Stubb, an adviser to the European Commission, wrote: 'In the past few weeks, we have been subjected to an unprecedented European foreign policy cacophony. The Union had a unique chance to show that Europe can speak with one voice in international crises. The failure was as fantastic as the opportunity, and it seems that everyone is to blame' (*Financial Times*, 13 March 2003). In even more striking tones, Anatol Lieven declared that it 'may be time to admit that there will never in fact be a common European foreign and security policy' (*Financial Times*, 3 February 2003). Meanwhile Stanley Hoffmann (2003: 21) concluded gloomily that in 'his determination to give wholehearted support to the US over Iraq ... Blair scuppered his own Saint-Malo initiative'.

ESDP after Iraq

Once again, however, inaction during a major crisis provided a fillip for further progress in building an EU defence capacity. While the bitter arguments that characterised the run-up to the war in the Gulf certainly had a negative impact on intra-European relations – not least in terms of the damage they did to personal relations between several of Europe's political leaders – the conflict has also had several salutary consequences for European defence policy aspirations. Not only has ESDP, events in Iraq notwithstanding, become operational but also the impact of Iraq has been to make explicit tensions within the design of EU security policies that hitherto had been implicit, yet potentially highly damaging, and capable of undermining the whole project.

Many of these tensions were a consequence of inflated expectations on the part of certain member states about ESDP, some of which were reflected in the draft constitutional treaty produced by the Convention on the Future of Europe. British officials were quick to voice their opposition not only to the idea of a mutual defence clause in the treaty (*Daily Telegraph*, 31 July 2003), but also to the notion of 'structured cooperation' whereby those states that so wished could collaborate more closely on defence matters. As Peter Hain, the UK's representative on the Convention, put it, 'we have to get rid of the nonsense that France, Germany, and Luxembourg, with all due respect, and Belgium can go off and launch a defence initiative in Europe's name on their own by bypassing NATO' (*The Times*, 9 September 2003).

Operational ESDP
Paradoxically, as the crisis over Iraq raged, ESDP took the final steps towards becoming operational. The European Union Police Mission (EUPM) in Bosnia-Herzegovina, which was given a three-year mandate, took up its role in January 2003. Certainly, one should not exaggerate the significance of the EU first police mission. It was a rather unchallenging debut for civilian ESDP in that it followed in the footsteps of a UN mission that had been on the ground since 1995, and the EU had twelve months warning before taking over. Early indications from interviews in London and Brussels, however, are of a high level of satisfaction with the way the mission has worked out in practice (Interviews, London and Brussels, December 2003, January 2004, March 2004).

Second, Operation Concordia, the small-scale military intervention in FYROM, was launched immediately after the Iraq war started (31 March 2003). Following the successful resolution of the 'Berlin Plus' issue in December 2002, approximately 250 troops from all fifteen EU member states participated in the Berlin Plus mission under the operational command of German Admiral Rainer Feist, Deputy Supreme Allied Commander Europe, with the objective of overseeing the agreement reached in 2001 between the Macedonian government and Albanian rebels.[2] France, which sent the bulk of the troops, assumed most of the responsibility on the ground. On 21 July it was decided that the initial six month mandate of the mission be extended until the middle of December 2003. Despite the far-reaching and highly publicised political disagreements between member states that occurred during the Iraq crisis, the Union proved its operational mettle on the ground in FYROM. Growing unrest in the country in September presented the EU force with a direct challenge, one that it proved well able to handle (*Christian Science Monitor*, 9 September 2003).

Finally, in June 2003, EU Operation Artemis landed in the north-eastern town of Bunia in the Democratic Republic of Congo to maintain peace between the government and rebels, remaining there until the beginning of September. Bunia was the capital of the flashpoint Ituri province, where clashes between the Hema and Lendu tribes had claimed some 50,000 lives. The EU force consisted of 1500 men, of which 900 were French troops (*BBC News online*, 12 June 2003). Again, it is important not to exaggerate the scale or scope of the mission. Critics were quick to point out that the force would be powerless to prevent the massacres that were occurring outside Bunia within the Ituri province (*EUobserver*, 13 June 2003; *Guardian*, 13 June 2003). However, Artemis represented the first autonomous EU mission (that is, without the use of the Berlin Plus formula which allowed the Union to act under NATO auspices), and the first time an EU mission had been deployed outside Europe.

ESDP has thus become an operational reality, and it did so at the very moment that intra-European divisions seemed more profound and bitter than ever. Yet, at the same time, the member states were, in the wake of the Iraq crisis, forced to confront head-on the various wrangles that had, before 2003, threatened to undermine its effectiveness.

The EU and NATO

Perhaps most clearly in this regard, Iraq forced the member states to address the issue of the relationship between the EU and NATO. Clearly, the Iraq crisis had intensified debate on this point, related, as it is, to the broader question of relations between the Union and the US. At a series of bilateral and trilateral meetings involving the British, French and Germans, attempts were made, in the context of the IGC that had, in September 2003, succeeded the Convention on the Future of Europe, to secure consensus, or at least agreement, on a text on defence. Some progress was made at an informal trilateral summit of Heads of State and Government in Berlin in September 2003, with Tony Blair agreeing on the need for the creation of an EU Headquarters and acceding to the notion of 'structured cooperation', on condition that all member states enjoy a veto over EU military operations (*Financial Times*, 22 September 2003; *EUobserver* 16 October 2003). Washington reacted angrily to what were seen as unnecessary concessions made by Tony Blair over the issue of structured cooperation, with the American Ambassador to NATO, Nicholas Burns, claiming that developments in ESDP represented the 'most serious threat to the future of NATO' (*International Herald Tribune*, 17 October 2003). The British Prime Minister's willingness to compromise, however, was matched by a softening of German rhetoric, with Foreign Minister Joschka Fischer appearing to back away from the more ambitious position his country had adopted at the mini-summit of April: 'I do not believe you need another big operational headquarters such as SHAPE. You have a NATO planning headquarters and there are [military planning] headquarters in Britain, France, and Germany' (*Financial Times*, 13 November 2003).

Discussions in early November made further advances, emphasising that capabilities and interoperability should be the relevant criteria for involvement in ESDP initiatives rather than simply a political desire to participate. This had been the case with the 'chocolate summit', which had seemed to privilege political aspirations for European integration in the defence sphere over military capabilities as a criterion for participation (*Financial Times*, 12 and 13 November 2003; *Guardian*, 25 November 2003). Final agreement came a step closer at a further meeting between Blair, Chirac and Schröder on 28 November at which the three leaders agreed on the need for the creation of at least an embryonic EU military planning capability (*Financial Times*, 26 and 28 November 2003). The meeting also provided the basis for broad agreement between Foreign Ministers meeting in Naples later that week (though the British were embarrassed when it transpired that *Le Monde* had leaked details of the agreement before they had had the chance to consult with Washington over the details) (*International Herald Tribune*, 29 November 2003).[3] On the Thursday before the European Council meeting scheduled to sign up to the new constitutional treaty, agreement was finally reached between the three large member states on a text (*Independent*, 12 December 2003; *Financial Times*, 12 December 2003). The following day, the summit itself signed up to the deal.

Under the terms of the final agreement, the member states agreed on the creation of a permanent civilian/military cell with a staff of around thirty to carry out strategic advanced planning on civilian/military issues. From this, an *ad hoc* operations centre could be set up to plan and run an autonomous EU operation (*Financial Times*, 12 December 2003; *International Herald Tribune*, 23 December 2003; Interviews, London, March 2004). The cell was established in January 2005 within the existing European Union military staff in Brussels, whose task is to advise the European Council on strategic developments. SHAPE has a liaison mission to it, and, reciprocally, a small EU liaison cell has been created in SHAPE, whose international staff continues to have the responsibility for planning Europe's NATO-assisted (Berlin Plus) operations.

Crucially, the outcome of the long and tortuous negotiation process was one that is closer to British preferences for an EU military capability closely tied to NATO structures than it is to the more 'autonomous' vision of ESDP propounded by the four in Brussels the previous April. The Council paper is clear that what was to be created was not a standing headquarters – as had been planned for Tervuren – but, rather, a capacity to generate an operations centre for a particular task. The main option for running autonomous EU military operations, therefore, would remain national headquarters. As one senior British official commented, 'We've put a British stamp on this in a way that does not undermine NATO' (*Financial Times*, 11 December 2003). In particular, by stressing capabilities as opposed to political will as the determinant of participation, London succeeded in limiting the 'ideological' aspect of

ESDP. Thus, European Council approval would be necessary for the initiation of structured cooperation, with membership dependent on the fulfilment of certain military criteria – notably an ability to mobilise, by 2007, in between five and thirty days, an intervention force capable of being deployed for 120 days.

Publicly voiced American concerns notwithstanding, the experience of the crisis over Iraq had had the effect of reinforcing the position of pro-NATO member states in the negotiation process. In discussions immediately following the cessation of hostilities in the Gulf, the negative reaction spawned amongst the EU-25 by the ill-fated mini summit of 29 April undermined the position of the four. The majority of the twenty-five[4] expressed hostility to the initiative, not least the impression given by its timing that it was an attempt to build ESDP on the basis of opposition to the US. Consequently, their room for manoeuvre in pressing for a model of ESDP more autonomous of NATO was considerably restricted. In a parallel set of negotiations over the Union's security strategy, the UK, backed by the EU candidate countries, secured a further victory. More prominence was in fact given in the final text to NATO (not mentioned in early drafts) and the relationship with the US than had been the case in the initial text of the document produced in April (*Financial Times* 4 December 2003).

The nature of EU security policies
The Iraq crisis also proved important in terms of helping to resolve the ongoing debate within the Union concerning the most appropriate form that EU security policies should take. For one thing, and reinforced by parallel developments in the EU's relationship with NATO, practical discussions on ESDP came to focus more on capabilities than political ambitions. The idea of an EU military capacity intended for relatively small-scale missions – though enjoying the necessary capabilities for these – was reinforced by discussions early in 2004 on the idea of battle groups, first raised at the Franco-British bilateral summit of November 2003 (*Guardian*, 25 November 2003). The idea was for units consisting of 1500 troops, capable of being deployed within fifteen days and of operating under a UN mandate. Missions would last up to thirty days and be 'appropriate for, but not limited to, use in failed or failing states, (of which most are in Africa)'. London and Paris announced that they hoped the plan would be accepted by all member states by the end of June, and implemented by 2007 (*Financial Times*, 9 February 2004). The following day, Berlin announced its support for the initiative (*Financial Times*, 10 February 2004). Again, in contrast to the political underpinnings of attendance at the April summit, participation in battle groups was based on interoperability, with the 'overriding' criterion for joining being military effectiveness (*Financial Times*, 9 February 2004).

In addition, the 'war on terrorism', and particularly the Iraq crisis have helped clarify ongoing debates about the relative utility of 'soft' and 'hard' power. For one thing, the Scandinavian states have become more supportive of the idea of the Union taking on an explicitly military vocation. The terrorist attacks of September 2001 in the US altered Norwegian attitudes towards EU defence cooperation, with 69 per cent of respondents in a poll carried out in 2002 supporting the idea of Norwegian participation in ESDP (*EUobserver*, 3 June 2002). At the same time, both Sweden and Finland have come to look more favourably upon the development of an EU military capability. In a joint article in the Swedish daily *Dagens Nyheter*, the two Foreign Ministers (Laila Freivalds for Sweden and Erkki Tuomioja for Finland) declared that they were 'prepared to study proposals to strengthen the EU common foreign and security policy'. Certainly, there were still limits to such support – the two states maintained (and continue to maintain) their opposition to either structured cooperation or a security guarantee. Yet both now emphasise their interest in seeing the EU develop the full gamut of security policy tools, including a defence capability (*EUobserver*, 12 November 2003, 8 and 9 December 2003).

The Iraq war has thus convinced some previously sceptical European states about the utility of an EU military capability. More broadly, the crisis convinced the member states of the need for a more 'muscular' approach to security affairs, reflected only a matter of weeks after the end of the conflict as EU Foreign Ministers, for the first time, held discussions about the threat posed by weapons of mass destruction (*Financial Times*, 13 April 2003; *EUobserver*, 15 April 2003). Meeting in June, they agreed on a declaration on weapons of mass destruction which included the phrase: 'in case political and diplomatic measures have failed, coercive measures, including as a last resort, the use of force in according with the United Nations Charter will be considered' (*Financial Times*, 15 June 2003; *International Herald Tribune* 17 June 2003). Conversely, the member states also increasingly came to recognise that security implied far more than simply force and coercion. Experience in Iraq and Afghanistan served to illustrate not only the utility of non-military security tools, but also the need for coordinated use of hard and soft tools, raising the necessity for the Union to address the fundamental question of the nature of the security policies it wishes to pursue. The clearest illustration of the emergence of a new and explicit consensus about the various strands of EU security policy aspirations was provided by the drafting and subsequent approval – at the Brussels summit of December 2003 – of an EU security strategy. As the Director of the EU's Institute for Security Studies has written:

> Before Iraq, raising the question of a European strategic concept amounted to either heresy or utopianism: among the Fifteen a combination of indifference, deference towards the US and national preference jeopardised the very idea of the EU having its own security concept. Since Iraq, all members of the enlarged Union of 25 are enthusiastically involved in drawing up a common vision of the world and also an agreed strategy on the Union's actions in it. (Gnesotto 2003: 21)

Not only was the 'common vision' drawn up reflecting a renewed determination on the part of the member states to ensure EU effectiveness in the security policy domain, but it arguably presented a less ambitious vision of the Union's security ambitions than had earlier drafts, with its emphasis on 'effective multilateralism' (European Council 2003). In this sense, the document mirrored a general tendency. As one informed observer has put it: 'It is striking that whereas the rhetoric in the EU only three years ago was couched, at least by implication, in terms of power projection ... and the use or threat of force for political objectives, it is now all about crisis management and conflict prevention' (Crowe 2003: 540).

In combination with the more explicit reliance on NATO, the current direction taken by EU security policies is inherently realistic. The Union is not an appropriate forum for the large-scale deployment of military forces (Menon 2002, 2003). In this sense, criticisms of Union inactivity in the Balkans and Iraq were misplaced in that ESDP was never going to be equipped to play a role in major conflicts of this kind. However, it does require the ability to supplement its undoubted strengths as a soft security actor with minimal military capabilities, in order to ensure the prospect of successful small-scale interventions along the lines of Macedonia or the Congo. Developments in the early part of the twenty-first century provide grounds for optimism that a more pragmatic approach than was implied by much of the exaggerated rhetoric of the past has been adopted.

Leadership

Finally, there are signs that the Iraq war has altered attitudes towards attempts on the part of the three largest EU member states to play a leading role in the formulation of ESDP. As illustrated above, such attempts had spawned concern amongst the other member states about the possible creation of a directorate. Yet no sooner had conflict in the Gulf ended then the larger member states started to work together closely in order to try to reconcile the differences between them, which had led to such public and damaging disagreements during the crisis itself. At the Athens European Council meeting held in April 2003, negotiations between British, French, German and Spanish representatives preceded the formal meeting in an attempt to reach agreement on the text of a declaration (*Le Monde*, 17 April 2003). As discussions over the constitutional treaty gathered pace, Berlin, London and Paris, as we have seen, kept up a dialogue in an attempt to resolve their differences over the defence dossier.

Crucially, shifting attitudes following the Iraq crisis altered the perception of such activity on the part of those member states not included within it. When it became clear, in December 2003, that London, Paris, and Berlin intended to work together closely on security matters, the dominant reaction was one of relief in that the other member states perceived this as a way of avoiding further damaging splits within the Union (*Financial Times*, 29

January 2004). The sheer bitterness of the divergences between the big three over Iraq had led to a realisation that consensus between them was necessary in order that EU external policies function effectively. As a Dutch diplomat put it: 'If Britain, France, and Germany can work together to make Europe stronger and more coherent, we could have a stronger security doctrine' (*Financial Times*, 4 December 2003).

Moreover, a further incentive for many member states to support trilateralism was their unease, particularly since the Iraqi crisis, about Franco-German leadership within the Union. Partly, this stemmed from the total disregard shown by Paris and Berlin, in November 2003, for the rules of the stability pact, which incited an angry reaction on the part of the other member states. One EU diplomat commented acidly that there 'is a real distrust now, especially with France and Germany' (*Financial Times*, 26 November 2003). Partly, too, the partnership between Paris and Berlin had lost legitimacy because of their actions during the Iraq crisis, and particularly the 'chocolate' summit. Hence, British participation in trilateral discussion was widely viewed as reassuring by many of the other member states (Interview, Brussels, February 2004).

Certainly, trilateralism will have to be handled sensitively. Attempts to use it as a way of exercising leadership across all issue areas will provoke only hostility, as illustrated by the tripartite summit of mid-February 2004, which focused on economic policy. It is also, moreover, necessary to distinguish between consultation and consensus between the three on security matters, which are now generally accepted as necessary and desirable in order to avoid future public disagreements and ensure progress in the implementation of ESDP, and efforts on their part to create a position of institutionalised leadership for themselves, which is not. Yet, as long as the issue is handled sensitively, there is arguably now greater scope for leadership by London, Paris and Berlin than was previously the case. Given the superiority of their military forces, such a situation can only help in rendering ESDP more effective in the future.

Thus, whilst the Iraq war undeniably drove a wedge between EU member states, its medium-term effects for ESDP were, in the main, both transitory and possibly even salutary. The eagerness with which commentators rushed to proclaim the death of the Union's security policy ambitions during the Iraq crisis notwithstanding, it is distinctly possible that EU defence policies will emerge strengthened from the conflict.

Conclusions

There are striking parallels between the ways in which the Union reacted to the crises in the Balkans and the Gulf. Its inactivity during each of them spawned a period of reflection amongst the member states, which in turn led to a period of increased activity in equipping the EU to play a greater role in defence matters. Crises have therefore had, in recent times, a salutary medium-term effect on EU defence policy aspirations if only, as in the case of the war with Iraq, in terms of limiting previously inflated expectations. It is impossible to imagine Saint-Malo without the Balkans, or the EU's security strategy without Iraq. More broadly, it is interesting to ponder the extent to which European integration as a whole has been driven by crisis; both the creation of the Single Market and the move towards the Euro can be explained in these terms.

Certainly, all manner of potential pitfalls lie in the way of a successful ESDP, not least the need for continued political will on the part of the member states to bring this about. However, this chapter has argued that crises have served both to launch and to re-launch ESDP. As things stand, the Union has accepted the need for its defence policies to be closely linked to NATO, and has rejected the more ambitious aspirations of some of its member states. Broad agreement on a more limited ESDP has thus sidestepped the potential for disagreements over ambitions undermining the policy altogether. Yet again, it would seem, the Union has shown an ability to make an opportunity out of adversity.

Notes

1 'Last Monday we were getting somewhere with the [second resolution]. We very nearly had majority agreement ... Then, on Monday night, France said it would veto a second resolution whatever the circumstances ... Not just opposed. Vetoed. Blocked. The tragedy is that had such a Resolution been issued, he might just have complied' (Prime Minister's statement opening the Iraq debate: www.number-10.gov.uk/output/Page3294.asp).
2 Altogether twenty-seven countries were involved in the mission, their soldiers wearing national uniforms with insignia bearing the letters 'EU for' and badges with the European colours – blue with gold stars – on the right shoulder.
3 One EU official remarked caustically to the author that London was embarrassed by not being able to 'seek permission' from Washington before details of the deal were leaked (Interview, Brussels, December 2003).
4 British officials speak of twenty states, i.e. all those member states that did not participate in the 'chocolate summit' (Interviews, London, December 2003, March 2004).

FRANCIS K. ABIEW

5

Kosovo, Iraq and the evolution of the theory and practice of humanitarian intervention

Introduction

Post-Cold War developments, and in particular the intervention in Kosovo by NATO, have rekindled the debate surrounding military interventions to protect human rights. Such debates generally suggest a gradual change in attitudes and challenges to the principles of state sovereignty and non-intervention in the domestic affairs of states.[1] The fact that absolute notions of sovereignty are no longer defensible is increasingly becoming evident (Independent Commission on International Humanitarian Issues 1988; Abiew 1999). Sovereignty is and will remain a central pillar in international relations, but as Nanda (1992: 38) remarks, 'to insist on adherence to its absolute dimensions flies in the face of international realities'. The conclusions of a 1991 international conference on human rights protection for internally displaced persons are that sovereignty confers responsibility on governments to protect the inhabitants of their territories. Failure to meet those obligations means that governments risk undermining their legitimacy (Refugee Policy Group 1991; Arnison 1993; Caney 1997). In essence, there is the tendency to restore notions of responsibility to state sovereignty (Deng 1995). When human rights violations that cause outrage in the international community occur, outside intervention is often one of the most important tools that can be employed to halt these tragedies. Yet it remains unclear whether the international community will support such action in every case.

The trend towards collective intervention in the post-Cold War era has not been without controversy. In light of the varying international responses to various humanitarian tragedies, the debate surrounding the legitimacy of humanitarian intervention continues unabated. In the 1990s, Adam Roberts (1993a: 429) posed two important questions:

- Is humanitarian involvement in conflicts – in the form of provision of food, shelter, and protection, under international auspices – a step on a ladder, which can or should lead to much more direct military involvement, even to participation in hostilities?
- Can we conclude from recent and contemporary practice that a new consensus is emerging on humanitarian intervention, that is, military intervention in a state, without the approval of its authorities, and with the purpose of preventing widespread suffering or death among the inhabitants?

It is in this context that differing views emerge. Some observers argue that a significant change is under way which is creating precedents in support of humanitarian interventions. Others maintain that collective actions are not to be expected under United Nations Security Council (UNSC) authorisation in every instance. Yet still, some contend that this is a special period and is unlikely to continue in the future. This chapter assesses contemporary developments in the principle and practice of humanitarian interventions in the post-Cold War period and argues that a notable shift seems to be under way.

Assessment of post-Cold War practice by legal scholars

Recent practice seems to suggest that there is a shift in the willingness to undertake action that has implications for both humanitarian intervention and sovereignty. Humanitarian crises resulting either from governmental acts or internal conflict have become amenable to outside intervention. These cases, as Damrosch (1993b: 105) suggests, are evidence of 'a newly emerging consensus that the Security Council's enforcement powers may be invoked in purely domestic situation[s]'.[2] First, according to these emerging principles, massive or widespread violations of human rights or humanitarian law arising from governmental acts or internal conflicts, and the human suffering that they engender, can constitute a threat to peace and security that the UNSC need no longer ignore. These matters, in other words, do not fall solely within the domestic domain of states. The UNSC, in these situations, can respond appropriately, even authorising the use of force, grounded in Chapter VII of the United Nations Charter for the protection of humanitarian relief operations and the creation of a secure environment for such operations. Second, abandonment of victims of man-made or natural disasters, especially the deliberate withholding or impeding of food and medical supplies necessary for survival of civilians trapped in the throes of internal conflict, constitutes a threat to human life, and ultimately peace and security. In these situations, necessary measures including force can be used to get much-needed humanitarian relief supplies to such victims. Third, states have a duty to support international organisations or humanitarian organisations working to provide humanitarian assistance to the victims of complex emergencies. Fourth, state sovereignty will not prohibit action to protect and sustain the lives of large numbers of civilians trapped in situations of internal conflict. Along with these new principles in support of intervention is the principle of individual responsibility for war crimes, and grave breaches of international humanitarian law, including interference with humanitarian assistance.[3]

International responses to the various humanitarian tragedies have, however, been less consistent than these principles might suggest. For some, this casts doubts on the legitimacy of humanitarian interventions. Nonetheless, the various responses have been grounded in the principle that massive human rights deprivations do constitute a threat to peace and security either through trans-boundary refugee flows or the spread of internal strife across borders. On this basis, international action, including the use of force, has been held to be legitimate. The euphoria generated in the aftermath of the Gulf War did eventually subside and was replaced with the expression of frustrations and disillusionment by the mid-1990s in the wake of the failure to take vigorous international action to deal with humanitarian crises. Even though this era is still unfolding, it would seem nevertheless important that emerging international principles and practices be sorted out, if only to serve as signposts for the future.

Various actors and writers have sought to interpret these trends. First, an increasing number of scholars view these developments as establishing the right to intervene for humanitarian purposes, thus creating significant precedents (Weiss 1994a; Falk 1996; Tesón 1996; Wheeler and Morris 1996). Scheffer (1993) interestingly summarises the new sense of urgency with regard to the need for international response by stating that a new standard of intolerance regarding the violation of human rights has taken hold. He argues that sovereignty and non-intervention cannot take precedence over the collective human rights of people whose lives are at risk. To ignore this new reality is to ignore the march of history. Similarly, Greenwood (1993: 40) has noted: 'It is no longer tenable to assert that whenever a government massacres its own people or a state collapses into international anarchy international law forbids military intervention altogether.' Finally, even a realist such as Hoffmann (1995/6) argues that military intervention is justified when domestic unrest and massive abuse of human rights threatens regional or international security.

Opponents of humanitarian intervention are, however, sceptical. They insist that sovereign states and their prerogatives remain fundamental even when humanitarian issues arise. Donnelly (1993), for instance, suggests we should not expect the imminent emergence of an international practice of humanitarian intervention. Others (e.g. Roberts 1993a; Booth 1995) have also expressed doubts and concerns about the viability of humanitarian intervention as a mechanism for enforcement of the will of the international community. Some (e.g. Ayoob 1995) even argue that humanitarian interventions may be counterproductive and selective, casting doubts about the real motives of interveners. However, as Whitman (1994: 167) argues, 'the deployment of military forces abroad is always founded on a hard-headed calculation of risk, and there is nothing to preclude humanitarian objectives on an agenda framed by more determinedly self-interested motivation'. If states conduct their affairs based on national interest, then the trends in post-Cold War humanitarian interventions can be explained on the basis that national interest is being redefined in such a way that humanitarian crises cannot be ignored, since they affect all nations. This is especially evident when humanitarian tragedies result in wider regional conflicts, and when the flow of refugees destabilises states, as in the Kosovo crisis. Thus, states have begun to redefine national interests more broadly, and in ways that acknowledge the relationship between humanitarian crises, and national, political, and economic security. Instances of less consistent responses or the selection bias in these cases of intervention can be explained by the assignment of various priorities to other interests at any particular time.

Attitudes of states

Not all states are supportive of an active international interventionist stance. International support has been forthcoming mainly from Western states. At the outset of the Clinton administration, a policy of 'assertive multilateralism' was proclaimed. This policy sought a US–UN cooperation in addressing intractable global problems. The then representative to the UN, Madeleine Albright (1993), outlined the relationship that the US would forge in the UN. She noted the fusion of peacekeeping and peace-enforcement operations with the delivery of humanitarian assistance, as examples of what the US would support. The US experience in Somalia, however, resulted in the passage of 'Presidential Decision Directive 25' (PDD 25) which represented the first comprehensive framework for US decision-making on issues of peacekeeping and peace-enforcement in the post-Cold War period. PDD 25, which stated that peace operations were not and could not be at the centre of US foreign policy, had implications for ruling out the deployment of ground troops in Bosnia until the Dayton Accords, the refusal to act in Rwanda, and hesitation about intervention in Haiti. With its involvement in Haiti and in Bosnia, the US sought to define new forms of participation in global conflict management, which Blechman (1996: 287) described as 'combining UN peace operations with parallel, but separately managed, multilateral interventions'.[4] In Kosovo, the US emphasised the aims of the campaign as that of expelling Serb forces from Kosovo, and the deployment of an international security force into the province, thus enabling the refugees from Kosovo and the internally displaced to return to their homes. With regard to NATO action, the US asserted that the UN affirmation of a threat to peace and security in the region and concern for the humanitarian situation were sufficient grounds for intervention. For President Clinton, the US 'act[ed] to protect thousands of innocent people' and 'prevent[ed] a wider war' (quoted in Egan 2001). Although US foreign policy was not very consistent, characterised as it was by a range of responses from doing something to doing very little, this multilateral approach in using international institutions has been beneficial in terms of capacity for dealing with humanitarian problems.

Following the intervention in Northern Iraq, former British Foreign Secretary Douglas Hurd proclaimed that 'recent international law recognises the right to intervene in the affairs of another state in cases of extreme humanitarian need' (*Guardian*, 20 August 1992). Britain has thereafter consistently supported UNSC resolutions dealing with various humanitarian crises. In October 1998, when it appeared that military action in Kosovo was imminent, the British Foreign and Commonwealth Office in a note to allied governments pointed out that UNSC authorisation to use force for humanitarian purposes is now widely accepted and that a UNSC resolution would give a legal base for NATO action. The note further suggested: 'Force can also be justified on the grounds of overwhelming humanitarian necessity without a UNSC Resolution' (quoted in Roberts 1999/2000: 12). Thus, in the British view, if action through the UNSC were not possible, NATO intervention would be lawful on grounds of overwhelming humanitarian necessity.

France has been at the forefront of those countries which have argued in favour of 'the right and duty' of humanitarian intervention (Sandoz 1992; Torrelli 1992; Garigue 1993; Guillot 1994; Bowring 1995). In a speech in 1991, President François Mitterand stated: 'France has taken the initiative of this new right, rather extraordinary in the history of the world, which is in a way the right of intervention within a country, when part of its population is a victim of persecution' (quoted in Bettati 1992: 5). Humanitarian issues have thus become a major theme of French diplomacy.[5] It is therefore not surprising that given the context of collective efforts aimed at alleviating human misery and suffering, France has been actively involved in UN humanitarian operations in the post-Cold War period. Recognising the gravity of the Kosovo crisis and disappointment with various diplomatic efforts aimed at finding a solution, France supported the call for the use of force by NATO, although it had reservations about whether it was appropriate to dispense with UNSC authorisation. Macleod's chapter in this book notes the French insistence that the NATO intervention be construed as an exception and not precedent-setting. Italy favours the idea that human rights protection must take precedence over state sovereignty. As shown more in detail by Croci's chapter in this book, for the Italian government, however, the use of force for humanitarian purposes requires the development of clear, realistic, and widely accepted criteria.

Appalled by the response to the Rwandan genocide, the Danish Foreign

Ministry convened a study group to evaluate emergency assistance, which resulted in a five-volume report (*The International Response to Conflict and Genocide: Lessons from the Rwanda Experience*) that Hindell (1996) characterises as essentially an interventionist manifesto. Thus in the context of the Kosovo crisis, Denmark did not hesitate to issue threats against the Federal Republic of Yugoslavia, and subsequently contributed troops towards NATO military intervention (Møller 2000). Both Germany and Belgium expressed similar sentiments and played an active role in the Kosovo crisis. Hans-Dietrich Genscher, the former German Foreign Minister, in a speech at the UN General Assembly, expressed Germany's conviction that 'where human rights are trampled upon, the family of nations cannot be confined to a role of spectator'. The Belgian Foreign Minister, for his part, declared: 'The international community should help states to respect human rights and to force them to do so, if necessary' (Møller 2000). This statement emphasises the idea that governments must be held accountable for the human rights violations of their citizens. Thus, forcible measures should, if necessary, be employed in extreme situations. Indeed, in Kosovo, Belgium's support for military intervention was based primarily on humanitarian grounds even if the proximity of the crisis and fears of it spreading were also mentioned as justifications (Haglund and Sens 2000). The Dutch ambassador to the UN acknowledged that his government preferred action based on a specific USC resolution regarding the use of force to protect human rights. Nevertheless, he added, if due to 'one or two members' rigid interpretation of the domestic jurisdiction clause such a resolution is not attainable, we will not sit back and simply let the humanitarian catastrophe occur ... we will act on the legal basis we have available, and what we have available in this case is more than adequate' (cited in Wheeler 2000a: 153).

The Canadian government laid the foundation for a significantly different approach in dealing with sovereignty, internal conflicts, and human rights violations abroad. Former Canadian Prime Minister Brian Mulroney suggested that it is unacceptable for the international community to ignore violence and repression within national borders (Gillies 1993). Canada supported NATO use of force in Kosovo. Former Canadian Foreign Minister, Lloyd Axworthy, for instance, was one of those Haglund and Sens (2000) have characterised as 'the vanguard of the humanitarian hawks' while the Canadian Ambassador to the UN claimed: 'Humanitarian considerations underpin our action. We cannot simply stand by while innocents are murdered, an entire population is displaced, and villages are burned' (cited in Wheeler 2000a: 153). Canada's role in the air campaign was comparable to that of Britain and France. Such activism was not, however, without controversy (Keating and Gammer 1993; Department of Foreign Affairs and International Trade and the Department of National Defence 1995; Haglund and Sens 2000). Justifications provided by other NATO countries similarly cited concern for regional stability, reference to UNSC resolutions, and the grave humanitarian situation in Kosovo as providing legitimate reasons for the use of force.

Opposition to humanitarian intervention has mainly come from states in the South. Many of them are sceptical of the motives of Western countries in advocating humanitarian intervention. Furthermore, concerns have been expressed about the expanding definition of 'international peace and security' by the UNSC (Weiss 1994b: 240). The ever-increasing powers of the UNSC have created some apprehension among Southern states. They fear becoming subject to, in the words of Dallmeyer (1995: 20), a 'hegemonic directorate'. Nafziger (1994: 230–1) has described it as 'the spectre of a modern Holy Alliance of the Great Powers' that could dispense with the principle that the basis for UN action in a state's domestic affairs must be subject to that state's consent. Some Southern states have thus argued that the General Assembly should maintain a greater involvement in decision-making processes regarding humanitarian intervention lest the UN become dominated by the major powers using it for their own ends. In essence, these states view international intervention with suspicion and fear.

Attitudes of IGOs

International governmental organisations (IGOs) have also played a role in opening the door to a more vigorous approach to humanitarian interventions. Within institutional secretariats, former UN Secretary-General Boutros Boutros-Ghali (1992) argued that the time of absolute and exclusive sovereignty had passed. His successor Kofi Annan pointed to the 'universal sense of outrage' provoked by the Milošević regime in Kosovo and stated that 'emerging slowly, but I believe surely, is an international norm against the violent repression of minorities that will and must take precedence over concerns of sovereignty'. For him, 'the UN Charter was there to protect individual human beings, not to protect those who abuse them'.[6] Similarly, Jan Eliasson (1995: 492–3), then Undersecretary-General of the UN Department of Humanitarian Affairs stated: 'The concept that solidarity does not end automatically at a border but rather with a human being in need has broken through in the humanitarian area.' About the definition of conditions under which humanitarian intervention could be undertaken, he writes:

> In interviews with representatives of member states at the United Nations and in discussions at various seminars, there is no objection to humanitarian intervention where there is overwhelming evidence that many people are starving and those involved in the conflict are deliberately preventing the international community from delivering humanitarian assistance to those who need it ... There is a consensus that under such conditions efforts must be made to overcome obstacles and to override the objections of the warring parties. There is also a consensus that these efforts should not be carried out unilaterally – either by

one country or a coalition of countries – but that such a situation should be brought to the attention of the international community to obtain a clear mandate for humanitarian intervention. (Cited in Jonah 1993: 70)

Thus, there appears to be a consensus supporting multilateral intervention in situations of extreme human rights deprivations and suffering.

International regional organisations have also been active regarding issues concerning humanitarian action. The Haitian problem helped the Organization of American States (OAS) overcome its reservations about what it regarded as interference in the domestic affairs of states. If the lessons of Haiti are anything to go by, then it seems the OAS will be prepared to take similar kinds of action in future, even if they fall short of the use of force where democratic rule – and the consequent violations of human rights – is truncated. The Somali tragedy has influenced the African Union in rethinking its approach to issues of sovereignty, human rights and intervention. The creation of the new African Union looks to the future and seems to signal an era of better governance on the continent.[7] It remains to be seen how the African Union will react to future cases involving egregious human rights violations.

It should also be pointed out that the UNSC authorised member states, 'acting nationally or through regional organisations', to enforce a no-fly zone over Bosnia, and to protect the Bosnian Muslims through the concept of safe havens. And that these actions were undertaken by NATO and the Western European Union. As Javier Solana, former NATO Secretary-General, pointed out, 'NATO helped bring the war to an end through its support over several years to the United Nations through its limited, but effective use of airpower'. Furthermore, 'not to meet the challenge of Bosnia would have been a profound failure of collective will and an abdication of moral responsibility by the entire international community' (Solana 1996). From this perspective, the situation in Kosovo resurrected the problems of Yugoslavia in a more vicious form. The Serb reaction to the terrorist activities of the Kosovo Liberation Army (KLA) produced significant civilian casualties and a flow of refugees and displaced persons. In this situation, NATO intervened in a bid to end the alleged atrocities against the Albanians of Kosovo and stop the flow of refugees. Justifying its use of force, NATO cited concern for regional stability and the humanitarian catastrophe, as well as UNSC resolutions, and argued that Yugoslavia's use of force against the civilian population of Kosovo was responsible for the crisis. In a press conference on 13 October 1998, NATO Secretary General, Javier Solana affirmed:

The unrestrained assault by Yugoslav military, police and paramilitary forces, under the direction of President Milošević, on Kosovar [sic][8] civilians has created a massive humanitarian catastrophe, which also threatens to destabilise the surrounding region ... These extreme and criminally irresponsible policies, which cannot be defended on any grounds, have made necessary and justify the military action. (Quoted in Egan 2001: 42)

In essence NATO argued that its action was both legal and morally justified since it was aimed at averting further humanitarian catastrophe, and was consistent with UNSC resolutions 1199 and 1203 which were made under Chapter VII of the UN Charter, which demanded that Serb forces end their violations of human rights in Kosovo.

NATO intervention essentially underlined the debate between universalism and regionalism in security matters, and the ambiguities involved in regional action when peace and security are threatened. The certain use of the veto in the UNSC by Russia, and possibly China, to kill any proposal for robust intervention, meant that the Council was unable to authorise NATO action explicitly even if a majority of its members were inclined to do so. This revived the *ius ad bellum* argument under the Charter, when the UNSC is unwilling or unable to act in situations of threats to international peace and security, as had often happened during the Cold War. The far-reaching implications of this development, as Wheeler (2000b: 159) aptly suggests, is that 'the limited prospects of the Security Council acting as a global posse means that enforcement of global human rights standards depends upon particular states acting on behalf of the society of states'.

Does action in Kosovo represent a watershed or create a precedent? Some commentators are of the view that this example is not a good one on which to base proposals for future action since explicit UNSC authorisation was not obtained. There is a sense that it is an exceptional case, not likely to be repeated in a hurry by NATO. Support may however be grounded in the approval by the UN of the Rambouillet accord. This agreement implicitly envisaged the possibility of enforcement action to stop the 'ethnic cleansing', and as McCoubrey (1999: 34–5) suggests, 'it may be thought that the United Nations has by implication embraced that possibility – and therefore actuality'. Moreover, 'the refusal of the Security Council to condemn the NATO action as unlawful when so requested by Russia may be seen as supporting this form of argument'. Furthermore, the Genocide Convention of 1948 states in article 1 that 'the Contracting Parties confirm that genocide, whether committed in time of peace or in time of war, is a crime under international law which they may undertake to prevent and to punish'. Thus, always according to McCoubrey, a strong case may be made that Serb policies in Kosovo did constitute genocide within the meaning of the Genocide Convention and therefore justified NATO action. The end result of NATO action was the return of Kosovo Albanian refugees, and the eventual fall from power of President Milošević, whose trial at the Hague International Criminal Tribunal for the Former Yugoslavia on charges of, among others, war crimes and crimes against humanity, represent a watershed in the accountability for such crimes by heads of state. In conclusion, the Kosovo intervention can be, and has been, justified on the basis of the customary international law right of the unilateral or collective use of force to end atrocities that incite the outrage of the international community.

The controversial US-led military intervention in Iraq has also raised, to a lesser extent, the justification of intervention on humanitarian grounds. In March 2003, a US-led force invaded Iraq with the stated objective of overthrowing the regime of Saddam Hussein. The major rationale for the invasion was that only regime change would provide the guarantee of disarming Iraq of its weapons of mass destruction. Furthermore, the Bush administration argued that the construction of a stable and democratic Iraq would promote reform and security in the Middle East at large. Having failed to secure the necessary support from France, China, and Russia – all permanent members of the UNSC – for an explicit resolution authorising the use of force, the US and Britain claimed authority for the action under the earlier UNSC resolution 1441, which at the time was the latest of numerous resolutions calling for Iraqi disarmament (Dobbins et al. 2003). Humanitarianism was one of the grounds, a comparatively minor one, on which the US-led coalition justified the Iraqi invasion after the fact. It is argued that since the Iraq war was not mainly about saving the Iraqi people from imminent or ongoing mass slaughter by the Iraqi government – such mass slaughters having happened, but a decade earlier – the invasion of Iraq cannot be justified on humanitarian grounds. Although Saddam Hussein's treatment of Iraq's citizens was deplorable, it might be argued that it did not rise to the threshold level 'shocking the conscience of the international community' or 'staggering the conscience of mankind' in the classical notion of the doctrine warranting the extraordinary response of military force. Humanitarian intervention must be guided primarily by a humanitarian purpose, or at least humanitarianism should be the dominant, or one of the dominant, reasons for military action. As Roth (2004: 13) poignantly notes: 'At a time of renewed interest in humanitarian intervention, the Iraq war and the effort to justify it even in part in humanitarian terms risk giving humanitarian intervention a bad name. If that breeds cynicism about the use of military force for humanitarian purposes, it could be devastating for people in need of future rescue.'

Attitudes of NGOs

Nongovernmental organisations (NGOs) are also becoming central to international responses to internal conflicts, performing important humanitarian tasks alongside other actors in the post-Cold War era. Their views on the use of force are thus becoming increasingly important. NGO support in using military forces in the complex humanitarian emergencies appears to be mixed. UN military actions have been the 'objects of a loud chorus of criticism or mixed messages from parts of the NGO community – some calling for military intervention one day and then castigating it the next' (Slim 1995). Some NGOs like Save the Children (1994) believe that the injection of UN military forces in humanitarian emergencies actually worsens the situation. In the former Yugoslavia, NGOs were initially hostile to the idea of armed protection for humanitarian convoys, but as the situation deteriorated, they accepted the idea (Guillot 1994). Other NGOs like the International Commission of the Red Cross argue that the use of force has a role to play in preventing massive violations of human rights (International Federation of Red Cross and Red Crescent Societies 1996). NGOs played a crucial role in the Kosovo crisis by exposing the killings and other human rights violations, and by communicating with decision-makers and lobbying governments in the West. Gaer (2000) argues that 'there were continuing demands from the NGO sector for international action' in light of evidence of atrocities by Serb forces in Kosovo. They lobbied Western governments and were instrumental in mounting pressure, which eventually led to NATO intervention. Albeit there were disagreements on the issue of whether to use force, Hermet (1995: 95) affirms that for NGOs the level of human suffering has come to mean that 'there could be no qualms about the methods used'.

Conclusions

A shift seems to be under way in terms of the principle and practice of humanitarian intervention in the post-Cold War era. There is the belief that state sovereignty connotes responsibility and cannot be used as a shield to perpetrate massive and systematic violations of human rights. Human rights have been a recurring normative theme in international relations. The Treaty of Westphalia, which introduced the idea of the sovereign authority of the state thus marking the inception of the modern international state system, as well as subsequent peace treaties, all contain significant clauses limiting sovereign prerogatives vis-à-vis the rights of populations inhabiting their territories. Post-1945 developments have also seen an elaborate international human rights regime from the UN Charter, and the Universal Declaration of Human Rights, to the 1966 UN Covenants on Human Rights, the Genocide Convention, and beyond. These documents spell out responsibilities of governments toward their citizens in terms of promoting and protecting their human rights. The Commission on Global Governance (1995) has acknowledged that global security extends beyond the protection of borders, ruling elites, and exclusive state interests to include the protection of people.

These policies and practices suggest adherence by governments to certain principles in their domestic practices. Interventions to protect human rights should thus not be seen as incompatible with state sovereignty but rather affirming it. Support for humanitarian intervention is on the rise among scholars, states (to a lesser degree among Southern states), in IGOs' institutional secretariats, and, so it seems, in the NGO community, at least in cases of intense violence and human suffering. The trend, however, is still unfolding, and if the international community should move towards an entrenched notion of humanitarian intervention, the UN can use recent cases to provide a framework for laying down some general principles or guidelines on when an internal situation warrants international action, either through authorisation by the UNSC or regional organisations. It is apparent that although support for humanitarian intervention is gaining currency, various actors are still opposed to its use. Getting closer to an international consensus will require a clear articulation of principles to further enhance issues of legitimacy. To this end, some analysts have proposed that the UNSC and the General Assembly jointly adopt a standard operating procedure for humanitarian intervention.[9] Concerns in the aftermath of the debate over the Kosovo War have led the Secretary-General of the UN to make compelling pleas at the General Assembly in 1999, and again in 2000, to the international community to try to forge consensus on an agreed doctrine of humanitarian intervention. He asked:

> If humanitarian intervention is, indeed, an unacceptable assault on sovereignty, how should we respond to a Rwanda, to a Srebrenica – to gross and systematic violations of human rights that affect every precept of our common humanity? (Cited in International Commission on Intervention and State Sovereignty 2001: vii)

The Canadian government took up this challenge by sponsoring an 'International Commission on Intervention and State Sovereignty' to deal with the whole range of issues posed by interventions to protect human rights. The Commission's work, after consultations with the widest possible range of actors around the world, resulted in the production of a report (International Commission on Intervention and State Sovereignty 2001) that would form the basis of further debate at the UN. At the very least, some kind of general declaration or statement analogous to those contained in the 'Copenhagen Document'[10], for instance, would be appropriate and represent significant progress towards finding some common ground on these issues. While international consensus, understood not necessarily to mean unanimity, but eliciting the widest possible support to bring this about, will be a difficult undertaking given the resistance of some Southern states in such matters, it is nevertheless worth exploring.

In the absence of specific criteria that guide the UN, or regional organisations, or the community of states to intervene for humanitarian purposes, it is incumbent, especially in the aftermath of Kosovo and to a lesser extent Iraq, to set out criteria along with the development of the means and will to intervene in all, or most, of the situations that may occur. The conditions that would justify intervention to protect human rights have been enumerated in various scholarly works, which deal with substantive and procedural issues and are considered either absolute or preferential prerequisites (e.g. Lillich 1967; Fonteyne 1974; Annan 1999; Wheeler 2000b). The aim will be to reduce the dangers of abuse by enunciating a standard against which to judge humanitarian interventions.

The Kosovo crisis revealed the extent to which there is still disagreement surrounding humanitarian intervention. Within NATO, efforts to develop an agreed-upon doctrine are largely in abeyance, especially given the disagreement between the US and the European members. The refusal to commit ground troops during the Kosovo crisis and the general unwillingness of the US to risk lives, because of the 'Somalia syndrome', where egregious human rights violations situations call for intervention, might present a problem for the future. In the same vein, the absence of an international consensus on the criteria for such interventions means that governments can abuse the concept, as the US has done with its ex-post-facto efforts to justify the Iraq war. The one rallying factor should a situation reminiscent of Kosovo happen in the future, will be the need for action based on the threat to regional peace and security. The nature of increasing support around post-Cold War humanitarian interventions presents an opportunity to push forward the idea of codification. This undertaking is worth pursuing if the international community should build upon the present practice of humanitarian intervention for the future.

Notes

1. This is, however, not to suggest that state sovereignty and non-intervention are no longer important norms in international relations. They still are. After a comprehensive review of recent cases Damrosch, for instance, concludes: 'Instead of characterizing interventions in internal conflicts as presumptively illegitimate, the trend now is to take seriously the claim that the international community ought to intervene to prevent bloodshed with whatever means are available' (Damrosch 1993a: 364).
2. See also Rodley (1992). Donnelly (1993: 639–40) argues that 'human rights are ultimately a profoundly *national* – not international – issue' (original emphasis).
3. Falk (1996: 493), for instance, notes the 'emergence of a highly articulated international law of human rights, reinforced psychologically by ideas about government and individual accountability for their gross violation'.
4. For a detailed explanation of why the US hesitated in taking on the leadership role promised by the rhetoric of the new world order, see Daalder (1996).
5. France was responsible for the origins of the UN General Assembly Resolution A/RES/46/182 (1991), requesting the UN Secretary-General to establish the position of an emergency assistance coordinator to work with governments and insurgents to provide more effective humanitarian assistance. This ultimately led to the creation of the United Nations Department of Humanitarian Affairs in early 1992.
6. UN Press Release, 20 September 1999.
7. For details of the constitutive treaty of the new African Union created in July 2002, see www.au2002.gov.za.
8. It should be noted, that the use of term 'Kosovar' to refer only to Albanians from Kosovo was part of the KLA effort to depict the region as entirely Albanian.
9. According to Roberts (1993b: 11) 'one might even say that if a coherent philosophy and practice of humanitarian intervention could be developed, it could have the potential to save the non-intervention rule from its own logical absurdities and occasional inhumanities'. See also Nafziger (1994).
10. The 1990 Document of the Copenhagen Meeting of the Conference on the Human Dimension of the Conference on Security and Cooperation in Europe contained references to circumstances that should trigger action by the signatories.

LENARD J. COHEN

6

Managing multilateralism? EU–US relations and the challenges of regime building in South-eastern Europe

> Bosnia was a moral crucible for many people ... Europeans must bring force to the table. Money – as in the provision of aid is not enough, nor the most important thing. The ability to commit substantial force is. The posture of doing the aid while the US does the fighting is not sustainable ... We have a European policy in the Balkans, and that is quite impressive. We will stay in the Balkans: the cost is going down – we must give them a sense of a common future. (Robert Cooper, EU Director-General for CFSP – November 2003)

> [Concordia] was a modest mission but it played an important role in the future stabilisation of Macedonia. It was also an exceptional laboratory for other missions ... In Macedonia we cooperated very smoothly with NATO. This is also a good partnership between the United States and the European Union. The United States and the Union have the same agenda, the same objectives for the country, and that facilitates cooperation ... It was in fact more difficult to coordinate European players in a crisis situation than to coordinate with NATO or with the Americans. (Alexis Brouhns, Special EU Envoy in Macedonia – December 2003)

The Balkan region is an important testing ground both for European foreign policy and for transatlantic relations. For example, the 'European Security Strategy' adopted by the European Council in December 2003, proclaims that it is because of the EU's 'concerted efforts with the United States, Russia, the North Atlantic Treaty Organisation, and other international partners, [that] the stability of the [Balkan] region is no longer threatened by the outbreak of major conflict'. 'The credibility of our foreign policy,' the EU conceptual outline for security goes on to say, 'depends on the consolidation of our achievement there' (European Council 2003: 13). For both Europe and the US the Balkan region is of considerable geopolitical significance and concern, and what happens to the states in South-eastern Europe, including *de jure* and *de facto* international protectorates, and various pre-state or sub-state entities, has a major impact on the transatlantic relationship.

This chapter will explore various aspects of the European, American, and NATO engagement in the Balkans over the past fifteen years. In order to provide a context for examining recent linkages between Balkan development and transatlantic relations, it is useful to consider some of the salient factors that have shaped European and American perspectives regarding the South-eastern European area. Four broad phases can be identified in the recent evolution of the relationship between Europe and the US with respect to the Balkans:

1. The twilight of the Cold War that was the prelude and backdrop to the wars of the Yugoslav succession: roughly 1989 to 1995.
2. The period from the Dayton Peace Accords in the autumn of 1995 to 9/11, 2001.
3. The period from 9/11 through the Iraq crisis, and up to the end of the first stage of the war in Iraq launched by the US–UK-led coalition on 20 March 2003.
4. The most recent period of transatlantic relations, i.e. from the prematurely claimed 'end of hostilities' in Iraq on 1 May 2003, through the NATO Istanbul summit in June 2004, and ending with the transfer from NATO to EU command of peacekeeping forces in Bosnia at the end of 2004.

Phase 1: Imagining multilateralism – the meltdown of Communism and the dissolution of Yugoslavia

The fall of the Berlin Wall and the end of the Cold War opened a new period of world history and transatlantic relations. Initially, the European countries and the US cast about for new conceptual and strategic anchors to address the new international environment. As socialist Yugoslavia drifted towards dissolution, and then descended into war, the EU proved unable to develop a coherent or effective approach to crisis management in the Balkans. During the latter stages of the George H. W. Bush administration and early Clinton administration, the US was also unprepared to take the lead on the issue of Yugoslavia's crisis, and to address directly regional security problems in South-eastern Europe. The result was a major international failure to prevent Yugoslavia's break-up or to respond adequately to the warfare and humanitarian catastrophe that ensued in the Balkans. Undoubtedly NATO and the EU helped win the Cold War by bolstering Euro-Atlantic defence and economic prosperity. As the Cold War ended, however, there was little consensus or conceptual preparation in Europe regarding how to deal with the new international environment, or the inter-ethnic bloodletting presented by the course of events in the Balkans. In contrast to the relatively peaceful demise of the Union of Soviet Socialist Republics (USSR), or the later velvet divorce between the Czechs and Slovaks, the case of Yugoslavia's disintegration confronted Europe and the international community with a wrenching challenge. Looking back at this period, Chris Patten, the EU Commissioner for External Relations, has observed that those who criticise Europe's common foreign and security policy (CFSP) 'should study recent history: Europe completely failed to get its act together in the 1990s on the policy for the Balkans. As Yugoslavia broke into bits, Europe was largely impotent because it was not united. Some member states wanted to keep Yugoslavia together at all costs, some wanted to manage its break up, and others still felt we should stay out of the whole mess ... We had to do better, a lot better' (Patten 2004).

The failure of the EU in the Balkans is clearly a major factor that stimulated concern over the development of CFSP. Indeed, the Balkan wars of the 1990s have become the point of departure for European leaders when they encourage subsequent EU efforts to 'do better'. In the words of NATO Secretary-General Lord Robertson (2003):

> In the Balkans, we missed the point, at least initially. The Cold War had so shaped our thinking that we had no recipe for dealing with a regional conflict on our own doorstep. The US argued that they 'didn't have a dog in the fight' and tried to get out of it ... Some Europeans may have boasted that this was the 'hour of Europe' but they were premature. As Jacques Delors once put it, the EU's policies reminded him of an adolescent taking up an adult problem.

In 1994 and 1995, the Clinton administration finally decided to address the Balkan crisis. The decision was largely driven by US electoral politics and Europe's continued impotence on the matter and was taken after the United Nations Protection Force (UNPROFOR) failure to maintain peace in Bosnia. Hence the lead up to the Dayton Peace Accords, including intensified US diplomatic activity, covert assistance to both the Muslims in Bosnia and to Croatian forces, and more vigorous NATO bombing strikes against the Serbian side. This type of intervention did not stop Srebrenica (1995), and was far too late to prevent Vukovar (1991), but through the creative use of coercive diplomacy, the US finally engineered an end to the war in Bosnia. The new political architecture developed for Bosnia at Dayton certainly had many flaws, but it made a major contribution to ending the war. The Europeans were clearly frustrated by their failure in the Balkans, and somewhat resentful of the successful exercise of US power and unilateralism. Romano Prodi would later describe the situation: 'It is largely thanks to the US that the stabilisation of the Balkans has been possible. At the same time, the EU was not in a position to deal with a conflict that had blown up on its very doorstep. And that realisation was a major factor in further developing our foreign and security policy' (Prodi 2003b).

Phase II: From Dayton to 9/11 (1995–2001)

The deployment of the Implementation Force (IFOR) in Bosnia, and later the Stabilisation Force (SFOR) – the move from UN blue helmets to NATO green helmets – opened a new phase in transatlantic relations concerning the Balkans, which continued through and beyond the 1999 war in Kosovo, and the deployment of the Kosovo Force (KFOR). The Dayton agreement, NATO stabilisation of Bosnia, and the US-led Alliance's military support for the UN-coordinated reconstruction and policing efforts, allowed the US to demonstrate its role as a 'European force', much to the chagrin of some European states. But, because of the war in Bosnia, the EU was stimulated to give higher priority to developing its own ability to act on matters of defence and foreign policy.

The American success in Bosnia rankled some Europeans throughout the 1990s. The Kosovo crisis and war only added to the clear asymmetry between the EU and the US. As the result of the war in Kosovo, the US also confirmed the principle – with European approval – that international armed intervention in waging war for humanitarian purposes could be conducted *without* United Nations Security Council (UNSC) authorisation. Many Europeans in the Alliance regarded the manner of the intervention in Kosovo as an exception. Still, there were interesting differences on this issue within Europe, and within the US (where many neo-liberals approved using force against their earlier instincts). However, the significant military role of the US in a European theatre again provoked transatlantic tensions: over military targets in Yugoslavia, whether to deal with Milošević in order to end the war in Kosovo, how to cooperate with or exclude the Russians, and how best to manage post-conflict arrangements. Ultimately, the KFOR–United Nations Interim Administration Mission in Kosovo (UNMIK) governance structure for running Kosovo as a protectorate was modelled in large part on the scheme used in post-Dayton Bosnia.

Despite intra-alliance difficulties during the Kosovo war, the imperative of stabilising the Balkans created an opportunity for the EU. Indeed, an important sub-phase of the second period, from 1995 to 9/11, 2001, opens in 1999, following the end of the war in Kosovo. The Europeans improvised a major role for themselves in the Balkans with the adoption of the Stability Pact for South-eastern Europe (SPSEE) inaugurated in June 1999. The SPSEE was originally discussed in 1998, but the war in Kosovo propelled the project forward in earnest. Designed to enhance cooperation between South-eastern Europe on the one side, and the EU states, the US and Russia on the other, the SPSEE utilised a regional approach in order to build stronger and more prosperous regimes in the Balkans.[1] Yugoslavia, initially outside the pact, would join the SPSEE after the fall of the Milošević regime. The boundaries and jurisdictional lines between the SPSEE and the EU, as well as the lines between the Pact, and the Organisation for Security and Cooperation in Europe

(OSCE) and NATO, often appeared confusing, as did some of the Pact's organisational goals. The Pact, however, was based on the idea of promoting stability and cooperation within the region before the Balkans' wider integration in Europe, and EU membership.

Acting within the SPSEE framework, the EU – as the Pact's coordinating and facilitating agency – became more deeply involved in the Balkan region. The SPSEE includes both the successor states to the former Yugoslavia as well as Albania, and also Bulgaria and Romania, which were already in the forefront of the pre-accession process. As such, the SPSEE became a kind of 'ante-chamber of the Union'. At the Feira European Council meeting in June 2000, EU heads of government indicated that they regarded all the countries in the newly-established Stabilisation and Association Process (SAP) as potential candidate members of the EU. The development and signing of Stabilisation and Association Agreements (SAA) became the designated 'road to Europe'.

With the establishment of SPSEE, the EU had begun to dangle some attractive carrots before the South-eastern European countries as incentives for good behaviour. Indeed, over the next five years, the EU would assume a major role on the civilian side of nation building and development in the Balkans. The EU humanitarian office had already been deeply involved in helping displaced persons and refugees. For example, between 1991 and October 2003, when it wound up its twelve year humanitarian aid programme in the Balkans – and replaced it with economic development projects – the EU spent £1.7 billion in the region. In November 2000, the EU adopted the Community Assistance for Reconstruction, Development, and Stabilisation (CARDS) Programme to coordinate assistance to the Balkans, and earmarked 4.6 billion euros for that initiative over the period 2000–2006. EU elites and citizens might have remained rather ambivalent about the actual potential to stabilise the Balkans as well as about the eligibility of the countries in Southeastern Europe to achieve EU membership. The Balkan region, however, has become a core area where the EU might establish credibility outside its own borders, and conduct operations independently of the US. The EU had begun to pursue a policy designed to 'resist unilateralism from the US', as Chris Patten (2000) put it. The CFSP, his colleague Javier Solana emphasised in the same week, 'is about the European Union being able to project its value and its interests, the core of its political identity, effectively beyond its own borders' (Solana 2000). The troubled Balkans had clearly become an important venue for CFSP activity.

On the military and diplomatic side of the equation, the Macedonian crisis of 2001 provided the EU with an opportunity to project itself more assertively. Briefly, in the face of a growing Albanian insurgency against Macedonian security forces in 2001, which threatened to completely destabilise and politically fragment the country, EU officials conducted protracted negotiations and were able to prod Slavic-Macedonian and Albanian leaders to sign the Ohrid Agreement. The agreement provided measures on power sharing and language use designed to improve relations between Macedonian Slavs and Albanians. Under UNSC resolution 1371, both the EU and NATO were designated to help enforce the agreement. For the moment, however, it was the NATO Alliance (primarily composed of European troops), not the EU, which would manage Macedonian security; first under 'Operation Amber Fox', and then the smaller mission 'Allied Harmony'. In Bosnia, Kosovo, and in Macedonia during 2001, the EU still played a secondary role in military and security matters.

Phase III: 9/11 to the Iraqi crisis – a shift in US priorities

The terrorist attacks of 9/11 fundamentally altered US perceptions of the world, including its view of the Balkans. The 'war on terrorism' and the controversy surrounding the lead-up to the war in Iraq also deepened the US–European policy divide. One by-product of the transatlantic rift and post-9/11 developments was stepped-up EU assertiveness in developing the CFSP in a manner that exhibited real military capability and civilian crisis management activity. It was the Balkan region, earlier the crucible of failure for Europe, which now became the arena for demonstrating European potential. The growing Europeanisation of the Balkans in terms of EU attention, assistance and military involvement, was directly linked to the shift in US priorities as well as to the logic of EU enlargement momentum. For example, although the US remained quite sceptical about European commitment to the kind of defence expenditures necessary to maintain security in conflict-ridden or post-conflict settings, the imperatives of the war in Afghanistan and Iraq required that Washington draw down its forces in relatively more stabilised regions such as South-eastern Europe. Earlier US concerns regarding the growing EU role in the region were gradually and grudgingly overcome during 2002 and 2003. The transfer to the EU of responsibility for Balkan security matters could now be rationalised in certain American quarters as composing part of the implementation of a broader 'strategic withdrawal', which was justified by the end of the Cold War, and the military requirements of both the war against terrorism and the war in Iraq.

Of course, some matters pertaining to the growing transatlantic rift, such as the Bush administration's policy regarding the International Criminal Court (ICC), as well as the effort to combat terrorism and the struggle in Iraq, complicated US–EU cooperation in the Balkans. As the US endeavoured to recruit as many countries as it could find into a 'coalition of the willing' to assist in Afghanistan, and then in Iraq, some countries proved to be more Atlanticist in orientation, while others were more Europeanist. How a given country in Europe, and especially the various states in what Donald Rumsfeld called 'New Europe', came down on the question of support for the US depended on many internal factors, and should be considered on a case-by-case basis. In general, however, countries that were getting closer to joining NATO were moved to pay attention to pressure from Washington, while trying not to alienate European officials in Brussels (especially if a country was close to EU accession, or in the throes of pre-accession negotiations). The name of the game in the 'New Europe' and in South-eastern Europe in particular, was finding a way to balance the different pressures coming from Washington and Brussels.

American distraction with the war against terrorism and the crisis in Iraq, as well as the potential scaling down of American presence in the Balkans, provided EU decision-makers with an opportunity. Thus in the summer of 2002, the EU indicated a willingness to replace NATO peacekeeping forces in Macedonia, and take over responsibility for the task of security in that country. The EU mission, 'Operation Concordia', would operate under the 'Berlin Plus' framework, which permits EU forces to use NATO resources and planning capabilities.[2] Operation Concordia was launched in January 2003 at the invitation of the Macedonian government and continued its responsibilities until the end of that year when it was replaced by an armed policing mission. Looking back at the mission, the EU Special Envoy to Macedonia, the Belgian diplomat Alexis Brouhns, remarked:

> It was a modest mission [400 men] but it played an important role in the future stabilisation of Macedonia. It was also an exceptional laboratory for other missions... In Macedonia, we cooperated very smoothly with NATO. This is also a good partnership between the United States and the European Union. The United States and the Union have the same agenda, the same objectives for the country, and that facilitates cooperation... It was in fact more difficult to coordinate European players in a crisis situation than to coordinate with NATO or with the Americans. (*De Standaard*, 10 December 2003)

At roughly the same time as the Concordia mission was launched in Macedonia, the European Union Police Mission (EUPM) was launched in Bosnia, taking over policing in that country from the UN-run International Police Task Force (IPTF) that had functioned over the previous seven years. With the advent of EUPM, the European Security and Defence Policy (ESDP), which was launched in 1999, became operational. The EUPM built upon other earlier EU experiences with CFSP civilian crisis management operations such as the European Union Administration of Mostar (EUAM, 1994–1996).

The EUPM mission in Bosnia, as well as the EU military and police missions in Macedonia, along with Brussels' active diplomatic role in the Balkans, were major steps forward in the EU role in foreign and security affairs. Such activities complemented the important EU role in the economic development of the Balkans through the SPSEE, the SAP process, and various assistance programmes, such as CARDS. The Balkans had become a major arena of EU external relations. The development of the Common Security

Strategy for the EU during 2003 also illustrated that Brussels was no longer willing to abdicate strategic thinking and international security issues entirely to the US. As the new EU strategy statement underlined, the Union's 'first line of defence' lies in the zone of insecurity around Europe, and that European notions such as 'effective multilateralism' and 'pre-emptive engagement' are somewhat different from similar US strategic notions (European Council 2003: 18). The European approach combined political, economic, and military dimensions in an integrated manner. It derives from a generally similar appraisal of global trends as that prevailing in Washington, but represents a more diversified strategy to deal with identified threats, based on different priorities, and a greater emphasis on international law. Jean-Ives Haine, taking a shot at some American commentators, described the differences this way: 'Those with the fondness for simplistic comparisons will stress Mars and Venus, the mix of Hobbes and Kant, the marriage of soft and hard power. Yet, these comparisons will be misleading because the Union is not a nation-state. This is what gives the strategic concept its special characteristics and its greatest merit. Its significance will be measured by its ability to deal with upheavals in the world' (Haine 2003).

Despite EU–US differences, at the end of July 2003 the EU and NATO agreed on a 'concerted approach' to security and stability in the Western Balkans. The new approach aimed at 'consolidating stability' in an area acknowledged as still having serious problems with ethnic tensions, slow economic reform, criminal networks, and extremism. The two organisations committed themselves to an 'enhanced dialogue', meaning closer cooperation, and addressing certain core areas of concern in the Balkans, such as conflict prevention and crisis management, defence and security sector reform, strengthening the rule of law, preventing terrorism, border security and management, and arms control and the removal of small arms. At the same time, Washington also stressed areas of cooperation in the Balkans between the US and the EU's increasing region-wide initiatives, such as the SPSEE country-specific security and reconstruction initiatives, as well as Operation Concordia that had replaced the NATO-led operation as the international security presence in Macedonia.

The EU also played a major role in the troubled relationship between the two federal units in post-Milošević Yugoslavia. Thus, in 2003, EU diplomats were instrumental in negotiating an agreement to replace the rump federation that had been designed by Milošević after Yugoslavia's disintegration. The new 'state union' of 'Serbia-Montenegro', which began functioning in early 2003, was in large part a creation of Brussels. Javier Solana played such an extensive hands-on role in negotiating the agreement that in Belgrade the new state arrangement was jokingly referred to as 'Solania'. Under the agreement, which created a new constitutional charter, a referendum in Montenegro (and Serbia) on the matter of further association or division was postponed until 2006. It was hoped in Brussels that by that time, the two federal units could work out their difficulties, and that a common state could be preserved.

Phase IV: EU ascendancy in the Balkans and further developments, May 2003–Spring 2005

During early 2003, as the US became busy with the war in Iraq, the EU continued with its increasing diplomatic, economic, police, and military activities in the Balkans. As the EU prepared for the spring 2004 enlargement from fifteen to twenty-five members, considerable concern began to be expressed over what impact this expansion would have on the broader European 'neighbourhood'. For example, how would the exclusion of the South-eastern European countries from the next wave of enlargement – except for Slovenia that was about to join the Union – affect the internal political development of the Balkan region? Bulgaria and Romania were already candidate countries and on track to enter the Union in 2007, but the other states, conventionally referred to as the Western Balkans (Croatia, Bosnia, Serbia and Montenegro, Macedonia, and Albania) were in a far less advantaged position. For example, in Croatia, in July 2003, European Commission President Romano Prodi proclaimed 'the whole of the Balkans must come into the European Union. No wall, no barrier, must divide the Balkans. That would be unthinkable. We know only too well how much suffering such divides have caused' (Prodi 2003a). Croatia, Prodi assured his audience, was in the 'forefront' but would still have a long and arduous process before it could enter the EU. He did not mention the other cases in the West Balkans, which suffered from many serious obstacles to meeting the standards for membership in the EU. The danger perceived by some European leaders was that after the 2004 wave of enlargement, support for the entry of another group of countries that were even less politically stable and economically developed than the 2004 entrants, would wane within the EU. The fear was that such 'EU enlargement fatigue' might lead to a protracted period in which the Western Balkan states would constitute a 'ghetto' or 'black hole' surrounded by EU members. For many observers, the key question was which tendency would prevail: the 'Europeanisation of the Balkans', or the 'Balkanisation of Europe'? Another issue was whether EU attention to the region in terms of economic assistance and military missions could be sustained as the US role in the region diminished.

Throughout early 2003 and 2004, as the transatlantic rift over the escalating war in Iraq and other matters continued, the Balkan region appeared to be an area of relatively low intensity tension and occasional rhetorical skirmishes between the EU and US. Non-Balkan matters had clearly assumed more significance in the relationship between the European states and the US: the future of Iraq; the Israeli–Palestinian question; how to combat the sources of international terrorism; how to prevent Iran from developing more nuclear capability; stabilising and rebuilding Afghanistan; trade relations, and so forth. For example, survey research conducted by the US State Department office of research in late 2003 and early 2004 indicated that on most major international issues, German and French citizens tended to view their own country's policies as working in a manner starkly in the opposite direction from the policies of the US. In contrast, British, Italian, and Spanish citizens (prior to the Madrid bombings at least) saw their country's policies and those of the US as complementary. On the issue of stabilising and reconstructing the Balkans, however, there were only marginal differences in public opinion within Europe. British, German and Italian public views concerning the complementarity of Euro-Atlantic policies in the Balkans were very similar. French opinion exhibited the most divergence from the results in other countries with regard to all major international issues, including the Balkans, but even French public opinion perceived more complementarity on Balkan issues than on other international problems (US Department of State 2004). One might interpret such results by concluding that the less salient or volatile the situation in a given region (i.e. the less issues of power, money and the potential expenditure of blood relating to an area), the greater the extent of complementarity and consensus regarding that region found between US and European public opinion, or among different European countries. Another way of looking at the poll results is that the US and the European countries had worked out a *modus operandi* on Balkan matters, or a model of positive 'trans-atlanticism' that could prove useful in dampening EU–US differences in other areas.

By the last half of 2004, the EU was clearly playing a major role in Balkan affairs. The incentive of possible future membership in the EU provided Brussels with considerable leverage in dealing with the states and political actors in South-eastern Europe. The carrot of enlargement was utilised to make CFSP/ESDP a success. Many factors, such as budget insufficiencies, capability deficiencies, and intra-EU differences combine to hamper EU foreign and defence policy, but they are routine dimensions of a diverse, complex and enlarged multi-state organisation.

The US was ambivalent about the EU's growing role in the Balkans, and more generally at Brussels' ascendancy both as a regional and global actor in the area of foreign policy and security. On the one hand, Washington urged Europe to share the international community's financial burden in the area of security. On the other hand, the US worried that a more independent EU would challenge American views, and limit Washington's influence on various matters. Indeed, one very prominent school of thought in Washington encouraged US support for EU enlargement specifically because it potentially would reduce Europe's political unity and the EU's ability to speak with a united voice. However, despite its mixed feelings about the EU's increasing foreign policy and security posture, the post-9/11 environment and the continuing Iraqi insurgency contributed to and accelerated US disengagement from the Balkan area (and Europe more generally), and Brussels' willingness to assume responsibility for security management in South-eastern Europe. In 2004, EU countries were supplying approximately eighty per cent of the troops on the ground throughout South-eastern Europe. A good portion of those troops served in NATO missions, but that number was scheduled to decrease as the EU, under Berlin Plus, assumed active management of new missions.

The December 2003 EU security strategy statement concluded with a notion that 'the transatlantic relationship is irreplaceable' and aims at creating an 'effective and balanced partnership with the USA' (European Council 2003: 13). However, the challenge remained of how to achieve this aim of EU–US partnership in the Balkans, and elsewhere. The transfer of responsibility for military security in Bosnia – discussed throughout 2003 and 2004, ratified at NATO's Istanbul summit in June 2004 and implemented at the end of 2004 – illustrated the extent of the Euro-Atlantic cooperation that had developed over the past fifteen years on Balkan matters, but also the anxieties on both sides of the EU–US/EU–NATO relationship. The EU exhibited a far more optimistic view than the US regarding Europe's capability to assume an ambitious role in Bosnian security. The prospect of EUFOR replacing SFOR in Bosnia undoubtedly served American aims to share the burden of cost for Balkan security and to reduce its Balkan military commitment. Such a mission, however, also raised concerns in Washington (and among some Bosnian officials) regarding the EU ability to control a major crisis zone, as well as the consequences of the EU's growing influence. Meanwhile, the EU, already having had the experience of Concordia in Macedonia, and the peace-keeping mission in the Democratic Republic of Congo (Artemis), felt well prepared for an expanded role in Bosnia. At its meeting on 17 May 2004, the Council of the European Union affirmed its ability to develop 'force packages' that are 'militarily effective, credible and coherent'. The Council also emphasised the importance it attaches to the principles of complementarity and mutual reinforcement between NATO and the EU. Through NATO, the US would continue to maintain a military presence in Bosnia and the Balkan region after 2004 (for example, the large American bases at Tuzla and in Kosovo), and Washington planned to establish new 'lily-pad' bases in South-eastern Europe (Bulgaria and Romania).[3] By 2005, however, Balkan security had become a jointly managed enterprise with a predominant European role, although South-eastern Europe remained increasingly an issue subject to the routine vicissitudes of transatlantic discourse and discord.

Balkan challenges and transatlantic tensions

The character of transatlantic relations, and the respective roles of the US and the EU, will certainly have an important impact on determining whether or not the Balkan states will evolve in a stable, prosperous and democratic direction. Internal Balkan developments, however, will also influence the course of transatlantic relations. Thus, the state of inter-ethnic relations and territorial issues, and the extent of extremism and ultra-nationalism expressed by Balkan elites, along with other factors, such as the network of organised crime and corruption, will present challenges that can have an impact on the ability of the EU, the US and NATO to cooperate, and, individually or jointly, to manage affairs in South-eastern Europe. Of course, some states can also assist in the stabilisation of the Balkan region. For example, Slovenia became a member of the EU in mid-2004, and Slovene officials have expressed a special interest in assisting the countries of South-eastern Europe. Romania, Bulgaria and Croatia are also states that are well on track for EU accession, and no longer present serious crisis management challenges. Other cases in the region, however, are far more problematic.

The unresolved issue of Kosovo's 'final status' has created a potential waiting game in the protectorate that adds to the already troubled relationship between Albanians and Serbs. The intensified polarisation between those two ethnic communities spilled over into serious ethnic violence in March 2004.[4] How to deal with Kosovo's future remained an exceedingly difficult outstanding question on the agenda of the international community. Both EU and US officials tend to agree that it is necessary for status talks concerning Kosovo to begin. However, American officials appear more willing to accelerate Kosovo's road to eventual independence than do EU representatives. For most European officials the Albanians of Kosovo still have a considerable way to go before meeting the standards set for self-determination and eventual EU entry. Instead of becoming a laboratory case of multiethnic coexistence, the ethnic divide in Kosovo deepened significantly in 2004 and 2005 as tension mounted over the protectorate's future status (Rupnik, 2003; United Nations Security Council, 2005). Meanwhile, Albania itself remains a state with a very weak institutional capacity, which also has a high level of organised crime, smuggling and corruption. Albania has made considerable progress since the breakdown of authority in 1997 (which prompted intervention by an Italian-led 'coalition of the willing' outside of the EU framework) but genuine stability and democratic consolidation remain elusive.

The dissolution of Serbia and Montenegro in 2006 is also a real possibility. Such state disintegration will most likely be a peaceful separation, but even a 'velvet' process could complicate the regional situation and could have a negative spill-over effect on the future of Kosovo. Montenegrin public opinion remains divided but Montenegrin elites are mostly very committed to leaving the current state union. In mid-May 2004, Montenegrin President Filip Vujanovic expressed the dominant view of the ruling parties in Montenegro: 'I think it would be best if two countries, two governments, come to an agreement on separation, and then form an integrated relationship between two, independent internationally acknowledged countries' (*Balkan Watch*, 17 May 2004). Serbia, meanwhile, is going through a difficult period of political development under a coalition of conservative democrats and moderate nationalists elected in December 2003. Political stability and reform are hampered by fissures in the ruling coalition as well as by criminality and episodic violence that remain features of the Serbian political landscape. Separatist and autonomous strains are also apparent in other regions of Serbia such as the Sandzak, Vojvodina and South Serbia. Most troublesome for Serbia's future integration into the EU and NATO framework is the issue of dealing with war crimes and getting 'past the past'. Chris Patten put the dilemma bluntly to Serb leaders in mid-2004: 'Either you will be supporting those who were accused of war crimes ... or you will be on the path to joining Europe. You can't have both' (*Balkan Watch*, 17 May 2004). Serb Prime Minister Vojislav Kostunica and many non-extreme Serb leaders have a less benign view of The Hague tribunal than either EU or American officials, and this is very likely to delay and complicate Serbia's integration into Euro-Atlantic structures. The more liberal president of Serbia, Boris Tadić, elected at the end of 2003, is rather more pro-European than Prime Minister Kostunica but his Democratic Party (formerly led by Serbian reformer Zoran Đinđić, who was assassinated in March 2003) remained outside the Serbian government in mid-2005.

Macedonia also remains very fragile largely because of poor inter-ethnic relations, despite improvements in its constitutional arrangements, and the successful leadership succession and election following the accidental death of President Boris Trajkovski in February 2004. In his address following his inauguration as the new president, Branko Crvenkovski drew attention to his country's priority concern: 'Good inter-ethnic relations are the pillar of Macedonia's stability; good inter-ethnic relations are the prerequisite to economic growth and progress; finally good inter-ethnic relations are the shortcut to European and Euro-Atlantic integration' (*BBC News online*, 12 May 2004). However, despite the supportive efforts of the EU and local reformers, Macedonia's cohesion and stability remain problematic. As a United Nations Development Programme report concluded in early 2005: 'The gap in the perception of the reality and the values between the Macedonian and Albanian ethnic communities is very obvious and it can have serious consequences for the process of stabilisation of the country' (United Nations Development Programme 2005: 33).

Bosnia is slowly becoming a modern European state, but the country is still ethnically and territorially segmented. Though most of Bosnia's leaders realise the importance of quickly advancing on 'the road to Europe', serious internal problems persist. As High Representative Paddy Ashdown put it to Bosnia's legislators in September 2003: 'Perhaps one question you should be asking yourself is whether this country can get into Europe with a government that works so slowly, and a parliament that meets only one day a month ...

The European Union didn't dilute its standards for Hungary or Poland – and it won't for you' (Ashdown 2003).[5] Thanks to the presence of NATO forces and UN-directed (and subsequently EU-managed) international police, inter-ethnic violence decreased in Bosnia from 1995 to 2005, and the security provided for the return of refugees and the displaced was quite effective. But the overall crime rate in the country was on the rise during 2003–4, by 8 per cent in the Federation and 23 per cent in the Serb Republic, and during the same period Interpol processed 250 persons suspected of ties to international terrorist organisations. While problems related to governance, corruption and economic difficulties are serious in Bosnia, the even more fundamental issue of the country's future constitutional structure remains outstanding, and very difficult to resolve. As a March 2005 Venice Commission report indicated, the existing constitutional features of Bosnia and particularly the weak central government, 'makes effective government extremely difficult, if not impossible' (Venice Commission 2005). The EU-controlled military force (EUFOR), which acquired security responsibilities for Bosnia at the end of 2004, has been working effectively (with 6300 troops in March 2005), but until Bosnia and the international community comes to grips with its political–constitutional problems it will be extremely difficult for the country to make a genuine transition to viable self-government.

The Balkan countries continue to be an 'interesting' area of opportunity for the EU to assert its role as an international actor and develop its CFSP/ESDP activities, but renewed violence and instability in the Balkans could quickly make the region a potential threat to Brussels' credibility. For example, this problem might arise for the EU if future local conflicts overwhelm its capabilities, and require a substantially upgraded NATO and US presence. Given the intense transatlantic rift that developed surrounding issues related to the war in Iraq, it might be argued that the record of relatively successful EU–US cooperation in the Balkans from 1995 to 2005 constituted a rather exceptional case of 'limited discordance', a unique situation not typical of the general issues that trouble the relationship between Washington and Brussels. Clearly, each regional and topical arena of EU–US relations is different. The fact that the Balkan region is in Europe's backyard, that it has not involved nuclear weapons and strategic resources, and has not served as a major base for international terrorism (at least not on a scale comparable to the Middle East), might be factors explaining why the area is less contentious in transatlantic relations than other zones of crisis. Of course the EU and the US will continue to have differences over how best to promote Balkan progress towards Euro-Atlantic values, and the details of how best to maintain regional security. Moreover, the salient conflicts and issues – many still related to ethno-political extremism – that emerge within the still troubled and volatile region, and particularly the intensity of the crises that arise, will also influence the opportunities and success of transatlantic cooperation with respect to South-eastern Europe. The many security threats posed by the continued internal fissures in the Balkan region, as well as the area's role as a potential breeding ground and transportation route for trans-national terrorism, and a major conduit for refugee flows and trafficking in people, arms and drugs, are all significant challenges that will require the EU, NATO and the US to address carefully South-eastern Europe in the future, and to seek new modes of cooperation in dealing with the region.

Notes

1. SPSEE has three 'working tables': for human rights and democratisation, economic reconstruction and development, and security issues.
2. NATO–EU military cooperation was facilitated through an embedded EU planning cell at NATO's Supreme Headquarters Allied Power Europe.
3. In May, 2004, Colin Powell remarked that when the George W. Bush administration took office, it began to review US commitments to nation building: 'We started to see how many of these we really should be doing and at what level. The first one we faced was, should we have troops in Bosnia, in Kosovo. We took a look at it, realised our international obligations, and I think I was the first one to coin the phrase at a NATO meeting, "Hey, we went in together to Bosnia and Kosovo and we'll come out together. The United States is not going to walk away from our obligations." And the President supported that and began using the same phrase. And we're still there. We're not walking away from our nation-building obligations in Bosnia, and Kosovo. We've been able to do it with fewer troops as we have scaled down over the last several years, but we're still there' (Powell 2004).
4. Prior to the March riots in Kosovo – which killed 19 people and led to widespread suffering and property losses by the Serbian minority community – KFOR had approximately 17,500 soldiers serving in the protectorate (including some 2000 American troops). Following the riots, troop reinforcements were rushed in, primarily from the European states, and by May 2004, KFOR had approximately 22,000 troops.
5. The lethargy exhibited by Bosnian and Serb authorities in dealing with the apprehension of indicted war criminals was one factor behind a NATO decision not to admit Bosnia and Herzegovina to the Partnership for Peace Programme at the June 2004 Istanbul summit.

ISABELLE FACON

7

Kosovo and Iraq: two test cases for the partnership between post-Soviet Russia and the West

Introduction

'We disagree with Russia on the legality of the war, and the tensions will last as long as the military operations which we hope will be of short duration. This is a disagreement about principles as was the case concerning the intervention in Kosovo.' These comments, from US diplomatic sources (*Le Monde*, 28 March 2003), identify the two events which have created the most acute strains in US–Russia relations since the end of the Cold War. Both crises offered interesting perspectives on the evolution of Russia's ties with the US and the Euro-Atlantic community as a whole in the post-Cold War environment. The first decade after the collapse of the Soviet Union was marked by the deep concern that Russian political, diplomatic and military elites feel as a result of the loss of their country's status as a superpower. The line pursued by independent Russia's first foreign minister, Andrei Kozyrev, had as its objective the creation of a 'strategic partnership' with the West with a special and equal relationship with Washington at its core. This effort represented the positive embodiment of the nostalgia for the times when Moscow was Washington's main enemy but also its chief international partner.

Faced with the painful realisation that this 'strategic partnership' had failed to materialise, Russian leaders tended to interpret any international development that did not meet the Kremlin's expectations or interests as reflecting Washington's determination not to let its former 'arch-enemy' become strong and influential again. Most important among these were the enlargement of NATO to former Warsaw Pact countries, NATO's new Strategic Concept which enlarges the functional scope of the Alliance, and the growing doubts about the relevance of the UN. Such an interpretation ignored the fact that the US was downgrading the importance of Moscow among its foreign policy and security partners primarily because of Russia's weaknesses and lack of diplomatic muscle. It betrayed Moscow's quasi-psychological difficulty in accepting the growing power gap between itself and the US – in economic, diplomatic, technological and, above all, military terms.[1] As argued by an observer of Russian foreign policy, 'the longevity and recentness of the Cold War has spawned a strategic culture that is fundamentally America-centric', and has indeed made the US become 'the natural point of reference for Russian foreign policy' (Lo 2004: 47). This posture has been a key factor in the policies that Moscow has developed towards other major international players, including the EU and individual European powers. Russia, in fact, has tried to use its ties with European partners as a counterweight to US ever-growing power in the international system. This instrumental approach has had a negative impact on these ties.

Russian top leaders have always opposed the US tendency to use 'coercion, up to and including the use of force, particularly in the Persian Gulf and in the Balkans' (Ivanov 2002: 112). Both NATO's military intervention in Kosovo and the Iraq war mobilised Moscow's anxiety about Washington's leadership in world affairs. The two events, however, triggered quite different reactions by the Russian government. Putting these reactions in perspective allows us to draw a picture of the continuities and changes that have marked Russia's policy towards the Euro-Atlantic community since this country became independent.

Russia faces Kosovo and Iraq: same arguments for two different crises

Through its energetic reaction to both NATO's military intervention in Kosovo and to the US military intervention in Iraq, Moscow revealed core principles of its diplomatic agenda. Even though the two situations were different, Russia resorted to similar arguments. Such similarity provides tangible indications of the issues that Russia sees as the most crucial in its efforts to re-establish itself as an influential international player.

Defending the traditional world security order to protect Russia's international voice
One of the key Russian arguments in the periods preceding the military interventions in Kosovo and Iraq concerned the risk that they represented to the stability of the international security system. The two interventions challenged the basic principles that have been at the core of the international system since the end of World War II, most importantly non-interference in the domestic affairs of sovereign states, and the regulation of the use of force by the international community through the United Nations Security Council (UNSC). As viewed from Moscow, such challenges to the UN-centred international security order might endanger its own interests and positions on the world scene.

In both cases, Russian officials denounced the intervention as constituting interference in the domestic affairs of a sovereign state. Russian official foreign policy and security documents adopted after 'Operation Allied Force' emphasised the destabilising effect of the growing tendency of 'certain countries' and 'organisations' to resort to military force to solve international problems, and to do so outside the UN framework.[2] After Kosovo, Russian officials, strategists and experts increasingly emphasised the danger posed to Russia by peacekeeping and humanitarian operations used as pretexts to infringe on the sovereign rights of states. In essence, Moscow's apprehension was that 'Operation Allied Force' might be the first example of a type of operation that NATO could be tempted to carry out in the post-Soviet space, or even on Russian territory. As a consequence, Russia's new 'Security Concept' and 'Military Doctrine', which were adopted in the first part of 2000, indicated in substance that military threats to Russia were on the rise, and Western policies had produced a 'remilitarisation' of international relations (Arbatov 2000). The military intervention in Iraq confirmed these approaches in Russian strategic thinking.

Even more importantly perhaps, Russia saw both crises as detrimental to its international influence and as undermining – concretely or potentially – its ability to play a significant role in world affairs. This concern was a key factor in Russia's fiercely negative reaction to the beginning of NATO's military campaign against Serbia in March 1999. As viewed from Moscow, NATO's initiative was evidence of a new world order dominated by the US and its closest European allies which deprived Russia of any significant voice in international security affairs. Russian officials and intellectuals argued that NATO's 'aggression against the sovereign nation of Yugoslavia' (Ivanov 2002: 105) proved that their country could no longer influence European security affairs. The West, in fact, had clearly shown that it was prepared to circumvent those institutions that provided Moscow with voice and hence ability to protect its interests. Many in Moscow concluded that 'Operation Allied Force' meant that 'equal partnership was a slogan, that the Founding Act and Permanent Joint Council [were] mere gestures and that Russia [had] become expendable in the eyes of the West' (Sherr and Main 1999: 1). Indeed, within the NATO–Russia Permanent Joint Council, Moscow had vehemently opposed any military option to solve the Kosovo conflict. Hence, NATO's intervention convinced most members of the Russian diplomatic and military elite that the West was determined to weaken Russia's international positions and was read as a patent failure of the policy of engagement in Western institutions which they had pursued 'in order to protect Russian interests, institutionalise a Russian voice in Europe and constrain Western actions that might threaten Russia' (Lynch 1999: 58). The fact that NATO intervened without a UNSC mandate and that NATO's new Strategic Concept, adopted in April 1999, opened the possibility for the Alliance to conduct peace operations without a UNSC mandate irritated the Russians even more. Indeed,

Russia's permanent membership in the UNSC constitutes one of the only relatively weighty remnants of Moscow's past superpower status. This is stated bluntly in manuals that are recommended to students in international relations by the Russian state education authorities. The following is an example: 'It is impossible not to agree with the opinion that for Russia, whose role in international affairs is not comparable to the importance of the USSR's, this organisation [the UN] remains one of the few international institutions, if not the only one, within which we can act relatively decisively. Thanks to our position of permanent member of the Security Council, we have the ability to really influence decision-making processes of international importance' (Zhirnov 2004: 240–1). This means that Moscow has an interest in emphasising anything that promotes the centrality of the UNSC in international security affairs. NATO's intervention in the former Yugoslavia without a UNSC mandate was therefore viewed by Moscow as yet another attempt by Western countries to reduce Russia's standing in world affairs.

This same overall analysis was at the basis of Russia's opposition to the war in Iraq a few years later. Russian officials condemned US intervention as interference in a sovereign state's domestic affairs because it aimed not only at destroying Iraq's WMD potential but also at toppling its political regime which they regarded as legitimate and posing no immediate threat to international security. US intervention was presented as illustrating the 'remilitarisation' of international relations and, as stated by Konstantin Kosachev, Deputy Chairman of the Duma's international affairs committee, and many other Russian politicians, Russian opposition to it stemmed from the country's willingness to defend 'the modern world order that has existed throughout the post-war period and is based on the fairly simple tenet that the world community's only body authorized to take decisions to use force, to use military force in international relations, was, is, and will evidently remain the United Nations Organisation' (*BBC Monitoring*, 30 January 2003).

Nostalgia for the bipolar world order: the US-centrism of Russia's diplomacy

Both in the case of Kosovo and that of Iraq, Moscow's denunciation of the growing trend of the US to resort to the 'indiscriminate' use of force to promote its interests betrays Russia's trauma of having lost its status of military superpower. Russian reactions also revealed how hard it is for the Russian leadership to acknowledge the end of the superpower-to-superpower relationship of the Cold War, and the impressive gap in resources, especially in the military area, which used to be the central field for competition between the USSR and the US. The Kremlin's nostalgia for the times when it used to be responsible, together with the White House, for the world strategic balance, is strong. This phenomenon finds its expression in the conviction, often expressed by Russian diplomats, that 'Russian–American relations continue to have a substantial influence on the world's political climate', that the two countries continue to 'bear particular responsibility for upholding international peace and security', and that 'there is scarcely a single important global problem that can be solved without involving both Moscow and Washington' (Ivanov 2002: 110).

The failure of Andrey Kozyrev's project of developing a 'strategic partnership' with Washington caused great alarm in Moscow and was perceived as a sign of US willingness to exploit Russia's weakness and to ensure that its former principal competitor would never become a threat to Washington's global ambitions again. Hence all the changes that NATO underwent in the 1990s, and that Moscow disliked (its Eastern enlargement, its new Strategic Concept, 'Operation Allied Force'), were systematically interpreted, even though they were supported by many European countries, as part of a US strategy to erode Russia's residual influence on the world scene, starting from the zones of its traditional influence – Central and Eastern Europe and the Balkans. This is why Russian politicians and academics have regarded US willingness to use military force outside the UNSC framework as evidence of Washington's attempt to prevent Russia from playing any role in decisions concerning international security. This approach is a key factor behind the Russian call for multipolarity and multilateralism. Such a call rests on the idea that a world facing global and multifaceted threats would be better off if it were able to devise cooperative and inclusive solutions by rallying the contributions of all members of the world community on an equal and democratic basis. The UN, of course, should have the leading role in structuring and coordinating such multilateral cooperation. However, throughout the 1990s, this part of Russia's discourse on multipolarity was more often than not superseded by declarations about the unacceptable nature of a world dominated by the US, a prospect that is unpleasant to many other states but that bears an especially painful meaning to the state that was the 'other pole' of the vanished bipolar world order. It was therefore not surprising that in the aftermath of the Kosovo crisis, the Russian leadership adopted new security and foreign policy documents that stressed the need to fight the dangers attached to the 'growing trend towards the emergence of a unipolar world order dominated by the economic and military power of the US'.[3] Such a wording was used again during the US-led war in Iraq.

Such an approach has put European countries, even those such as France and Germany that are the most sympathetic to the project of an EU–Russia strategic partnership, in a delicate position since they wish to avoid being used by Moscow in its policy towards Washington. Indeed, during the 1990s, Russia's interest in the EU was primarily instrumental, that is largely depending on the leverage that – from Moscow's point of view – developing ties with the EU could provide in dealing with the US and NATO – the latter being regarded in Moscow as Washington's tool for keeping the Europeans in line.[4]

Indeed, Russia has made it clear that it is interested in the development of a European Common Foreign and Security Policy (CFSP) and in the European Security and Defence Policy (ESDP) primarily in terms of their potential to lessen 'NATO-centrism' in Europe.[5] The concept of a 'multipolar world order' that Russia claimed to be defending in its opposition to the Kosovo intervention is not attractive to most European states since it has been excessively associated with anti-American feelings. These exist but are not widespread within Europe, and most European countries wish to avoid any initiative that threatens to widen the transatlantic gap. Even countries that are convinced that a strong relationship with Russia could only benefit Europe are very cautious in promoting the view that a solid EU–Russia partnership can constitute a serious 'pole' in a 'multipolar' security order. France and Germany, for instance, are well aware that the idea of a Moscow–Paris–Berlin axis which Moscow has tried to sponsor is too closely associated with Russia's negative, anti-US approach to multipolarity. Consequently, they have remained very guarded towards Moscow's 'triangular proposals'.

During the Kosovo crisis, Kremlin officials relied heavily on the rhetoric of the unipolar versus multipolar world order. This was less the case during the Iraqi crisis. As Hélène Carrère d'Encausse (2003) notes, Putin's 'rare interventions' during the diplomatic contest over Iraq 'suggested that Russia presented itself as a European country, able to integrate into Europe, not as a champion of a really multipolar world'. Contrary to all expectations, since Moscow had systematically criticised all Anglo-American air-strikes against Iraq, Russian leaders seemed to be willing to display much more restraint in expressing their criticism of US policy. Absent from official speeches was the kind of strong anti-American language that had characterised Russian attitudes during the Kosovo crisis. This is a good illustration of the changes in foreign policy decision-making that Vladimir Putin introduced when he became Russia's president.

Between Kosovo and Iraq: the emergence of new parameters for Russia's foreign policy

The Kosovo crisis marked a turning point in Russian foreign policy. The choice of constant opposition to US policy, in fact, had not paid off. Not only it had not prevented NATO from enlarging or from intervening militarily in the Balkans but had also led to the relative isolation of Russia both in Europe and in the world. As argued by Bobo Lo, the Kosovo crisis 'was a disaster for the Yeltsin presidency whose strident criticism of allied military intervention established an image of Russia in the West as an annoying and increasingly irrelevant international actor' (Lo 2004: 49). Some domestic critics charged that Russian insistence on the centrality of the UNSC was misguided as well. Their argument was that the failure of the attempts to generate a common position within the UNSC against the military campaigns proposed by NATO not only diminished Russian influence in matters concerning European security but contributed also to undermine the very credibility of the UNSC.

These considerations led the Kremlin to decide that it should take part, both diplomatically and militarily, in the Kosovo post-conflict processes. They also became the driving force behind Vladimir Putin's efforts to alter the basic paradigms of Russia's foreign policy. Quite rapidly after the new Russian president's election, cooperation with NATO, which Moscow had frozen because of 'Operation Allied Force', resumed and was strengthened.[6] A few months after Putin was elected president, it became clear that he regarded a *rapprochement* with the Euro-Atlantic community as a key foreign policy goal important for both stimulating economic development and ensuring that Russia becomes a major international power again. The aims of the new Kremlin were not different from those pursued by the Yeltsin administration: Moscow should enhance its role in international politics by 'mak[ing] Russia indispensable to the West' (Sherr and Main 1999: 1) and make it heed its interests. The means to pursue those aims, however, had changed.

Russia in the pre-Iraqi war period: Moscow's new foreign policy pragmatism
An important element of the new Russian foreign policy was the downplaying of the multipolarity slogan, or at least an effort 'to divorce multipolarity from confrontationist and anti-American tones' (Kononenko 2003: 23). Russian officials have instead increasingly used the terms 'multivectoriality' and 'multilateralism' to frame their new foreign policy line. This change of language accompanied a change in policy towards the US, which under the Bush administration was threatening to downgrade the relationship with the Russian Federation. President Putin considered it necessary to reduce the importance of the 'American factor' in foreign policy-making in order to lessen the confrontational mood that such an attitude on the part of Washington could trigger among the Russian elite. Therefore, several times President Putin stressed, early in his first presidential mandate, that the US was to be treated as *one* priority, not as *the* priority, of national diplomacy. If Russia wanted to get the support of the US to achieve some key goals (e.g. WTO, Chechnya) then it should accept a lower profile in the bilateral relationship. In Putin's opinion, giving up the illusory strategic competition with the US and accepting the role of 'junior partner' could only bring benefits – a chance to make Washington more attentive to Moscow's interests and to widen the options of Russia's foreign policy on other fronts by enabling Russian diplomacy to devote more strategic thinking and energy to other important partners.

By that time, indeed (2000, and the first half of 2001), the idea was gaining ground in Moscow that 'America-centrism' and the obsession with negative multipolarity (negative because focused primarily on counterbalancing the US) in Russian foreign policy had spoilt relations with many other players, notably the EU. Indeed, the change in postures towards Washington was instrumental in Putin's strategy to develop a broader, more substantial relationship with Brussels. By downplaying the anti-US tonality of its foreign policy, Moscow made it possible to reassure Washington's European allies and to convince them that Russia's policy towards them would now become less closely dependent on its relationship with the US. The EU was put at the top of new priorities of Russian diplomacy not only on paper – it came in second after the Commonwealth of Independent States (CIS) in the new 'Foreign Policy Concept' that Vladimir Putin signed in June 2000 – but also in deeds. Putin tried to heighten the attention of the Ministry of Foreign Affairs towards the EU, and became himself very active in relations with Brussels. In general, Russia's new foreign policy came to concentrate on the belief that differences of view, even strong differences, should be managed so as not to endanger Moscow's foreign economic and political interests.

The careful and balanced position that Moscow took in the pre-Iraqi war period was therefore no surprise to those who had observed the changes in Russian diplomatic behaviour since 2000. In Putin's view, America's 'Iraqi project' could only be detrimental both to the stability of the international system and to Russian interests. The US was once more willing to circumvent the UNSC and use force without international consensus. Moscow opposed US intervention against Iraq, arguing that UNSC resolution 1441 was not enough to legitimise military action and stressing that it would not support a second resolution seeking to authorise the use of force. Moscow favoured instead the continuation of UN inspections. The Russian president, however, was also convinced that the Iraqi issue should not become a cause for ruining the efforts made since 2000 to enhance Russia's political and security partnership with the Euro-Atlantic community in the fight against the new global threats. 9/11 had helped Moscow consolidate its efforts for a *rapprochement* with the West, in making its European and US partners more reactive to its cooperation proposals.[7] The stake for the Russian leadership was to preserve this still fragile accomplishment. This is why Russia proved much more cautious in its diplomatic manoeuvring during the Iraqi diplomatic crisis of 2002–3 than in the Kosovo context. This was an additional and critical illustration of Putin's lucid 'reluctance to fight un-winnable battles' (Lo 2004: 57).

Russia's 'new' foreign policy: the Iraqi crisis as a playing ground

The Kremlin paid special attention to the need to safeguard the new partnership with the US. During the pre-Iraqi war period, President Putin mentioned several times that Russia should not jeopardise its relations with the US which had considerably improved after 9/11 because of Washington's considering Russia as an important partner in the fight against terrorism and the proliferation of weapons of mass destruction. Of course, the two Ivanovs (Russian foreign and defence ministers) delivered speeches which were critical of the US but these were more pre-electoral efforts[8] to appease segments of Russian public opinion and representative of the diplomatic and security apparatuses which clamoured for tougher reactions against the US. President Putin adopted a much more conciliatory tone, which is very important since the Russia–US partnership relies very much on the personal bond between the two presidents. When the US launched the intervention he reacted in a 'calmly negative' way. This was the same way he reacted to Washington's withdrawal from the Anti-Ballistic Missile (ABM) treaty and to NATO's decision to welcome the Baltic States into its fold, two events that Putin labelled as 'mistakes' and not 'tragedies'. There were no threatening speeches of the kind Russian officials had delivered in 1999.

Thus, the Russian–American relationship did not come under severe strain. Of course, the intervention in Iraq convinced the Russian leadership that after 9/11 the US would not hesitate to use force in international relations without UNSC authorisation and that the partnership with the US would be determined primarily by American interests and would never be a partnership of equals. The main goal of Moscow officials, however, was to make sure that the war in Iraq would not hurt the anti-terrorist US–Russian partnership which the Kremlin regarded as a key instrument to regain visibility and weight on the world scene (Smith 2003). In a speech in which he elaborated on the reasons why Russia was opposed to the US waging war in Iraq, President Putin went as far as to recognise candidly that 'the economy and currency of the United States have a global significance and their development directly influences the development of the economies of Russia and Europe' (*NewsMax.com*, 5 April 2003). Once the war started, President Putin declared that a US defeat was not in Russia's interest. After the war, Moscow voted for UNSC resolution 1483, lifting the sanctions against Iraq and granting the US and the UK the right to act as the legitimate authority in this country for a definite period.

The Iraqi war was also an opportunity to measure the semi-failure of one of Putin's key foreign policy ambitions, which was to shore up the partnership with the EU on the eve of its 2004 enlargement. Many analysts stressed that Russia had used the Iraqi crisis as an opportunity to show the world that it had made a distinct pro-European choice and that in defending positions that were close to those of such European heavyweights as Paris and Berlin, it marked – as Andrew Jack put it in a piece for the *Financial Times* (3 April 2003) – 'the start of a shift away from its *rapprochement* with the US in favour of a closer alliance with Europe'. As Dmitri Trenin (2003/4: 76) indicated, 'many observers believed that Putin was returning to his pre-9/11 emphasis on relations with Europe', especially as Washington at a given point in the diplomatic dispute over Iraq addressed harsh criticism of Moscow's policy towards Saddam Hussein's regime.[9] Things, however, were much more complex than that. First, as it was previously stressed, Russia was careful not to disturb too much the 'new' relation with the US. It was not before February 2003 that its position on the US line hardened significantly. As a result, many

French and German decision-makers had become frustrated, charging that Russia tended to 'hide itself' behind Berlin's and, above all, Paris's, back.[10] The stance of Russian officials was never as hard-line as that of Berlin and Paris. Up to the end of the diplomatic crisis that preceded the war in Iraq, the French and the Germans doubted whether or not Russia was prepared to use its veto. Thus, there was no 'Russian–European' alliance to confront the US. There was an alliance *de circonstance* whose members had different perspectives and goals. For Russia, there was an obvious opportunity to try to benefit indirectly by France's and Germany's determination against the war, which significantly helped Moscow appear as defending the authority of the UN, while not being too rude to Washington. Besides, this is exactly why the US subsequently decided, according to Condoleezza Rice's widely quoted quip, to 'forgive Russia' while 'punishing France and ignoring Germany'.

Thus, the temporary Paris–Berlin–Moscow axis was not devoid of ambiguities, which reflected the status of Russian–European ties after 9/11. Trenin (2003/4) is right when he points out the perspective of Russia 'returning' to the pre-9/11 emphasis on relations with Europe, as the terrorist attacks in the US had led Russia's foreign policy to concentrate again on the 'US first attitude'. Indeed, many Russian officials and experts hoped that the new alliance against terror could rejuvenate some kind of 'special partnership' with the US, especially since representatives of the US administration went as far as to hint that Russia might prove a more compliant and useful partner in the war on terrorism than older European allies. The result was a Russian foreign policy that became not only less focused on developing relations with the EU but also less open and flexible when faced with the new problems that were appearing in these relations because of the forthcoming enlargement. This showed, among other things, that a substantial change occurred in Russian perspectives of Europe in the period between the Kosovo crisis and the Iraqi war. In the Balkans crisis context, Russia 'forgave' the European countries that took part in the military campaign. This was a reflection of its feeling that first, Europe was not threatening to become a major political and security player able to challenge Moscow, and that, secondly, Europe was prepared to mend the ties with Russia[11] and was more respectful than the US of its 'special role' and 'great power status'. Nowadays, Russia feels not only that the partnership with the US is more useful in terms of promoting its interests on the world stage (Lo 2004) but also that Washington may prove more understanding towards Moscow than Brussels. Indeed, on the eve of its enlargement, the EU became increasingly critical of Russian domestic developments and became more assertive in the post-Soviet space. This probably influenced Russia's choice during the Iraqi crisis: to remain as open as possible with the US, although its policy was in so many ways opposed to Russia's key foreign policy goals, and despite the fact that Moscow had an opportunity that it did not have in the Kosovo crisis context i.e. that it shared common goals with major European countries. When the war in Iraq loomed in late

2002/early 2003, the 'European prospect' was not clear and promising enough for Russia to engage more resolutely with its European friends.

Conclusion

The Kosovo crisis marked the culmination of Russia's deteriorating ties with the West after a decade of tensions caused by NATO's enlargement and transformation and by Moscow's US-centrism that caused Russian diplomacy to become very hectic, emotional, and reactive. However, Kosovo was also a turning point in the foreign policy of the Kremlin, which realised that a completely new approach was required if Russia wanted to make a comeback on the world scene. If 9/11 served to consolidate the efforts that Moscow had made since the inception of Putin's presidency to improve significantly the relationship with the West, the US intervention in Iraq provoked new tensions and dilemmas for Russia. Moscow felt that its international position was threatened because the war was not sanctioned by the UN whose credibility and importance were being challenged again by US unilateralism. The war in Iraq was interpreted in Moscow as a major setback in its efforts to promote its vision of the post-Cold War international order which sees the UNSC at its centre.[12]

In both cases, Russia had 'little choice other than to accept the outcome of US actions' (Smith 2003: 3). However, in the time span between Kosovo and Iraq, Moscow had changed its foreign policy focus and behaviour with a view to getting the most out of its weakened situation, which meant building stronger relations with Western industrialised nations, because they have a determining influence over international economic and political processes. One of the steps that were taken to achieve this goal was making Russian policy towards the West more balanced, i.e. less heavily and negatively focused on the US. Such a balancing act resulted from the Kremlin leadership's awareness that something had to be changed, as the Kosovo crisis had blatantly revealed the deficiencies of the previous policy, and that the illusory quest for strategic equality with the US had not only antagonised Washington, but also prevented Russia from developing its relations with other major partners, including the EU, on a sound basis. Kosovo triggered new approaches in Russia's foreign policy. Iraq revealed the limits of these new approaches and the constraints on Moscow's policy towards the West.

A few years after 'Operation Allied Force', Russian reactions to the US intervention in Iraq demonstrated that the balance in its partnership with the various poles of the 'Euro-Atlantic community' had been modified again. Moscow obviously tried not to alienate Washington, which was visible in the extreme cautiousness that it displayed in opposing the war and the skill with which it 'used' Paris and Berlin's resistance to Washington's line. This gave some credibility to Putin's claims that in joining France and Germany in opposing the US line, Russia was not yielding to its traditional tendency to try to drive a wedge in the transatlantic relationship, but defending international law and the resolution of crises and conflicts through international diplomacy. But this also testified to the fact that Russia's foreign policy had not managed to become less 'US-centred'. One reason for that is that 9/11 produced strong hopes in Russia that the fight against terrorism and the proliferation of WMD might be instrumental in recreating some kind of a new privileged relationship with the US. Another, more unexpected reason was probably Moscow's lack of confidence in the stability of EU–Russia relations, increasingly tested by tensions related to the EU's enlargement and Russian domestic politics. This approach is compounded by the Kremlin's realisation that Paris or Berlin's interest in developing good relations with Moscow might prove helpful tactically (as was the case in Iraq) but not necessarily strategically, i.e. in terms of lessening the US influence in world affairs and of anchoring Russia to Europe. Both Germany and France, in fact, have their own diplomatic and security agendas and interests that do not necessarily coincide with Russia's. Anything that Paris and Berlin do with respect to Russia is aimed at strengthening the EU as well as their country's position within it. That means they will promote the idea of bringing Russia close to Europe for the sake of the stability of the continent; and that they will try to offset the potentially negative inputs of some EU members, including the new ones, that may not be too enthusiastic about such a goal. The French and German leaders, however, also know well that over-emphasising a desire to create a 'special relationship' with Moscow might affect negatively the intra-EU consensus, as anything that may look like efforts to build a *directoire* in Europe would be rejected by other European players, including the new EU members that favour a tougher policy towards Russia.

Russia's position on Iraq showed that the 'outcome of the Euro-centrism versus America-centrism debate in Russian foreign policy' may not end in Euro-centrism. It also showed that the 'cultural-civilisational affinities' between Russia and Europe 'are all very well, but ... are subordinate to concrete realities', among which, in particular, is 'the United States' position as the primary external actor in relation to Russia's major external policy priorities' (Lo 2004: 60), which compels Russia to devote a great deal of energy to consolidating its relationship with Washington. However, there is also another no less concrete reality, namely that Russia has to work to preserve its position as a European power. This was after all one of the major stakes Russia had in the Kosovo crisis. In the early part of the twenty-first century, again, Russia feels increasingly threatened in its European identity by the EU's enlargement to its former Central and Eastern European 'satellites', by Brussels' ambition to develop a more active policy towards its 'new neighbourhood' that includes several former Soviet republics such as Ukraine, and by the EU's assertive position in promoting its values and standards over the European political, security and economic space. All these developments,

Russian leaders feel, might marginalise Russia on the European stage if the two sides do not manage to devise creative ways to integrate Russia into a European landscape that is increasingly structured by the EU's norms and values.

This delicate, and quite new, situation has certainly been a major factor behind the 'non-choice' – as Jacques Amalric called it in a piece written for *Libération* (27 March 2003) – that Russia made between the US and Europe in the Iraqi crisis, even though its position was shared by key EU members. As viewed from Moscow, the current dynamics within the EU do not allow Russia to count on its European partners to act as a counterweight to the US in a joint effort, on a structured, permanent basis. In years to come, Russia's foreign policy might become more Euro-centric, in the sense that Moscow will have to devote a lot of energy and inspiration to invigorate its partnership with the EU, thereby consolidating its place and role in Europe. Until then, Russia may view its relationship with the US, with whom the political and security dialogue appears less intricate, if only because it has more ancient roots and pragmatic goals (Medvedev 2004), as the stable factor in its still complex partnership with the West.

Notes

1   Moscow's unease in this connection finds its expression in Russian officials' calls for the establishment of a 'democratic world pattern' which avoids 'an oligarchic model ... determining the rights and responsibilities of states towards each other and toward the world community as a whole solely according to their financial-economic and military strength' (Ivanov 2003).

2   These are the 'Security Concept' (Presidential decree No. 24 of 10 January 2000), the 'Military Doctrine' (Presidential decree No. 706 of 21 April 2000), the 'Foreign Policy Concept' (28 June 2000) and the 'Russia's Middle Term Strategy towards the EU – 2000–2010'. The first three of these documents are available in Russian on the website of the Russian Security Council: www.scrf.gov.ru/documents/documents.shtml. The fourth can be found on the website of the European Commission's delegation to Russia: www.delrus.cec.eu.int/en/p_245.htm.

3   See note 2, above.

4   For instance, when Russian diplomats and international relations experts discussed the EU and its enlargement, it was more often than not to stress that NATO's 'expansion' was possibly threatening to Russia's interests and destabilising for the whole of Europe while at the same time asserting that the integration of Central and Eastern European countries into the EU constituted a much better option from the point of view of these countries' security and of Russian interests.

5   'Middle Term Strategy on Relations with the EU, 2000–2010' (see note 2 above).

6   Experts note that even at the height of Russia's resentment over 'Operation Allied Force', several aspects of its foreign policy demonstrated that Moscow was not prepared to sever completely its relations with the West (Lynch 1999; Sherr and Main 1999).

7   At first, the West did not really react to Moscow's new cooperative spirit. Western leaders probably had doubts over Moscow's sincerity, and their attention was

distracted by other priorities. It was only after President Putin expressed his full support to George W. Bush after 9/11 that the West started thinking that maybe the time was ripe to answer Moscow's cooperation calls (Medvedev 2004). And indeed, it was only then that the EU and the US recognised Russia as a market economy and that Moscow was granted fully-fledged membership within the Group of Eight (G-8) countries. In October 2001, the EU strengthened the mechanism for defence and security dialogue with Russia. NATO, for its part, established a new Council with Russia, in May 2002, which gives Russia a voice equal to that of NATO members on a number of issues that are supposed to be of common security interest.

8   Parliamentary elections were held in 2003 and a presidential election in 2004.
9   When Putin called the start of the war in Iraq a 'great mistake', Washington accused Russia of having violated the arms embargo imposed on Iraq. In retrospect, however, the general impression is that Washington shared Moscow's view that the bilateral relationship, which was under reconstruction, should be protected from the negative effects of the dispute over Iraq (Medvedev 2004).
10 Timmins (2005: 66) notes that when V. Putin and G. Schröder met for bilateral consultations in St Petersburg in April 2003, 'neither leader had wanted to find themselves ... badly estranged from the US, but wasted any opportunity for reconciliation when Jacques Chirac found his way into the summit and media misinterpretation of the meeting as having been called specifically to discuss the Iraq crisis placed Germany and Russia in the context of an unholy, anti-American political alliance with France'.
11 This impression was connected to the EU adopting its 'Common Strategy on Russia' (European Council 1999) right after 'Operation Allied Force' (4 June 1999).
12 This explains Moscow's insistence that the UNSC should take the lead in settling the situation in post-war Iraq, as well as being reformed in such a way as to improve its effectiveness.

PART II

The domestic contexts

MICHAEL WALLACK

8

From compellence to pre-emption: Kosovo and Iraq as US responses to contested hegemony

Introduction

This chapter examines the US role in the Kosovo and Iraq wars in the context of evolving strategic and foreign policy doctrine. The conclusion reached is that the George W. Bush administration has made a significant change in US strategic and foreign policy doctrine exemplified by its use of force in Afghanistan, and particularly clearly in Iraq. The change is the move from a central doctrine of defence by deterrence, containment, stable alliances and alignments, to a policy of expansion of influence and consolidation in areas of contested hegemony by means of pre-emptive war and regime change. In the new diplomacy, temporary coalitions take the place of alliances and the 'revolution in military affairs' provides graduated dominant unilateral force in preference to compellence. Cooperation with allies is primarily seen as a means to provide pre-conflict temporary staging areas and ports and post-conflict stabilisation and reconstruction support. The United Nations Security Council (UNSC) is considered as a source of post-conflict legitimation rather than a locus of decision on the legitimacy of the use of force before the fact.

The George H. W. Bush Administration's foreign policy was a continuation of the alliance-based approach which reflected the pre-Reagan internationalist worldview constructed by Truman, Acheson and Marshall at the start of the Cold War. With the collapse of the Soviet Union and the opening to the world of China, US policy-makers in the George H. W. Bush Administration cautiously tested the limits of multilateralism in response to the Iraqi invasion of Kuwait and ceded to Europe the problems posed by the break-up of Yugoslavia. Their tools were UN and regional diplomacy, embargoes, and finally in Iraq, war authorised by the UNSC.

The Clinton presidency focused on domestic affairs. Weakened by a newly-energised and unified Congressional Republican party, it reluctantly and haltingly edged into Bosnia and Kosovo within the highly circumscribed limitations that were set by the regional context, the flickering attention of the President and the internal power struggle among all the players: the White House staff, the Departments of State and Defence, the Armed Services and Congress. Their tools were diplomacy, the UN-sanctioned NATO stabilisation force in Bosnia, and the NATO-authorised compellence and UN-authorised stabilisation force in Kosovo.

The attack on the US by al Qaeda crystallised the George W. Bush administration's alternative to the existing defence and foreign policy paradigm – an alternative that originated in neo-conservative policy discussions during the 1990s. Among it strongest advocates were Richard Perle, Paul Wolfowitz, Donald Rumsfeld, and Vice-President Richard Cheney. Until the 9/11 attack on the US, the rationale for an assertive use of force to support US interests, rejection of Alliance commitments, force-limiting treaties, and constraints by international institutions lacked an urgent threat-based rationale that could serve to dampen objections from the military, Congress and the Department of State. The slow pace of change in the armed forces toward the goals implied by the so-called 'revolution in military affairs' (RMA) was set by the sceptical defence establishment, by budgetary limitations and by a lack of commitment to it by George W. Bush. These impediments were swept away by 9/11.

Kosovo: compellence in a multilateral framework

The Kosovo air war was the endpoint of the Clinton administration's conflicted interest in maintaining its dominant role in the Atlantic Alliance. For better and worse, it reflected the evolution of policy that began with Clinton's first-term effort to change the Bush presidency's non-engagement in the Balkan wars. The most important change in US policy that was produced by the Balkan conflicts during the Clinton administration was the realisation that the US post-Cold War commitment to Europe could impose serious political and military costs on the US, divide its European allies, and pose difficult domestic political choices for the administration. The context in which these realisations became evident was the confrontation between Clinton's pre-election policy on Bosnia and its rejection by Europe, the security and foreign policy bureaucracy, and Congress.

The Clinton administration's Bosnia policy

In the election campaign that brought him to power, Clinton criticised the George H. W. Bush administration's refusal to become engaged in Bosnia against what he regarded as the Milošević regime's expansionary war. In so doing, Clinton the candidate seemed to be continuing the Carter administration's human rights idealism, while at the same time prompting a split between neo-conservative Republicans who favoured such an approach and the pragmatic George H. W. Bush's realist coolness to Bosnian engagement (Halberstam 2001: 307; Wolfowitz 2003). At the same time, however, that election strategy presented the newly-elected Clinton administration with a seemingly intractable dilemma – 'the problem from hell', as Vice-President Albert Gore called it. NATO allies, particularly France under President François Mitterrand and the UK under Prime Minister John Major opposed the Clinton 'lift and strike' initiative[1] and favoured the Vance-Owen plan for the ethnic cantonisaton of Bosnia as well as the continued UNSC-approved arms embargo on all parties. They would agree to military pressure on the Serbs only if the US would insert ground forces to bolster the safety of their 9000-man peacekeeping forces serving in the United Nations Protection Force (UNPROFOR). A policy deadlock ensued. The policy preferred by Clinton and seen as necessary to the preservation of US leadership of NATO was blocked by the opposition to it by key NATO members.

However, Clinton's interest in advancing a more forceful approach to Bosnia was tempered by the reality of the White House's perennial need to reconcile its position with those of the Departments of State and Defence, and Congress. Secretary of State Warren Christopher was not a supporter of the 'lift and strike' initiative, and Defence Secretary Les Aspin and the Joint Chiefs of Staff (JCS) opposed it, as did a significant number of members of Congress of both parties.[2] Almost no one in the administration, the President included, would contemplate the use of US ground forces in anything but a limited and temporary role. The compromise adopted by the NATO allies was an agreement to protect the UN designated Muslim 'safe areas' by force if necessary, but without US ground forces. Ivo Daalder (2000: 18) writes: 'In what would become a pattern in the administration's approach to Bosnia in these early years, the failure of a US policy initiative was soon followed by Washington's adopting the approach favoured by the Europeans.'

In December of 1994, the US had agreed to supply as many as 25,000 ground troops to support a withdrawal or redeployment of UNPROFOR or the supervision of a peace agreement. The extraction force would have NATO command, not 'dual-key', and would operate under rules of engagement determined by the US. The difficulty however was that with this agreement, the US was obligated to respond to a UN request to NATO to withdraw, rather than by any subsequent decision of the President. According to Daalder (2000: 55), 'everyone [in the administration] knew that if the UN request[ed] assistance, the operation would be approved [by NATO]'.

The prospect of a US force having to extract NATO UNPROFOR forces from the midst of a civil war was not a happy one for the Clinton administration. It would pay a heavy political penalty if it sent ground forces in, and it would get little credit from its association with a continuing Bosnian humanitarian disaster (Halberstam 2001: 306). At the same time, the value of the US role in NATO, and NATO itself, would be seriously questioned if the US did not help to resolve the Bosnian crisis. It was this argument, made by Madeleine Albright in a memo to Clinton and the National Security Council (NSC), which formed the basis of the Clinton administration's 'endgame strategy' and the Dayton Accords. Continued Bosnian Serb attacks, including the massacre at Srebrenica, and the attack on Gorazde and Zepa produced an agreement at the London conference of the UNPROFOR and NATO member states to use decisive air power.³

Air-strikes would be used with streamlined dual key restrictions to force Bosnian Serbs to give up attacks on safe zones. At this point Chirac and Clinton were almost on the same page. They had got there because Chirac challenged Clinton to do something about Bosnia at the G-7 Summit in Halifax (June 1995) by declaring that 'the position of leader of the free world [was] vacant' (Halberstam 2001: 305). Rising to the challenge, Clinton called for a new plan for Bosnia, and his national security advisor Anthony Lake responded by circumventing the deadlock among domestic policy actors. Rather than passing on the variety of discordant views from the Departments of State and Defence, the Lake 'endgame' called for the use of air-strikes to force the Bosnian Serbs, Bosnian Muslims, Milošević and the Croats to negotiate a comprehensive settlement. The key external ingredients for the success of US policy were the pressure on decision-makers produced by public outrage at Bosnian Serb atrocities at Srebrenica, and the effective Croatian and Bosnian Muslim attacks on Bosnian Serb enclaves. As Halberstam (2001: 307) has noted, 'Clinton was infuriated by the images of US helplessness that had been shown on network television, and his aides witnessed some of the worst of his private rages'.

If local actors could force a settlement, the size of US forces could remain within parameters set by Congress and the Defence Department. The JCS were determined not to fight a major conflict in the Balkans because, in part, they were wedded to their strategic commitment to be ready to fight two 'major theatre wars' elsewhere: Iraq and Korea. These were the conflicts that had driven planning, and force sizing and basing decisions for the last ten years. They would accept a much smaller commitment, as they had in the Bosnia UNPROFOR extraction agreement provided it was either non-hostile or if hostile, temporary. Otherwise the logistical demands and mission creep would undermine planning for the two theatre wars and jeopardise success in them should they have to be fought at short notice. As General Wesley K. Clark (2001b) described his problem as NATO Supreme Allied Commander during the Kosovo conflict:

> The real problem was that there was a conflict between the Pentagon's institutional interest and what it thought it needed and what NATO needed. So there was, the hardest struggles weren't with the French, not for me. The hardest struggles emotionally for me were with my own chain of command. That was because

they were weighing things off. They were still concerned about Operation Northern Watch. I pulled a lot of the aircraft out of Northern Watch. I wanted to use them in the operation that NATO's future depended on. If Saddam Hussein got frisky for a couple of days, I didn't think that was a big deal. But to Washington it looked like a big deal, so they were trying to balance off both of my operations.

In the aftermath of Srebrenica, Clinton and Chirac spoke on the phone, agreed to 'do something' and a few days later in a Bastille Day speech, Chirac compared the events to the West's response to Hitler's occupation of the Sudetenland and implied that French forces would be withdrawn rather than continue as passive observers (Daalder 2000: 69; Halberstam 2001: 316). On 26 July 1995, the US Senate voted to lift the arms embargo against Bosnia that was imposed on all of the former Yugoslavia in September 1991.

The US Defence Secretary, now William Perry, and the new Chairman of the Joint Chiefs of Staff, John Shalikashvili, were sent to Europe to propose an extensive air campaign as the best military option to force a peace negotiation. They stressed the effectiveness of air power and precision weapons brought about by the RMA since the Gulf War (Halberstam 2001: 318, 327). Since Chirac had already changed the debate from the question of whether to use force to the question of what kind of force to use, and since a failed air campaign would require extraction with US forces already committed, the decision was all but made. According to Daalder (2000: 74, n.96), Chirac agreed to support the US air campaign strategy in a phone call to Clinton on 18 July, three days before the London Conference at which the decision was officially made and announced. On 21 July 1995 after leaders met in London, NATO threatened to use air-strikes to protect the safe area of Gorazde.

National Security Advisor (NSA) Anthony Lake gained formal approval for the 'endgame' strategy at a meeting of the principals (i.e. Defence and State) on 7 August, and made a tour of European capitals to delineate the new policy. At each stop, according to Daalder, Lake outlined the policy of seeking a comprehensive settlement, using air-strikes to prompt agreement and lifting economic sanctions on Serbia. What followed was the beginning of the negotiations led by Richard Holbrooke, the shelling of Sarajevo by the Serbs, the ten-day NATO bombing of Bosnian Serb military positions, a ceasefire, the approval of a NATO-Russia Implementation Force (IFOR) mission in Bosnia, and the Dayton Accords.

The compellence policy that brought Milošević to the negotiations that ended the Bosnian conflict reflected the Clinton administration's conception of the problem of responding to humanitarian concerns generated by television news coverage of the war, and the central political objective of maintaining US leadership of the Atlantic Alliance. The limiting domestic factors in the choice of means were the strong opposition from Congress and the Defence Department (and JCS) to the use of US ground troops in large numbers in a hostile environment. Clinton thought he had those domestic limitations covered in his 'lift and strike' policy proposal, but found as President that NATO could not be convinced to accept it. Compellence became possible when NATO objections to it ended, but this change required Clinton to give some evidence that he was ultimately willing to go beyond compellence if air-strikes proved ineffective.

The policy, as spelled out by NSA Anthony Lake, made it clear that failure of the policy of air-strikes, whether caused by the unwillingness of NATO or its ineffectiveness, would result in US disengagement after nine months of bombing. We simply do not know whether Clinton's willingness to use US ground troops to help extract UNPROFOR would have led to a larger military role for US forces – along side a multilateral force – in the absence of success at Dayton. In retrospect, the formula proposed by Lake – massive air-strikes, armed indigenous forces and a (possibly) US-led multilateral force – resembles an early version of George W. Bush's Afghanistan conflict.

Kosovo

The US participation in the Kosovo war was a product of the success of Clinton's Bosnia effort and the evolution of thinking that was taking place in Europe. It represents an important evolution of US security policy because it offers a clear example of an acceptance by the US of multilateralism in the use of force in circumstances where core US security interests were not threatened. It represents a possible future paradigm for the US and Europe if the George W. Bush policy of pre-emptive unilateralism does not become the *de facto* policy paradigm in Washington.

However, the decisions that led the way to Kosovo were the product of the temporary ascendancy in the Clinton administration of officials who were advocates of a continuing US leadership role in European security, particularly Secretary of State Madeleine Albright and, for a brief time, civilian and uniformed military leaders. It also was enabled by the unlikely and temporary alliance between Congressional foreign policy liberals and neo-conservative supporters of military intervention. While Congressional liberals favoured a multilateral alliance-based policy, neo-conservatives favoured bilateral support for Balkan allies, along the lines used in Central America during the Reagan administration and in Afghanistan. The acceptance of compellence by the JCS and the Secretary of Defence was predicated on its time and force-limited nature and by the results of the pre-Dayton compellence.

In the last days of the George H. W. Bush administration, President Bush warned Milošević that in the event of Serb political repression of the Kosovo Albanians, the US would be prepared to 'employ military force against the Serbs in Kosovo and in Serbia proper'. The new Secretary of State Warren Christopher reiterated this warning in a softer form ('We remain prepared to respond against the Serbs') in early 1993 (Daalder and O'Hanlon 2000: 9). As

Bosnia became the focal point of the Clinton administration's policy-making, Kosovo receded to such a considerable degree that the status of those warnings was uncertain. It may well have been the case that the original warning was an effort to forestall unwelcome policy initiatives by Serbia during the (likely) transition to a new administration, rather than a permanent commitment. Seen in that light, the softening by Warren Christopher might have been designed to put the Clinton administration's approach to the Balkans in better perspective – Clinton did not come into office with a policy of using force against Serbia. After Dayton, however, the enthusiasm of Secretary of State Albright and NATO's Supreme Allied Commander Wesley Clark for using compellence against Milošević, as well as the willingness of the new Secretary of Defence William Perry, and the new Chair of the JCS John Shalikashvili to use force in the Balkans – particularly air power and precision weapons – together with the distraction of Congress in the midst of the Clinton impeachment, combined to make a new policy possible. Responding to events in Kosovo in May and June of 1998, NATO formulated its common objectives and began to devise military responses to Serb attacks on Albanians in Kosovo. As the situation in Kosovo worsened, NATO issued activation orders for air-strikes and began a diplomatic effort to resolve the conflict, allow Kosovo Albanians to return to their homes and obtain the withdrawal of Serb forces from Kosovo. As air-strikes were about to begin, Milošević agreed to the substance of NATO's demands, which included a non-military Organisation for Security and Cooperation in Europe (OSCE) observation force and over flights by NATO to help the ground monitor. UNSC resolution 1203 endorsed the agreement. In the early months of 1999, however, fighting resumed and the reconvened Contact Group reinforced by a NATO Council approval of the use of air-strikes led to the Rambouillet and Paris negotiations. The failure of these negotiations and the increased use of force by Serbs in Kosovo in violation of the October 1998 agreement led to the withdrawal of the OSCE observers and the bombing campaign against the Serbs lasting seventy-seven days.

During the course of this exercise, it became clear that a significant difference of opinion was growing within NATO on the utility and conduct of the compellence strategy. It soon became apparent that bombing would not rapidly move Milošević to the bargaining table, end killings of Kosovo Albanians, or significantly degrade the Serb forces in Kosovo. In effect, the most important objectives of the new bolder compellence strategy were being called into question, but unlike the earlier limited compellence aimed at Bosnian Serbs, this effort was intended to force a sovereign state to change its objectives as a test case for the continued value of NATO as a security community.

These factors prompted the escalation of the campaign to military, political communication and economic targets within Serbia proper. While this escalation divided the leaders of the alliance and generated strong negative effects on European public opinion, it did change the dynamic of the conflict. By their continued participation in the Kosovo war, despite opposition in public opinion NATO members endorsed the continued importance of a transatlantic European security policy. While it is not possible to say with assurance that the extended air war was the decisive factor in producing a negotiated settlement, it was certainly one of the major factors, along with the increasing strength of the Kosovo Liberation Army (KLA), the pressure by the Russians on the Serbs to accept an agreement, and the suggestions that ground forces were being readied for deployment to Kosovo (Daalder and O'Hanlon 2000: 200–6; Hosmer 2001).

Conclusions on Kosovo and compellence

The compellence strategy, that seemed to be leading to a commitment of ground forces, finally adopted by the Clinton administration was not its preferred option. The Defence Department and much of Congress was opposed to the use of force by the US in the Balkans in what could become a protracted conflict with an uncertain result. Force planning had not identified the region as one of high national interest and consequently the military opposed such a commitment. Only the political decision that the US leadership role in NATO required some response to Milošević, together with the change in the policy positions by its major European allies, led the US into a policy decision to commit itself to war in the Balkans. That the result proved to be a positive one from the US perspective was more a product of the particular circumstances of regional politics than it was a demonstration of the success of compellence as a tool for NATO or the US. By negotiating war aims and carefully delineating the military strategy to be used within NATO and the Contact Group, the Clinton administration was able to put together a multilateralist compellence policy that overcame the differences with the Alliance and within the US government itself.

Iraq as a test case for pre-emption

Iraq policy in the Clinton administration
The Clinton Administration's policy toward Iraq essentially continued the George H. W. Bush containment policy using UN sanctions, over-flights, the oil for food trade embargo, and haphazard support for both internal and exile efforts against the regime. One goal of containment was to protect Saudi Arabia, the Gulf States and Kuwait from another oil grab by Iraq. Another goal was to prevent Iraq from either attacking, or provoking an attack by, Israel. US military planning assumed Iraq containment as a central feature in the design of its force structure and deployment policy. Iraq and Korea were

the two 'major theatre wars' that were built into all military planning and therefore all military position taking in inter-agency decision-making.

These plans assumed that war would come as a result of an imminent threat or actual military move by Iraq. Hence the Bush–Clinton embargo, inspection and over-flight policy was consistent with Defence and JCS operational plans since that policy provided an internationally legitimated means to operate in Iraqi airspace, collect intelligence, and limit the military capacity of an important adversary. By 1998, however, Saddam's counter-efforts against the continued UN inspection regime and the trade embargo were gaining ground and world and US support for containment was slipping. As Joseph McMillan (2003: 24) notes:

> It was time to choose one of two options: take more direct action to bring about a change of regime and the forcible resolution of the Iraq problem, or retrench into long-term deterrence and containment. Under the latter approach, the United States, as it has done on the Korean Peninsula, would accept the continued survival of a hostile regime in a vital region but defend against Iraq with a robust forward presence and deter it from egregious conduct with the threat of overwhelming retaliation.

Clinton, however, had to contend with the fact that the Republican Congress had adopted the 'Iraq Liberation Act', which pledged the US to aid those Iraqis who sought regime change using force. In what had become a typical Clintonesque approach to policy, the Administration found itself claiming to be committed to containment for the sake of maintaining its international coalition and UN-based mandate while at the same time claiming to support regime change for domestic political reasons. The incoherence of the two positions was not lost on either audience and only served to weaken efforts to maintain the embargo, over-flight and inspection regime.

Even though it was clear enough by 1999 that the Iraq containment policy could not be continued much longer, the lesson of the Gulf War was that the lead up to a regime changing war would necessarily be divisive and protracted if it was opposed by the military and Congress. There was simply no possibility that Clinton, an out-going impeached president, could initiate such a major change in security policy. It would be a problem for the next administration.

The Clinton administration policy on Iraq should be placed in a broader context of US policy toward the Middle East. Most important was the administration's effort to encourage a negotiated settlement of the Israeli–Palestinian conflict. In the long term, US security interests in the region require a political settlement of that conflict. The Clinton administration, taking a political rather than military point of view of the multi-faceted regional context, preferred to contain Iraq and Iran, postponing the security problems they posed, and regime change, until after a resolution of the Israeli–Palestinian conflict. The current policy of the George W. Bush administration is based on the assumption that regime change in Iraq will create conditions that will make a political solution of outstanding regional security issues possible – in effect the reverse of the previous analysis. While many critics of US policy see this change as the result of the long standing ideologically driven views of the so-called Bush administration Vulcans (i.e. Cheney, Wolfowitz and Rumsfeld), there are at least two sets of factors that are more important: the RMA and the collapse of the US–Saudi alignment.

The Bush administration chooses regime change

The 'Revolution in Military Affairs'

The first policy of the Bush administration was the so-called 'smart sanctions' initiative proposed at the UN in the first months of the administration. Imports into Iraq would be tightened, oil smuggling out would be interdicted, and Iraqi assets in foreign banks would be more closely controlled. Russia indicated that it would veto the proposal in the UNSC and it was shelved in favour of an extension of the existing sanctions on 3 July 2001. In retrospect it might be seen as a treading of water until a more robust military regime change policy could be designed, built and rolled out, perhaps in a second Bush administration after 2004. Events would change this timeline.

While Secretary of State Colin Powell was following the diplomatic track to its defeat (with the help of Russia and France), Rumsfeld was in the midst of a Quadrennial Defence Review (US Department of Defence 2001) that was substantially altering US world military strategy. While the Department of Defence had been engaged in a continuing modernisation debate on the implications of new information and communication technology for a decade under the heading RMA, the last years of the twentieth century saw the actual capacity of available hardware catch up with futurist discussions.[4] Perhaps more importantly, the new Secretary of Defence was prepared to use a lifetime of bureaucratic infighting skills to eliminate uniformed officer objections to the RMA driven changes.[5] Under the new doctrine, the specification of the core objectives of US military policy would no longer be built on a 'two major theatre war' doctrine. Technology would allow a flexible and interoperable set of military capacities to be assigned to a wide variety of conflicts in additive steps from low-level, sub-national conflict to general war against future superpower rivals (US Department of Defence 2001: 6).

This was, in effect, a conventional war doctrine updating the Cold War nuclear strategy of graduated response that had been the revolution in nuclear strategy in Rumsfeld's youth. In that doctrine, tactical nuclear weapons would add leverage to US technological superiority to compensate for the comparative disadvantage in numbers of soldiers under arms enjoyed by China and the USSR. In the new RMA armed forces, US advantages in information technology, communications and other weapons technology would allow a global reach at a manageable cost and without the need for large permanent troop deployments and long standing commitments of forces and bases by regional allies. This would be a force designed for concerts of the willing rather than standing alliances. Few allies could match the technology at the level necessary for multilateral force integration. As a consequence and perhaps by choice, the US would do the fighting while willing allies would be limited to providing an after-conflict stabilisation force and humanitarian assistance. Precision weapons, instant worldwide communications and the ability to deliver information to each soldier in real time would enable even a small force to engage an indigenous enemy without the usual information and communications disadvantages faced in the asymmetrical conflicts of previous eras (*Washington Post*, 18 November 2003).

The importance of this doctrinal shift to understanding the decision to move to a strategy of pre-emptive war in Iraq and elsewhere is that it provides a means (and perhaps an incentive) to choose military regime change in Iraq at a much lower expected cost, in a shorter time frame, and without extensive support by Alliance partners. At least, these are the suppositions driving the new 'quadrennial defence review' doctrine.[6] The Iraq war would accelerate force transformation and transformation would lower the costs of the war.

The collapse of the Saudi–US alignment
The second factor that helped facilitate the shift of policy from compellence and containment to regime change in Iraq was the deterioration in the US–Saudi alignment as a consequence of the success of Osama Bin Laden and the inability or unwillingness of the Saudi regime to face its own failing legitimacy. Quite simply, the Saudis could no longer act openly as a regional partner to the US, and the US could no longer count on the Saudi regime to continue to provide either a military access point for US forces or a secure supply of oil (*New York Times*, 9 February 2003). Iraq had to be moved from one side of the regional balance to the other.

If Iraq could be transformed by regime change into a friendly regime it could replace Saudi Arabia (if combined with Kuwait and the Gulf States) as an oil price and supply stabiliser and as a regional military access point for US forces (*New York Times*, 20 April 2003). Iraq is en route to everywhere else in the region, and unlike Saudi Arabia, Iraq has not been cultivating regional friends and is not the site of Mecca. It is, instead, the subject of numerous UNSC warnings, admonitions and sanctions. Of course, this set of factors only makes an argument for regime change if Iraq can be transformed into a stable and friendly state after a regime change (*New York Times*, 22 September 2002). Otherwise, the result would be an unstable Saudi Arabia and an unstable Iraq and perhaps even an intractably anti-US Iraq and Saudi Arabia. While the declaratory policy of the US envisions a stable and friendly unified Iraq, it might be the case that US regional objectives could also be achieved if

Iraq slips into a loose federation along communal lines, with only parts of it stable, friendly and rebuilt.

Time pressure

It is often the case that a decision to go to war is taken by policy-makers because they believe that the alternative of persisting in diplomacy, compellence, or delay will find their own capacities for war in the future weaker, and the capacities of their enemy stronger. Something of this was happening in the Bush administration, but not precisely this. The RMA, according to the 2001 Quadrennial Defence Review, would continue to favour the US for some time to come. Although it was said that Iraq was moving toward a nuclear capacity, at the time the war against Iraq began, no one seriously suggested that Iraqi military capacity was increasing. While many key decision-makers probably believed that Iraq had chemical and biological weapons, and that the Iraqi regime might pass them on to terrorists, it was also known that such weapons were also held by several other unfriendly regimes around the world. Hence, fears that terrorists might use these weapons against the US did not depend upon their possession by Iraq.

The deterioration of authority in Saudi Arabia, however, was expected to worsen with no obvious means to prevent it. According to a member of the Pentagon team planning the 'war on terror' quoted in an article by Priest in the *Washington Post* (13 March 2004),

> The strategic thinking was the Middle East is going down the tubes. 'It's getting worse, not better,' said one former senior Pentagon official who worked closely with [Undersecretary of Defence for Policy, Douglas] Feith's offices. 'I don't think we thought there was objective evidence that could be got from CIA, DIA, INR,' he added, referring to the Defense Intelligence Agency, the Pentagon's main intelligence office, and the State Department's Bureau of Intelligence and Research.[7]

The likelihood, therefore, of the collapse of that regime or its 'Talibanisation' by al Qaeda might well have lent weight to the decision to use force sooner rather than later.

The internal opposition and Blair

Evidence provided by the hearings of the 'Special Commission on 9/11' and by the publication of Bob Woodward's book on the Iraqi war decision provides additional insight into the decision to invade Iraq. It is clear that Rumsfeld, Wolfowitz and Cheney favoured war and regime change from the beginning of the Bush administration, and that Bush himself agreed that the question was not whether but when the war should be undertaken (*Washington Post*, 12 January 2003).[8] Rumsfeld, Wolfowitz, Richard Armitage (Powell's chief deputy) and others expressed their views on Iraq as far back as 1998, in an often quoted open 'Letter to President Clinton' (1998)

> The only acceptable strategy is one that eliminates the possibility that Iraq will be able to use, or threaten to use, weapons of mass destruction. In the near term, this means a willingness to undertake military action as diplomacy is clearly failing. In the long term, it means removing Saddam Hussein and his regime from power.

In the *Washington Post* (20 April 2004), Bob Woodward would later describe Cheney's view of the issue after the election thus:

> In early January 2001, before Bush was inaugurated, Cheney passed a message to the outgoing secretary of defense, William S. Cohen, a moderate Republican who served in the Democratic Clinton administration. 'We really need to get the president-elect briefed up on some things', Cheney said, adding that he wanted a serious 'discussion about Iraq and different options'. The president-elect should not be given the routine, canned, round-the-world tour normally given incoming presidents. Topic A should be Iraq ... After Sept. 11, 2001, Cheney said, the president understood what had to be done. He had to do Afghanistan first, sequence the attacks, but after Afghanistan – 'soon thereafter' – the president knew he had to do Iraq. Cheney said he was confident after Sept. 11 that it would come out okay.

It is also clear that the uniformed military was divided on when and how to deal with Iraq during the first year of the George W. Bush administration because not all of the uniformed service was convinced by the arguments on force size and strategy that flowed from the new RMA doctrine. The usual way that the military has to delay such a decision is to provide war plans that require a larger commitment in numbers and costs and a darker prognosis than those favouring the war are willing to defend to Congress or the President. This apparently happened during 2002 but Rumsfeld, Wolfowitz and others eventually beat it back. While some in the military disputed the plans and costs, the war itself, however, was not opposed. This was a foregone conclusion since Iraq had been identified and war-gamed for many years as a possible opponent in military planning. Hersh (2003) thus describes the bureaucratic infighting conducted by Rumsfeld:

> Rumsfeld's personal contempt for many of the senior generals and admirals who were promoted to top jobs during the Clinton Administration is widely known. He was especially critical of the Army, with its insistence on maintaining costly mechanized divisions. In his off-the-cuff memoranda, or 'snowflakes', as they're called in the Pentagon, he chafed about generals having 'the slows' – a reference to Lincoln's characterisation of General George McClellan. 'In those conditions – an atmosphere of derision and challenge – the senior officers do not offer their best advice', a high-ranking general who served for more than a year under Rumsfeld said. One witness to a meeting recalled Rumsfeld confronting General Eric Shinseki, the Army Chief of Staff, in front of many junior officers. 'He was looking at the Chief and waving his hand', the witness said, 'saying, "Are you getting this yet? Are you getting this yet?"' ... Gradually, Rumsfeld succeeded in

replacing those officers in senior Joint Staff positions who challenged his view. 'All the Joint Staff people now are handpicked, and churn out products to make the Secretary of Defense happy', the planner said. 'They don't make military judgments – they just respond to his snowflakes.'

What little opposition to the decision there was in the Administration came from Colin Powell. According to Woodward (2004) and other sources, it appears, however, that the Secretary of State was not asked for his opinion and probably understood that the train had in fact left the station unless a miracle removed Saddam before the US supply train arrived at Basra. He did remind the President that if he decided on war, the US would 'own' Iraq. Bush did not seem disturbed by the prospect at the time, having taken counsel not with his father – whose National Security Advisor Brent Scowcroft had opposed the war in a *Wall Street Journal* op-ed piece (15 August 2002) – he said, but with a 'stronger' father. Perhaps he was speaking through Woodward to his Evangelical electoral base, or perhaps he meant Cheney. Again, with the benefit of hindsight, it appears that Powell was never in the running as the source of policy ideas for the President but was being kept busy with make-work diplomacy so as to keep him on board as an administration supporter rather than having him operating on the outside as a critic and rival.

As a minor element of this aspect of Powell's role, his work in the UN was thought to be essential to keep Tony Blair in office and on side. However, according to Woodward (*Washington Post*, 21 April 2004), Bush offered to let Blair back out of his commitment if that was necessary to keep him in office. It must have been a bit disconcerting to Blair to learn that Bush did not actually think he needed to keep Blair on side but could accept a public disavowal of the US policy even from Blair at that late date. Of course, the implication of Bush's offer also meant that Bush did not need to accept any advice from Blair, since Bush had already, in effect, given permission to Blair to jump ship if necessary.

Congress, the Tonkin gulf ploy and terrorism

Having a regime change resolution in hand, and a solid and fervent Republican majority in Congress after 2002, and having delivered regime change in Afghanistan without finding Osama, the Bush Administration had little to fear from Congress as it moved toward war in Iraq (*Washington Post*, 12 December 2003). Democrats in the Senate generally supported the war, finding no way to counter the arguments proposed by the administration that Saddam Hussein had weapons of mass destruction; had challenged the UNSC by ejecting the UN inspectors; was deceiving the UN inspection team; was moving toward the an end of sanctions on a wave of support even among NATO members; and had provided refrigerators and washing machines and who knows what else to the families of suicide bombers. Sceptics had no way to counter the administration's contention that Saddam had gone into league with terrorists even if he could not be linked directly to the attacks on the US. The sticking point for Congressional Democrats was the role of the UN inspections – many Democrats wanted inspections to continue for longer, and then later, Democrats were sceptical about administration estimates of the cost of the war and reconstruction. Posen (2003: 31) reflects the views of dissenters in the uniformed services,

> The historical record suggests that stability operations require between two and twenty soldiers and/or policemen per 1,000 individuals, depending on the level of political instability. Prior to the commencement of hostilities against Iraq in March 2003, many warned that the post war occupation of the country could require significant troops. Gen. Eric Shinseki, then chief of staff of the US Army, estimated before the Congress in late February 2003 that several hundred thousand troops would be required for several years to occupy Iraq with its 22 million people.

Shinseki's estimates were derided by Wolfowitz and the general left active duty (Crane and Terrill 2003; *New York Times*, 28 February 2003; Fallows 2004).

Under such favourable circumstances, and in marked contrast to the fairly serious and substantive Senate debate that preceded the Gulf War and the close supervision exercised by Congress over Clinton in Bosnia and Kosovo, the Bush administration was able to get a Congressional resolution that was a virtual blank cheque. In addition, it was also able to disclose almost nothing of its plans for the war or post-war occupation.[9] The only explanation that can be offered for this lack of oversight by Congress is that Congress had been swept up by the fear of terrorism, and weakened by the debilitating Clinton impeachment scandal and by the voters' inclination to believe the suggestions by many in the Bush administration that Saddam was somehow behind the terrorist attacks on the World Trade Center and the Pentagon.[10]

Conclusions

The grand strategy with which Bush entered office amounts, in post-9/11 practice, to a defensive unilateralism that is at the core of the announced policy of pre-emptive hegemonism. The Clinton administration accepted the globalist soft power world model, and saw Kosovo as a necessary component of making that framework work in the post-Cold War environment. Bush is uninterested in, and even hostile to, European institutional transformation and global institutions, including NATO, the UN, and any new or proposed multilateralist responses to world problems that would restrict US freedom of action. The 9/11 attack on the US gave the RMA's transformation a politically powerful rationale. It also provided a counterargument to those in the uniformed military that wanted to keep the Powell doctrine and its implicit veto power on the use of US forces in compellence or in circumstances where US vital interests were not being challenged. George W. Bush and his compliant Republican majority in Congress were easy converts to the grand strategy of hegemonic primacy promoted by Cheney, Rumsfeld and Wolfowitz. A question that remains is whether the bitter experience of military victory in Iraq will cause the next administration to reconsider the policy of primacy.

Notes

1 Clinton favoured lifting the UN arms embargo on the region and using NATO air power against forces that challenged a UNSC sanctioned ceasefire (Halberstam 2001: 220–30).
2 Powell told Clinton that Bosnia would take 500,000 troops in a series of steps. When Madeleine Albright (then Ambassador to the UN) asked: 'What's the point of having this superb military that you're always talking about if we can't use it?' she was reminded of Vietnam (Blumenthal 2003: 62–3).
3 'Following the London Conference last Friday [21 July], a specific warning was issued that any attack by the Bosnian Serbs on Gorazde would be met with a substantial and decisive response. Last Saturday, the North Atlantic Council met and, in the light of the gravity of the situation, directed the NATO Military Authorities immediately to prepare plans to implement this warning' (Speech by NATO's Secretary General following the North Atlantic Council meeting of 25 July 1995): www.nato.int/docu/speech/1995/s950725a.htm.
4 Hogg (2002: 400) writes: 'Just winning battles will not win wars or effect regime changes. Clausewitz states that, to have victory in war, one must first destroy the enemy's army or force; second, one must occupy his country; and, third, one must destroy the enemy's will to fight ... RDO [rapid decisive operations] envisions being able to defeat the enemy's force, addresses breaking the will of the enemy to continue to fight, but it does not discuss occupying the enemy's territory.' RDO was called 'Shock and Awe' (Ullman and Wade 1996) in the Iraq war.
5 Cordesman (2001). To critics, the RMA in Rumsfeld's hands was the military equivalent of the tech bubble on NASDAQ.
6 President Bush first enunciated the 'pre-emption doctrine' in a speech at West Point in June of 2002: www.whitehouse.gov/news/releases/2002/06/20020601-3.html. See also White House, 2002.
7 According to Priest, 'the Pentagon operation was created, at least in part, to provide a more hard-line alternative to the official intelligence, according to interviews with current and former defense and intelligence officials. The two offices, overseen by Feith, concluded that Saddam Hussein's Iraq and al Qaeda were much more closely and conclusively linked than the intelligence community believed. In this sense, the offices functioned as a pale version of the secret "Team B" analysis done by administration conservatives in the mid-1970s, who concluded the intelligence community was underplaying the Soviet military threat. Rumsfeld, in particular, has a history of scepticism about the intelligence community's analysis, including assessments of the former Soviet Union's military ability and of threats posed by ballistic missiles from North Korea and other countries.'
8 The *New York Times* (22 September 2002) wrote 'On September 17, 2001, six days after the attacks on the World Trade Center and the Pentagon, President Bush signed

a 2¹/₂-page document marked TOP SECRET that outlined the plan for going to war in Afghanistan as part of a global campaign against terrorism. Almost as a footnote, the document also directed the Pentagon to begin planning military options for an invasion of Iraq, senior administration officials said ... Over the next nine months, the administration would make Iraq the central focus of its war on terrorism without producing a rich paper trail or record of key meetings and events leading to a formal decision to act against President Saddam Hussein, according to a review of administration decision-making based on interviews with more than 20 participants. Instead, participants said, the decision to confront Hussein at this time emerged in an ad hoc fashion. Often, the process circumvented traditional policymaking channels as long time advocates of ousting Hussein pushed Iraq to the top of the agenda by connecting their cause to the war on terrorism.'

9   Public Law 107–243, 107th Congress, Joint Resolution to authorise the use of United States Armed Forces against Iraq. 'The President is authorized to use the Armed Forces of the United States as he determines to be necessary and appropriate in order to: (1) defend the national security of the United States against the continuing threat posed by Iraq; and (2) enforce all relevant United Nations Security Council resolutions regarding Iraq.' The resolution passed the House (296–133) and the Senate (77–23).

10 President Bush said: 'The Iraqi regime has violated all of those obligations. It possesses and produces chemical and biological weapons. It is seeking nuclear weapons. It has given shelter and support to terrorism, and practices terror against its own people. The entire world has witnessed Iraq's eleven-year history of defiance, deception, and bad faith. We also must never forget the most vivid events of recent history. On September the 11th, 2001, America felt its vulnerability – even to threats that gather on the other side of the earth' (remarks by the President on Iraq, Cincinnati, Ohio, 7 October 2002): www.whitehouse.gov/news/releases/2002/10/20021007-8.html. See also former White House counter-terrorism expert Richard Clarke on President Bush's apparent beliefs about the connection: 'You know, the White House is papering over facts, such as, in the weeks immediately after 9/11, the president signed a national security directive instructing the Pentagon to prepare for the invasion of Iraq. Even though they knew at the time from me, from the FBI, from the CIA that Iraq had nothing to do with 9/11' (Clarke: 'White House is papering over facts', *CNN.com*: www.cnn.com/2004/ALLPOLITICS/03/23/clarke/index.html).

Alex Macleod

9

Competing for leadership in West European defence: France, Great Britain and the wars in Kosovo and Iraq

Introduction

The meeting on European defence between the French and British governments in Saint-Malo in December 1998 gave clear signs of convergence on European security policy between Western Europe's two major military powers. Since then, France seems to have abandoned, at least for the immediate future, the objective of establishing an autonomous European defence policy, while the United Kingdom of Great Britain and Northern Ireland (henceforth simply Britain) has appeared to accept the idea of a truly European defence policy, albeit still within NATO. These developments cannot hide the fact that France and Britain remain rivals for the leadership of European defence and continue to practise different strategies towards the US and the transatlantic relationship.

The chapter will first examine what leadership means for two middle-sized powers which both aspire to be recognised as states with global responsibilities, and the strategies they have used to maintain this status. It will then look at how Britain and France applied these strategies during two vital periods for the future of European defence, the conflict in Kosovo and the US–UK invasion of Iraq. It will be argued that in the final analysis, British and French aspirations to lead the emerging European Security and Defence Policy (ESDP) are closely linked to managing their relationship with the US.

French and British conceptions of international leadership

Britain and France have never accepted the idea that they no longer count as world powers. Permanent membership of the United Nations Security

Council (UNSC), possession of nuclear arms, a leading role in most of the important international institutions, and membership of the Group of Eight (G-8) are all attributes that both countries cite as proof of their international status. However, given the obvious wide gap between the great powers – the US, Russia and China – and the medium-sized powers – which France and Britain clearly are today – the concept of leadership needs to be carefully defined.

Leadership for a medium-sized power is located at two levels: the regional and the global. At the regional level, the one which relates most directly to the issues raised in this chapter, states can claim a leading position vis-à-vis local rivals, which will allow them to set the regional agenda, to bring other states to adopt their positions and to be generally recognised as indispensable for any decisions affecting the region.

The demand to be recognised as a global leader is much more difficult to establish since it usually conflicts with the interests of the acknowledged great powers. Both Britain and France insist that they have interests, or rather responsibilities, which go beyond Western Europe, not only because they are former colonial powers, but also because they remain major trading states. Global leadership for these two countries cannot mean setting the global agenda or being consistently called upon to solve international conflicts, since they possess neither the physical capacity nor the undisputed moral authority to intervene in such a way, except on a limited scale. They exercise their leadership in a more oblique way, usually in the form of influence, in the hope that they can have some vital input into important international decisions. In this situation, leadership means that others turn to the state in question, either for support or for help in ensuring a desired outcome. At both the regional and the global level, Britain and France have tended to adopt very different strategies.

For the British, leadership and the capacity to influence are very closely connected. They have tended to emphasise sovereignty and the right to defend a fairly narrow conception of the national interest as a way of maintaining their position in the world. In acting this way, they have effectively excluded themselves from the battle for political and economic leadership of Western Europe. They appear to be satisfied with simply protecting their economic and political interests in Europe without actively seeking a leadership role. However, in the area which they consider most vital to their foreign policy interests, that of security, they have never relinquished their claim.

On the surface, the British seem to have yielded leadership of European defence to the Americans, in the form of the so-called 'special relationship'. British leaders of both major parties have always viewed a European defence policy without the Americans as costly, inefficient and not particularly credible. The decision to defend Europe through an organisation dominated by the Americans, NATO, reflects a fundamental policy choice, which two observers have called a 'strategy of influence' (Touraine and Sabin 1990: 37). This policy is based on three ideas. First, Britain's international influence as a middle-sized power can only be enhanced by being closely associated with the world's most powerful country. Second, it is easier to influence the US by being perceived as a reliable ally. Finally, since, in British eyes, a US presence is vital for European security, the best way to maintain that presence is through support, especially by maintaining American leadership of NATO.

Traditionally, the French have preferred a 'strategy of power' (Touraine and Sabin 1990: 37), or, to be more precise, a 'strategy of autonomy', with emphasis on the capacity to lead a foreign and defence policy, which would be as autonomous as possible from that of the US. In the 1980s, French policy turned towards setting up a West European security structure, which met with some success, at least in terms of creating some combined European armed forces, but which could never seriously rival NATO. French policy has always insisted on maintaining France's international status as a leading power, a notion that can be summed up in one of the most important themes of that country's foreign policy, *rang*, or preservation of its position as a major power.

The Kosovo conflict

Britain and France had their first opportunity to show their commitment to Europe's post-Cold War security during the 1991–95 Bosnian conflict. France assumed a leadership role through its firm involvement in peace-making and peacekeeping operations, which it backed up by maintaining the largest foreign military force in the region. However, management of the war in Bosnia could hardly be called a success for a European solution to the endemic instability of the Balkans, since one European institution which should have played a major part in these operations, the EU, was almost totally excluded from the process throughout the war. President Jacques Chirac, freshly elected in May 1995, offered some tough rhetoric, forcing the G-7 to put the question on its agenda at the June 1995 Halifax meeting, and then successfully lobbying in favour of a rapid reaction force to support of UN forces in difficulty. Yet, in the final analysis, US diplomatic intervention was needed to put an end to this war. However, the French did manage to maintain themselves in the forefront of the fray and were instrumental in making sure the Americans assumed, much against their will, their international responsibilities in the Balkans. To the extent that they maintained a significant role in all the institutions involved in the conflict, the French established their claim to international leadership.

The British contribution to the search for peace in Bosnia began under even less auspicious circumstances. It was only after succumbing to intense international pressure that they agreed to send a token force of 1800 soldiers to Bosnia in August 1992. The French, for their part had already argued in favour of sending in troops to the region in July 1991 and actually sent them in April 1992. Though the British did fully commit themselves to the operations in Bosnia once they became militarily involved, they did not appear to share French enthusiasm for such forceful measures as air-strikes to counter Bosnian Serb attacks against Sarajevo. As for the issue of European defence, British participation in the Bosnian conflict only served to confirm their view that nothing of substance could or should be carried out without keeping NATO at the heart of any solution.

By the outbreak of the Kosovo conflict, the situation had evolved considerably. On the domestic front, government had changed hands in both countries. In France, power was now shared between a Gaullist president, Jacques Chirac, and a left-wing coalition government, headed by a Socialist prime minister, Lionel Jospin, but this did not affect France's ability to conduct foreign policy, because of the general consensus on foreign affairs and defence issues which had existed at least since 1981.

The British Labour government of Tony Blair, elected with an unassailable majority in May 1997, was a far cry from its Conservative predecessor, whose slim parliamentary majority was further weakened by a deep split within the ruling party between pro-Europeans and Euro-sceptics. Blair had more or less eliminated his internal opposition, had gained support for a more openly pro-European policy and seemed much better placed to make a credible claim to a British leadership role in international affairs.

When NATO launched its first air raids against Yugoslavia on 24 March 1999, France and Britain were well prepared for pursuing their respective leadership strategies. They had already taken a lead in the search for a solution to the crisis in Kosovo when they co-hosted the talks in Rambouillet, the failure of which precipitated the conflict. European security arrangements had progressed since the war in Bosnia. On the one hand, NATO had begun to give greater recognition to the notion of a European Security and Defence Identity (ESDI), and, on the other, the EU, especially since the signing of the Amsterdam treaty in 1997, appeared better equipped to be involved in European security matters. The most important development in this respect was the Franco-British agreement on European defence signed in Saint-Malo in December 1998, in which both countries made great strides towards accommodating each other's traditional position.

From the very beginning, both governments justified the operations against Yugoslavia on moral grounds, arguing that this was a battle for a 'certain conception of Europe and European values' (Jospin, 26 March 1999),[1] for 'a world that must know that barbarity cannot be allowed to defeat justice' (Blair, 26 March 1999) because it was the 'right, humane and civilised thing to do' (Blair, 14 April 1999) or, more simply, for the 'defence of European security and regional stability' (French Foreign Minister Hubert Védrine, 29 March 1999). However, from the French point of view, it was also necessary to establish both the legality and the legitimacy of this action against a sovereign state. This was achieved by referring specifically to the three UNSC resolutions on Kosovo adopted in 1998 – 1160, 1199 and 1203 – and by defending recourse to NATO as the only possible response to the urgency of the situation, since the Security Council was in no position to play its role of maintaining peace and international security.

Throughout the conflict, French leaders felt decidedly much less at ease than the British with the decision to bypass the UN, insisting that NATO's intervention represented an exception and not a precedent. Though French decision-makers agreed that the urgency of the Kosovo situation had called for rapid military intervention on the part of NATO, they declared that no international security operation could forego authorisation from the UNSC. This policy undoubtedly reflected French reservations about the US role in European security and the need for a counterweight to American power. It also expressed a more general French concern that the UN should be seen as the ultimate source of international law and legitimacy for the use of force. During the Kosovo crisis, France often clashed directly with the US over this question. In the words of Prime Minister Jospin, the UN had to regain its role and 'to have a central action in the search for a settlement' (Jospin, 8 April 1999). UN approval for NATO's actions and the need for the UNSC to take responsibility for the final settlement and peacekeeping within Kosovo became vital themes of French policy.

The question of the UN took on a different complexion in British thinking. Britain's leaders appeared much more concerned about its inability to act in time of international crisis than about whether it was effectively playing its role as a major source of international law. While Prime Minister Blair agreed that it was necessary to support the UN as the 'central pillar' of a 'world ruled by law and international co-operation', his speeches put much more emphasis on the need for its reform, otherwise there would a return 'to the deadlock that undermined' its effectiveness during the Cold War (Blair, 22 April 1999).

The Washington summit celebrating NATO's fiftieth anniversary in late April 1999 illustrates the different strategic approaches of the two states. For France it provided an excellent opportunity to use its influence to map out the direction NATO should take. According to a spokesperson of the French Ministry of Foreign Affairs (26 April 1999), France achieved four objectives in Washington: a clear definition of the geographical limits of NATO's military activities; NATO's recognition and acceptance of the notion of European defence; keeping the door open to future enlargement, especially for Romania and Slovenia; and reaffirmation of NATO's respect for the UN Charter and the role of the Security Council, in particular in peacekeeping operations. Despite these claims, most observers considered that the French somewhat exaggerated the true extent of their success in Washington (*The Washington Post*, 26 April 1999; *Le Monde*, 27 April 1999). In some ways, these claim indicate the depth of the desire to convince opinion at home that France's continued participation in NATO in no way jeopardised its autonomy, but they also confirmed that France could not really conceive of European security without NATO.

In their assessment of the summit, the British agreed there was a need for an 'effective European pillar' within NATO and that the Alliance had 'endorsed a comprehensive suite of measures' to strengthen it further in Washington (UK Ministry of Defence 1999: 5–6). They, however, saw no particular need to celebrate the meeting as a decisive step in reshaping NATO in any fundamental way, despite the adoption of a new Strategic Concept.

During the summit, President Chirac revealed the extent of differences between France and the US, supported by Britain, over the respective roles of NATO and the UN in Kosovo and any future conflicts. At a press conference, he talked of French disagreement with the position of some of 'our allies and notably our American friends' who advocated freeing NATO from UN authority. In his view, such a move would be tantamount to 'accepting or imposing the law of the strongest'. This was not just a quarrel about the conduct of this particular conflict. As President Chirac saw it, it was the 'whole international order put in place after the Second World War which was being questioned in this discussion. It was also our vision of the world, which was in some ways being discussed, even threatened' (Chirac, 24 April 1999). He later boasted that his country's diplomacy had scored a decisive victory by ensuring that the UN had been present from the very beginning and had found again 'the role and the place it must have in a world organised with a rule of international law' (Chirac, 10 June 1999).

The French also saw the Kosovo crisis as an opportunity to define the role of the EU as a security institution. It was here that they could make a claim to the leadership of European defence and security and put into practice their 'strategy of influence' with the greatest chance of success. At all stages of the conflict, French leaders stressed the need for the EU to play a full role in it. According to Foreign Minister Hubert Védrine, this meant that it should act as a 'designer and a leader' and not just as a 'counter for distributing subsidies for reconstruction' (Védrine, 21 April 1999). France attempted to translate these sentiments into a series of immediate, medium-term and long-term policies to be enacted through the EU.

In the short run, all the allies agreed that one of the most important measures for hastening the conclusion of the conflict was oil sanctions against Yugoslavia. French policy-makers argued, successfully, that there was no legal basis for an oil blockade within the NATO framework. Moreover, they claimed that the type of embargo envisioned by certain NATO members that would have involved boarding ships from third countries and blocking access to the ports of Montenegro, constituted an act of war, and, as such, needed authorisation from the UNSC. At a meeting of the European Council, the EU supreme decision-making body, in mid-April, France proposed and obtained unanimous backing for a policy of oil sanctions against Yugoslavia, which became binding on all its members. It also included a call for associate EU members to respect this decision. After some wrangling at the Washington summit, NATO also agreed to abide by the same rules.

As a medium-term measure, France advocated that the EU should assume full responsibility for civil administration over Kosovo once a settlement had been achieved. However, even before the conflict was over, it had begun to soften its position on that issue. Foreign Minister Védrine acknowledged that the decision was up to the UNSC, adding that the EU was 'in a way a candidate for this mission in liaison with the OSCE' (Védrine, 11 May 1999). As for NATO, France was determined to limit it to a strictly military role with absolutely no part in running civil affairs. Though it gained unanimous EU support for its position, it had to bow to the decision to create a UN-administered Kosovo. However, it did not give up the fight entirely and called for this administration to be headed by an EU personality. President Chirac then lobbied actively, and successfully, for the post to be filled by his country's own candidate, Health Minister Bernard Kouchner (*New York Times*, 3 July 1999).

French leaders felt they had advanced one of their most prized EU projects, a truly European defence policy. As we have seen, they considered that recognition of their efforts to formulate a truly European security and defence policy constituted one of the most important gains from the NATO summit in Washington. At the same time, they were compelled to acknowledge that the Kosovo conflict had revealed the very real weaknesses of a united European defence, yet saw reasons for optimism. The 1998 Saint-Malo Declaration had indicated a radical change in the British attitude, even though NATO remained a very important part of European military security in that document. The operations in Kosovo underlined how indispensable the Franco-British axis had become to any meaningful European defence policy in French eyes.

At the very moment when the end of the conflict was in sight, the European Council, meeting in Cologne, adopted the outlines of a common defence and security policy. Despite President Chirac's claim that this resolution represented 'an important moment in the construction of a European defence identity' (Chirac, 4 June 1999), his more cautious foreign minister, Hubert Védrine, warned that there was no reason to think that either a European defence policy or a common European foreign policy would come out 'fully armed' from the Kosovo crisis (Védrine, 18 June 1999). He also noted that the conflict had clearly demonstrated that only NATO possessed the military means for a large-scale operation (Védrine, 11 May 1999). Finally, in accordance with the French view of how security institutions should operate, Defence Minister Alain Richard declared, with obvious satisfaction, that the decision taken in Cologne had reiterated that a European defence policy would be intergovernmental (Frédet 1999: 32).

At every stage of the conflict, France attempted to exert its influence within the institutions involved and took full advantage of its potential veto power. Not only did French decision-makers insist on seeking general UN authority for the operation as soon as possible, and on giving the EU a leading role, they also claimed that the allies had 'recognised the importance of (France's) role' in NATO (Ministère de la Défense 1999). President Chirac claimed after the conflict that 'there was not one single target which was not agreed upon by France beforehand' (Chirac, 14 July 1999). Throughout the war, public statements by government leaders and official spokespersons confirmed that France had intervened within the Alliance to halt attacks on Yugoslav civil installations, in particular the bridges of Belgrade. It also took credit for steering air raids towards Yugoslav forces deployed in Kosovo itself, for sparing as much as possible Montenegro and for preventing NATO from proceeding to stage 3 of its operations, which would have entailed intensifying and extending air raids.[2] Prime Minister Jospin also explained to his government colleagues that NATO's five conditions for ending its operations were based on 'French proposals' (*Libération*, 8 April 1999).

The British appeared to give their tacit assent to French claims for European leadership within the main European institutions, but the picture is not quite as favourable to French claims as it seems. In the first place, the British had succeeded in eliminating the Western European Union (WEU) as an effective alternative to NATO, which remained – and on this point the French had, perhaps reluctantly, been forced to agree – the principal military arm of European defence. Secondly, though they backed such EU decisions as the oil embargo, the British had by no means given up their concept of a much wider and therefore looser EU, where cooperation between member states was to be preferred to integration.

ESDP and the Iraq effect

Between the Kosovo conflict and the war in Iraq, differences between British and French conceptions of ESDP became even clearer, though there was no question of going back on the progress that had been made. Despite profound divisions within the EU over Iraq, both the British and the French attempted to separate this issue from the question of European security and defence. However, during this period, the future of European defence provided a backdrop to one of the most contentious questions of recent transatlantic relations. Before analysing the effects of divisions over Iraq on the leadership of European defence, however, it is important to look briefly at how the 9/11 events affected French and British perceptions of the international system and relations with the US.

Both the British and the French expressed their shock and horror at what took place on 9/11 and declared their solidarity with the US. However, after the initial shock, the French suggested that little fundamental change in the international system had actually occurred. In their view, there was nothing essentially new about terrorism. Even more importantly, as President Chirac put it: '[Terrorism is] not the only threat in the world and the world must not just organise itself around the response to the challenge made on 9/11, for we would only be playing into the hands of those whom we are fighting' (Chirac, 29 August 2002). The British, on the other hand, without necessarily sharing the American view of a dramatic change in the international system, tended to see the main threats to international security basically in the light of 9/11. The world now had to deal with 'the proliferation of weapons of mass destruction; the scourge of global terrorism; and failed and failing states' (British Foreign Minister Jack Straw, 17 October 2002). The French had no fundamental disagreement with this assessment in itself, but rejected any attempt by the British or the Americans to relate this series of threats specifically to Iraq. The French talked in general terms of contemporary terrorism's 'capacity for devastation' (Chirac, 4 January 2002) and of an 'increasingly unstable environment' where terrorism, regional conflicts and proliferation of weapons of mass destruction 'are a constant threat to our security' (Chirac, 1 July 2002). The British, on the other hand, did not hesitate to point the finger, calling for the need to be ready to 'act where terrorism or weapons of mass destruction threaten us', and stating that to allow a state like Iraq to develop weapons of mass destruction without any hindrance would be 'grossly ignoring the lessons of the 11th of September' (Blair, 7 April 2002).

For the French the most pressing question facing the international system remained the same as before 9/11: how to deal with what former foreign minister Hubert Védrine had dubbed America's 'hyperpower'.[3] In the immediate aftermath of 9/11, French leaders emphasised their solidarity with the US. President Chirac declared that France intended to be 'on the front line against terrorist networks ... beside America' (Chirac, 21 September 2001), but more traditional views of the Franco-American relationship soon came to the fore. Jacques Chirac resumed the delicate position of his country when he told an American paper that 'France is not an aligned ally but it is a faithful ally' (*International Herald Tribune*, 20 March 2002). Obviously, France had no illusions about competing with American power but it demanded to be treated as an equal, seeing itself as a friend in times of crisis. 'When it comes to solidarity, France has never failed,' President Chirac stated (21 September 2001). Foreign Minister Dominique de Villepin, however, added that France was also a moderating influence on American temptation 'to go it alone, to yield to selfishness, with the eye glued to the uncertain compass of too short-sighted interests' (*Le Figaro*, 9 September 2002).

Between March 2002 and February 2003, President Chirac gave three long interviews and wrote an article for the US press, which indicated just how preoccupied the French were with their relationship with the US (*International Herald Tribune*, 20 March 2002; *New York Times*, 8 September 2002; Graff and Crumley, 2003). Among the most important points that the

French tried to convey was the idea that their reservations about American foreign and security policy should not be confused with anti-Americanism. This meant that even at the height of Franco-American tensions, as during the period after Foreign Minister Dominique de Villepin had suggested that France could possibly use its veto against the US in the UNSC, they insisted: 'We are the friends of the United States. We have been friends for centuries. We are friends today and will remain so, whatever happens' and that their relationship with the US was driven by 'the spirit of solidarity' (de Villepin, 5 February 2003).

If many of these concerns could be construed as a bilateral matter between the US and France, which the British could choose to ignore, they strongly rejected the French conception of how to manage American power. While agreeing to a large extent with French insistence on multilateralism, the British could not accept the French preference for a multipolar world, in which Europe would play a central role, because it was 'the first economic power of the world and there is no balance in the world without a very good and strong relationship between Europe and the United States' (Chirac, 26 May 2002). This was a theme to which the French would return repeatedly as the Iraq crisis deepened.

The British remained totally opposed to an idea that went against their own strategy of influence. For Tony Blair, any attempt to create a Europe which deliberately set out to counter the US would not work and would be 'dangerous and destabilising' and would simply push the Americans towards unilateralism (*Financial Times*, 27 April 2003). The British, in fact, feared much more. According to Minister for Europe, Denis MacShane, the French project would simply play into the hands of 'the ideological fundamentalists who want a world not of partnership but of subordination'. Multipolarity, as proposed by the French, would simply create the conditions for a new Cold War, which, this time, would pit Europe as a whole against the US (MacShane, 15 May 2003).

It is in this context that the British and the French found themselves on opposite sides of the international debate leading up to the war in Iraq; a debate which not only presented two opposing visions of the direction that the newly-enlarged Europe should take on questions of international security, but also exposed the limits and the weaknesses of British and French leadership strategies. Nothing illustrates better the limits of French and British capacity to sway the US than the battle over Iraq fought out in the UNSC. French Foreign Minister Dominique de Villepin probably summed up the difference between the French approach towards the need for UN support for any armed action against Iraq and that of the US and Britain when he said that the latter 'speak of a vital role' for that body, whereas France is convinced of its 'central role' (de Villepin, 5 February 2003).

When the Security Council finally adopted Resolution 1441 authorising the resumption of arms inspections in Iraq in November 2002, both the

French and the British claimed a victory. The British had coaxed the Americans into submitting a draft resolution and into negotiating with the French on the exact wording of the final version, and thereby avoided isolating the US. The French, to quote one of their diplomats, saw the whole question as 'about the rules of the game in the world today, about putting the Security Council in the centre of international life and not permitting a nation – whatever nation it may be – to do what it wants, where it wants' (*The Los Angeles Times*, 10 November 2002). They got what they wanted most, a resolution which would not allow the US to automatically declare war on Iraq without involving the UNSC. Less than three months later, relations between France, on the one hand, and Britain and the US on the other, entered their worst crisis since the 1960s, when Dominique de Villepin announced, during a press conference at the UN, the possibility of a French veto against any resolution allowing for armed intervention against Iraq (de Villepin, 20 January 2003).

There is no need to go into the story of the threat of a French veto here, except to point out that this whole incident underscored the limits of the British strategy of influence. Clearly, the Americans had never felt the need for a second UNSC resolution to defend what they considered to be a matter of national security and only agreed to one to help Tony Blair to stave off opposition from the Labour benches in the House of Commons. They let it be known they would go ahead regardless (Stothard 2003: 85). Between the adoption of UNSC resolution 1441 and the de Villepin bombshell, Europe had become one of the battlegrounds for the fight over Iraq.

Backed by Britain, the US had attempted to influence the vote on Turkish membership of the EU at the European summit in Copenhagen in December 2002, a gesture that the French had not appreciated. In January 2003, France used the fortieth anniversary of the Elysée treaty between France and Germany to reaffirm the role of these two countries as the pivot of European integration, which was another way of confirming France's bid for European leadership, given the political, economic and military frailty of present-day Germany. These celebrations were followed a week later by the famous letter signed by eight European countries, led by Britain, Spain and Italy, and including Hungary, Poland and the Czech Republic, which was followed by another letter from ten Eastern European countries, supporting the Bush administration's Iraq policy, which were both clearly meant to be a response of the other major EU powers to France and Germany (*The Times*, 30 January 2003; *Daily Telegraph*, 6 February 2003).

When it came to the more specific issues of European defence and ESDP, a definite 'Iraq effect' could be felt, with both direct and indirect consequences. Some effort was made to separate the question of Iraq from the debate over ESDP. Meetings over ESDP between Britain and France, and then Germany, continued both before and after the war, with progress being made on some essential questions. However, even if the influential French daily *Le*

Monde claimed that Tony Blair had come 'indisputably strengthened' out of the war in Iraq, the British Prime Minister had to make important concessions on points over which he had been adamantly opposed to the French.

The first public sign of the 'Iraq effect' on European defence came with what most observers consider one of the most serious crises in the history of NATO. In February 2003, France, supported by Germany and Belgium, opposed its veto against a decision to deploy NATO equipment to Turkey to defend it in the case of war with Iraq, because it considered that such a measure involved entering into a 'logic of war' which it steadfastly rejected (*Le Monde*, 12 February 2003). The crisis was finally resolved by persuading Germany and Belgium to back down, and taking the decision in the Defence Planning Committee (DPC), which France had boycotted since 1966.

On the more specific question of ESDP, at first glance everything seemed to be back to normal. The British and French held another summit in February 2003, in Le Touquet, at which they agreed on several major issues concerning European defence, including further pooling of military assets, pressing ahead with the creation of an EU rapid reaction force, French leadership of the first EU military operation in Macedonia, a proposal to establish an EU defence procurement agency, and the possibility of British cooperation on building a second French aircraft carrier. However, once American and British forces actually invaded Iraq, European defence and the war became inextricably entwined. British and French leaders clashed directly over Iraq at the Brussels European summit held on 20 March 2003. Then, on 29 April, France, Germany, Belgium and Luxembourg met to discuss their own particular plan for European security and defence. Apart from the obvious decision to call a meeting of the four European states openly hostile to the war in Iraq, the meeting was significant for pushing forward the idea of creating a core of EU member states which, together, would adopt the concept of a European Security and Defence Union (ESDU), an idea which had been launched during the celebrations of the fortieth anniversary of the Franco-German partnership in January. ESDU would bring together 'the member-states which are ready to go faster and further in reinforcing their cooperation in the area of defence' (joint declaration of the four governments after the Luxembourg meeting on 20 April 2003). It would also entail creating a 'nucleus of collective capacity for planning and conducting operations', which would in fact be a separate EU military headquarters to carry out operations not involving use of NATO resources. Finally, the four countries called for extending the Petersberg tasks[4] that had determined the limits of ESDP.

However much British and American leaders disliked the ideas adopted by what they called the 'gang of four', these now shaped the debate on ESDP. The British attempted to counter the most unpalatable part of these proposals, establishing a separate EU military centre, with one of their own, which called for setting up an EU military planning cell, but as part of NATO, and to be housed at NATO's military headquarters in Mons, Belgium

(*Independent*, 29 August 2003; *Le Monde*, 4 September 2003). As the initiative on ESDP appeared to be slipping further and further from British hands, Britain sought a compromise that meant bringing in the Germans. Thus at an informal summit between Blair, Chirac and Schröder held in Berlin on 20 September, the British Prime Minister made some crucial concessions. According to an unpublished internal document, it was agreed that the EU 'should be endowed with a joint capacity to plan and conduct operations without recourse to NATO resources and capabilities' (*Financial Times*, 22 September 2003). This 'joint capacity' could be achieved 'either in consensus with the 25 [member states] but also in a circle of interested partners'. In other words, the British had accepted three ideas they had always resisted: some form of an independent EU military centre; an embryo of a two-speed security and defence body, which could be the basis for ESDU; and EU military operations without NATO. The latter suggested the possibility of abandoning NATO's 'right of first refusal', on which the British and French had always been at odds. In return, the French and Germans made what amounted to symbolic gestures: the 'circle of interested partners' would always remain open to others; and there would be an EU military headquarters located within NATO's military headquarters (*Le Monde*, 23 September 2003).

At the following November's Franco-British summit meeting in London, Blair set out to reassure the Americans, stating that European defence cooperation was not incompatible with NATO and that it 'makes complete sense in circumstances where NATO is not engaged, for Europe to have the capability and the power to act in the interests of Europe and the wider world' (*BBC News online*, 24 November 2003). The British had yet to convince the Americans that the 'Berlin compromise' did not involve any decoupling of European defence from NATO. This was achieved just before a European summit in Brussels met and endorsed the main points of the Anglo-Franco-German agreement in December 2003, and which had been set out in a short note published by the EU Presidency, at the time held by Italy (EU Presidency 2003). This document spelt out how autonomous EU military operations would be carried out. For the British, the sequence to be followed was clearly established. In the words of Minister for Europe, Denis MacShane: 'There is a hierarchy of NATO first, then European Union Member States agreeing to participate in a mission but requiring to use NATO assets ... and finally there would be completely EU-only operation mainly in the carrying out of Petersberg tasks' (UK House of Commons 2003). In fact, the presidency note was not quite so explicit on the question of such a hierarchy and said nothing specific about the limits of EU-led operations.

Instead of a fully-fledged separate EU military planning centre to prepare and carry out purely EU-led operations, as outlined by the 'gang of four', the summit established a 'cell with civil/military components' within the existing European Union Military Staff (EUMS), to 'conduct early warning, situation assessment and strategic planning'. There would also be, as the British had insisted, a 'small EU cell' within SHAPE, and liaison arrangements between the EUMS and NATO. As for the actual conduct of autonomous EU military operations, they would normally be based on national armed forces, 'which can be multi-nationalised for the purpose'. In other words, operations would be *ad hoc*, and there was no question of creating a permanent structure, on which some form of ESDU could take shape.

Both the British and the French could find satisfaction in the decisions made at the Brussels summit. Most of the measures laid out in the Berlin compromise had been adopted. For the British, the vital point was to clarify the EU–NATO institutional arrangements and to limit both the evolution towards the setting up of a totally autonomous EU military headquarters and a two-speed ESDP. The French had gained recognition for the need for some form of a purely EU planning unit, and for the possibility of what were called 'structured co-operations' between states which wanted to act together – what a French journalist referred to as 'countries forming a *vanguard* for cooperating on defence' (*Le Monde*, 12 December 2003). But perhaps the main French achievement was to gain further legitimacy for the idea of EU-led operations outside of NATO.

Conclusion

Whatever the ambiguities and the tensions between Britain and France over the direction ESDP should take, after these two very important conflicts, European defence policy has tended to progress and to take shape. Looked at from the focus of this chapter, that is competing strategies of influence and their impact on Franco-British rivalry for the leadership of ESDP, the reviews are mixed. Both states can feel some satisfaction about the success of their conduct in the Kosovo conflict. However, Britain succeeded in gaining a certain edge by managing to ensure that NATO played the leading role in it. Neither, however, can be totally happy about their capacity to exercise global influence, and especially influence over the remaining superpower, before, during and after the war in Iraq. The British quickly realised the Americans would go their own way, whatever this meant for the political fate of Tony Blair, and the French gambled and finally lost, at least in the short term, in their bid to stand up to the US. At the regional level, a more nuanced assessment is called for.

At the end of the two conflicts, just what can the two major European military powers chalk up in the wins and losses columns? The British can claim that they have held their ground and maintained NATO's place as the main force for ensuring Europe's military security. They can feel they have won support for their pro-NATO stance from all the former Eastern bloc states that joined the EU in 2004. They can also find some satisfaction in the fact that amongst the original fifteen EU members, only Belgium and Luxembourg were prepared to back openly the Franco-German position on both Iraq and the future of ESDP. This would appear to push the balance of forces within the enlarged EU security and defence policy towards Britain.

On the other hand, the French have maintained and strengthened their relationship with Germany, which is now an equal partner with France and Britain in the debate over European defence policy. They have also made some important gains on the question of autonomous EU-led operations. On this particular issue, the distance between the French and British positions has never been quite as wide as they both made it appear, at least since Labour came to power in 1997. Britain, like France, favours greater European military capacity and has worked for closer coordination on purely EU security tasks as set out at Petersberg in 1992, and has actively supported more decisive EU-led operations, including use of troops. Autonomy for the French does not mean abandoning NATO for ESDP, let alone creating some form of a balance of power between the US and the EU, but rather, it involves opening up the space for the EU to act on its own authority in security and defence matters. Franco-British differences, though very real, are by no means irreconcilable, as the Berlin compromise and the subsequent agreements made in Brussels in December 2003 showed.

Clearly the French, with German support, would still like to achieve an ESDU, and the British have indicated that this goal can be accommodated, if not wholly attained in the way the French would like. However, the Iraq effect has affected the British claim to leadership in European defence. Though the Americans insist on maintaining NATO as part of their general policy on international security, the rather curt refusal to allow NATO to invoke article V after 9/11, and their apparent tendency to see NATO more as a support force for their war on terrorism in Afghanistan and now Iraq, indicate that NATO no longer occupies quite the same place in US foreign policy as it did. Though any announcement of NATO's demise would certainly be more than premature, its dominant position in European defence arrangements would seem very dependent on its perceived continued usefulness for furthering US policy objectives. This situation obviously threatens a British policy that stakes so much on NATO. Such perspectives are of course as yet only on the distant horizon. More immediately, because of its desire to remain closely tied to Europe, Britain has had to make some significant concessions to France, as the Berlin compromise showed. As has been suggested, the capacity to set the agenda is a fundamental attribute of leadership, and it must be admitted that on the question of EDSP, France has tended to set the agenda during and since the war in Iraq. Of course, it has not achieved all its goals, but most of the important items within the Berlin compromise have forced the British to yield in areas where they had always insisted they would not budge. They have also been compelled to open their special relationship with France on ESDP to the Germans, which also strengthens the hand of the

French. Finally, the British may have felt justified in thinking that with enlargement, the balance of forces in Europe has irretrievably shifted towards themselves on security and defence issues. But, as the results of the Spanish elections of 14 March 2004 showed, a change in government can seriously upset the balance of forces. Britain can no longer count on the Blair–Aznar partnership to maintain Spain on its side of the ESDP–NATO debate. There is no reason why elections and change of government elsewhere in the EU could not have similar consequences.

Notes

1   Unless otherwise explicitly indicated, all the quotations in this chapter come from speeches or interventions made on the date indicated within parenthesis and reported on the websites of the French and British Ministries of Foreign Affairs: www.france.diplomatie.fr and www.fco.gov.uk respectively.
2   These examples are all taken from official statements, speeches, and interviews made during the conflict.
3   Védrine used this term for the first time in an interview with the magazine *Jeune Afrique* in February 1998 (Védrine 2003: 111–15).
4   The Petersberg Declaration of 19 June 1992, made by the members of the now-defunct Western European Union, predecessor of the EDSP, laid down three broad areas for EU security operations: humanitarian and rescue tasks; peacekeeping; and crisis management and peacemaking.

UDO DIEDRICHS

10

Between Kosovo and Iraq: changing paradigms of German foreign and security policy?

German foreign and security policy between continuity and change

The transformation of the international system after 1989 required new approaches and strategies of national foreign policy, but Germany remained firmly multilateral, embedded in international organisations such as the EU, NATO, and the UN (Peters 2001; Webber 2001; Risse 2004). Post-war Germany had cultivated the image of being a reliable partner acting in coordination with other countries in order to promote its foreign policy objectives (Maull 2004). Furthermore, Germany had pursued a policy of reconciling 'Atlanticism' and 'Europeanism', serving as a bridge between French aspirations for a 'Europe puissance', acting autonomously from the US, and British preferences for Atlantic solidarity and the pre-eminence of NATO in security policy (Regelsberger 2002). After 1989, Germany continued to regard NATO as the primary organisation responsible for European defence (Meiers 2002). The country also looked favourably upon the EU beginning to play a more active role in crisis management but rejected any attempt by the EU to replace the Alliance. Partnership with the US within NATO has traditionally constituted the key pillar of German security and defence policy, and Germany felt that an increased role for the EU in these areas should be kept as a complementary element to NATO's role. Until recently, the use of military force for purposes other than territorial defence had never been seriously taken into consideration to the point that some observers have referred to Germany as a 'civilian power' (Meiers 2002). While Germany does not exclude the use of military force *a priori*, it has favoured military restraint in international affairs (Miskimmon and Paterson 2003).

The first change to this traditional position came in the wake of Germany's refusal to take part in the Gulf War, when the UN, the US and NATO began calling for a more active foreign role for Germany.

Consequently, the federal government began, cautiously at first, to increase its level of activity participating in several international UN missions e.g. in Cambodia in 1992 (with a medical unit), and in Somalia in 1993/94 as part of a peacekeeping mission (Maull 2000). However, it was in the former Yugoslavia that Germany's military role in international affairs was fundamentally redefined. NATO's request for a military contribution to the task of monitoring the UN-imposed embargo triggered a controversial debate over participation in NATO 'out of area' operations. The federal government decided to let German military personnel take part in patrol flights over the Adriatic Sea and be part of the crew of AWACS planes that guided NATO fighters in the attacks against Bosnian Serbs. These decisions met with the criticism of opposition parties as well as the chagrin of some sectors of the ruling coalition (Nolte and Krieger 2003). In 1994, a Constitutional Court ruling marked a historic turning point in Germany's foreign, security and defence policy and thus opened the way for an enhanced German role in international politics. The ruling allowed for the deployment of soldiers in the framework of a 'system of mutual collective security' as defined by the Constitution (Art. 24.2), which meant that Germany could now participate in NATO's 'out of area' operations. The Court, however, also ruled that the *Bundestag* had to give authorisation to any such deployment (Nolte and Krieger 2003). In principle at least, the Court ruling opened the door for playing out the increased influence a reunited Germany enjoyed as a fully sovereign country. The Court also made it clear that Germany could no longer use the legal or historical 'uniqueness' of its situation to evade responsibility in the international arena. The first big test for German foreign policy under these changed operational parameters came with the Kosovo crisis.

Germany and the Kosovo conflict: normalisation and multilateralism

Germany during the Kosovo crisis: the real end of the Cold War foreign policy?

For German politicians as well as the public at large, Kosovo had remained in the shadow of other crisis-areas in the former Yugoslavia – particularly Bosnia, which absorbed a great deal of political, military and diplomatic attention. In 1997, however, when the situation in the province began to deteriorate rapidly, Germany had to tackle the issue. The German government from the very start avoided pursuing a national *Sonderweg* (a distinctive German way), having learned the lesson from the early 1990s, when it had angered its European partners by unilaterally recognising Croatia and Slovenia. This time it coordinated its policy closely with its main European and international partners within the Contact Group (of which Germany was part together with the US, France, Britain, Italy and Russia), NATO and the EU. At the same time, the German government also regularly emphasised the role of the Organisation for Security and Cooperation in Europe (OSCE) and particularly the UN, which it regarded as the primary body for legitimising any use of force at an international level.

The German government did not regard the secession of Kosovo as a viable option and believed that any solution had to emerge from negotiations between the Belgrade government and the representatives of the Albanian community. At the same time, however, it believed that the lesson from Bosnia was that a humanitarian catastrophe had to be avoided. Thus, for Germany, it soon became clear that it was essential to persuade the Milošević regime to stop taking actions that caused civilian casualties. From a broader international point of view, the German government was eager to integrate Russia as closely as possible into the efforts to solve the conflict. Russia was regarded as a key partner in Europe, for political as well as economic reasons. Finally, the federal government was particularly interested in a preventive strategy that would stop the flow of thousands of refugees pouring into the country (Krause 2000).

The Contact Group initially shared the German preference for a negotiated solution, but as hopes for a peaceful solution disappeared, Germany's position within the Contact Group became more difficult to maintain. In early June 1998, German Foreign Minister Klaus Kinkel, preoccupied by the escalation of the situation in Kosovo and by the rising numbers of refugees, came to regard military intervention as a viable option and urged NATO to begin preparing for the eventuality of air-strikes (Krause 2000). On 12 June 1998, the German government also agreed to the release of a stern warning by the Contact Group which threatened the adoption of 'further measures to halt the violence and protect the civilian population, including those that may require the authorisation of a UN Security Council resolution'.[1] The German government, however, was still hesitant about embracing a military solution for two reasons: first, it had doubts about the legality of a military intervention in the absence of a United Nations Security Council (UNSC) authorisation; second, it feared that Germany would probably be asked to play a military role much bigger than it had in Bosnia.

As the situation in Kosovo did not substantially improve during the summer of 1998, NATO began the planning process for a military strike which might include Germany. UNSC resolution 1199 of 23 September 1998 marked a watershed in explicitly identifying the events in Kosovo as a threat to world peace and international security. Shortly afterwards, the German government decided to offer NATO a number of Tornado fighters for suppression of enemy air defence and reconnaissance tasks as well as unmanned aerial vehicles in case of an intervention. This was one of the last acts of the government headed by Chancellor Helmut Kohl concerning Kosovo and it was carried out in close coordination with the next Chancellor Gerhard Schröder and the next Foreign Minister Joschka Fischer, the Social Democrats and the Green Party having won the elections on 27 September

1998. It was however, the old *Bundestag*, which, on 16 October 1998, voted by a large majority in favour of the deployment of the Tornados.

NATO plans notwithstanding, efforts to negotiate were still under way. The German Foreign Ministry was not overly disappointed when, in January 1999, US Ambassador Richard Holbrooke failed to reach an agreement with Milošević. Germany, in fact, considered the US approach as rather unbalanced in favour of the Albanian-led Kosovo Liberation Army (KLA) (*Financial Times*, 7 June 1999). During the Rambouillet talks, which began in February 1999, Germany stressed the role of the EU, and initiated the concept of regular meetings of the EU foreign ministers (*Frankfurter Allgemeine Zeitung*, 12 May 1999). This was in part a reaction to complaints by some EU members concerning the 'directoire' character of the Contact Group (*Neue Zürcher Zeitung*, 15 February 1999).

Rambouillet marked a turning point within the Contact Group. Coherence had been frail and the main actors seemed to prefer a bilateral approach. France was suspicious of the US for neglecting its allies, while Germany felt marginalised. The Foreign Ministry was sceptical about the results of the conference which seemed to encourage Milošević to intensify his operations. The prevalent perception was that diplomatic efforts had not only proven unsuccessful but had also triggered a new cycle of violence. Germany attributed the failure of Rambouillet mainly to Serb intransigence. In a common declaration by the EU Heads of State and Government, adopted at the Berlin summit on 24 March 1999, they singled out Milošević as bearing the main responsibility for the events and the consequences that would follow (*Neue Zürcher Zeitung*, 25 March 1999). In this regard, the Red–Green coalition acted in a less scrupulously legalistic manner than the former government which had been torn between the need to avoid a humanitarian catastrophe and the perceived requirements of international law. Surprisingly, the Red–Green coalition was ready to support German participation in the NATO strikes against Belgrade even without an explicit UN mandate.

Germany and 'Operation Allied Force': transatlantic solidarity
When NATO began its strikes against Serbia on 24 March 1999, the objective of the new German government was to demonstrate the country's reliability as an ally by providing political as well as military support. Shortly before the launching of military operations, the Chancellor informed the leaders of all major parties in the *Bundestag* about the role the *Bundeswehr* would play in them (*Süddeutsche Zeitung*, 24 March 1999). The government did not consider that a vote was necessary since Parliament had already agreed to the deployment of German forces on 16 October 1998. Some observers remarked that a delay of five months between authorisation and deployment was too long, but in the end the government's position prevailed (*Süddeutsche Zeitung*, 25 March 1999). Germany deployed eight Electronic Combat

Reconnaissance (ECR) Tornados, equipped with High-speed Anti Radiation Missiles (HARM) to destroy enemy air defence, while six Recce Tornados were used, as their name suggests, for reconnaissance; additionally, German CL-289 Unmanned Aerial Vehicles (UAVs) came into operation. German troops were stationed in Macedonia, but their tasks were carefully separated from military action in Serbia or Kosovo. Chancellor Schröder's comment: 'We have no choice' (*Die Welt*, 24 March 1999) was meant to convey the message to the German public that the attacks were unavoidable given the stance by the Milošević regime. The comment, however, could also be interpreted to mean that Germany had to take part in the military operations lest it would lose influence and reputation within the Alliance and in particular, vis-à-vis the US. The reasons for this stance were twofold: first, it signalled foreign policy reliability to NATO partners; secondly, Germany had an interest in stabilising South-eastern Europe since instability there could affect Germany, primarily through an influx of refugees (Maull 2000).

While military operations were under way, Defence Minister Rudolf Scharping repeatedly hinted at the proofs of 'genocide' organised by the Serb political leadership. At the same time however, he stressed the need to keep exercising pressure on Milošević and together with Foreign Minister Joschka Fischer stressed that no German ground troops would be deployed in the region (*Die Welt*, 29 March 1999). In late March, Chancellor Schröder rejected the suggestion transmitted by Milošević through Russian Prime Minister Yevgeny Primakov that he was willing to participate in new Kosovo peace talks and would allow the return of 'peaceful' refugees on condition that NATO stop its air-strikes (*Die Welt*, 31 March 1999). Schröder knew that acceptance of Milošević's proposal would be interpreted as a sign of political weakness, particularly by the US. As an official from the Chancellery put it, 'we are not going to be the wimps' (*Financial Times*, 24 April 1999). However, in early April, the number of critics within both the Social-Democratic Party (SPD) and the Green Party grew and became more vociferous, making the situation for Schröder and Joschka Fischer more difficult (*Die Welt*, 9 April 1999). The longer the campaign lasted without visible results, the more cases of collateral damage became public, and the higher the number of civilian victims grew, the more difficult it became to defend the operation. To make things worse, the Milošević regime did not appear ready to give up and accept defeat as had been expected (*Die Welt*, 7 April 1999). Public resistance to the reception of refugees, an issue to which the Centre-Right parties were particularly responsive, also grew. By May, around 680,000 people had fled Kosovo. Germany had taken around 10,000 of them. When Interior Minister Otto Schily announced that the government would be ready to take up to another 10,000 people, the opposition harshly attacked him (*Berliner Morgenpost*, 6 May 1999). The real fear was that the high number of refugees in neighbouring countries, primarily Albania, which had received 400,000 people, would lead to increasing problems and raise the pressure for migration towards

Western Europe. Meanwhile, several regional organisations of the Green Party called for a suspension of the attacks (*Frankfurter Allgemeine Zeitung*, 12 May 1999). The government thus came to face a difficult situation: domestic support for the intervention was becoming more fragile precisely at a time when the fact that the air-strikes seemed insufficient to bend Milošević was leading to stronger international calls for the deployment of ground troops. Parliament, however, had not authorised the use of ground troops in October 1998 and thus any such deployment would have required a new vote in the Bundestag.

The way to peace: the hour of German diplomacy
On 14 April 1999, Foreign Minister Fischer presented a plan aimed at stopping the air-strikes and paving the way towards a solution to the Kosovo issue. The plan provided for the Group of Eight (G-8) to draft a resolution for the UNSC specifying the conditions under which NATO would cease the air-strikes. The resolution would call for the withdrawal of all Serb security forces from Kosovo, a commitment by the KLA to stop all violent actions and surrender arms, and the deployment of an international force under NATO. It would also provide for the return of all refugees, the establishment of a provisional administration until the adoption of a final negotiated solution, and economic aid (*Financial Times*, 16 April 1999). In line with German preferences, the plan included Russia – now part of the G-8 group – in the process, brought the UN back into play, and carved out a role for the EU (whose Presidency Germany had taken over in January 1999) which would have the major responsibility in the reconstruction process. Germany used its parallel Presidency of the EU and of the G-8 to push the process of negotiations with the Milošević regime. Schröder held particularly close contacts with Finnish President Martti Ahtisaari who acted on behalf of the EU (*Financial Times*, 29 April 1999).

In early May, Italian Prime Minister Massimo D'Alema came up with a proposal of his own which called for a pause in NATO strikes as soon as Russia and China had agreed to the text of a UNSC resolution. The reaction of the German government was cautious. The problem from a German point of view was that the Italian plan did not exclude the option of a ground invasion should Serbia fail to comply with the UNSC resolution (*Financial Times*, 19 May 1999) and called upon NATO to take the first step. This issue was indeed central and the roadmap to peace agreed upon by the G-8 Foreign Ministers in early June provided for NATO to stop its air-strikes *after* the Serb forces had started to withdraw from Kosovo. This would be followed by a UNSC resolution, the draft having been prepared by the G-8, authorising the deployment of a UN peacekeeping force (*Financial Times*, 9 June 1999). Germany was pleased by the adoption on the part of the EU of the 'Stability Pact for South Eastern Europe' (SPSEE) which reflected the strategic perspective promoted by the federal government. The SPSEE was a 'comprehensive conflict-prevention strategy ... aimed at strengthening the efforts of the countries of South East Europe in fostering peace, democracy, respect for human rights and economic prosperity'. It also provided a 'framework to stimulate regional co-operation and expedite integration into European and trans-Atlantic structures'.[2]

These few weeks were considered the hour of German diplomacy which had proved capable of taking the initiative and laying the ground for an effective solution. German multilateralism i.e. the search for an adequate organisational context that would ensure a broad international consensus but also a pronounced role for the country itself, had been rewarded with success. The continued commitment to the region also became visible in the German participation in post-conflict stabilisation. After June 1999, German armed forces participated in the Kosovo Force (KFOR) operation, an essential element in the implementation of the UNSC resolution 1224 defining a post-conflict order for the province. In 2004, Germany had 3700 soldiers deployed in Kosovo, the bulk of German military presence in the Balkans.[3] These figures indicate the importance Germany attaches to the stabilisation of the region and underline the country's aspiration to play a key part in the solution of the conflict.

The domestic debate about military participation in Kosovo: opposing principles

The decision to participate in the military intervention in Kosovo was a momentous one for Germany since it touched upon its very identity in international politics, and required the reconciliation of conflicting principles. The deeply anchored foreign policy tradition of military restraint clashed with the need for taking action in the case of a humanitarian crisis. The Kosovo crisis decidedly moved the SPD and the Green Party towards acceptance of a military role for Germany after the end of the Cold War. In the early 1990s the SPD was split between 'pacifists' and 'moderate interventionists'. The 'pacifist' wing began losing ground in the mid-1990s when a majority of the SPD parliamentary group voted in favour of the participation of German soldiers in the Implementation Force (IFOR) in Bosnia (Maull 2000). From then onwards, most members of the SPD leadership looked favourably upon military deployments under UNSC authorisation or in support of NATO initiatives. During the Kosovo crisis, it was Defence Minister and former party leader Rudolf Scharping in particular who led the cause in favour of intervention, underpinning his plea with documents on alleged plans for ethnic cleansing by the Belgrade government known as 'Operation Horseshoe'. The impact on the German public was considerable as it helped to build a strong majority in favour of NATO air-strikes, at least in the first phase of the operations.

The Greens were also split between a 'fundamentalist' wing (the so-called *Fundis*) and the 'realists' (the *Realos*). The first regarded pacifism as one of their core values. Hence for them any compromise called into question the very identity of the party which had developed out of the peace movement. The latter favoured a more moderate stance on the use of military force. To them, the idea of 'Nie wieder Krieg' (Never again war) was no longer compatible with the idea of 'Nie wieder Ausschwitz' (Never again Auschwitz) (*Die Welt*, 25 March 1999; Hyde-Price 2001). Foreign Minister Joschka Fischer publicly defended military intervention, confessing to having dropped his own pacifist attitude in the wake of the events in the former Yugoslavia, namely after a visit to Srebrenica in 1994 which he described as a personal 'key experience' (*The Times*, 1 June 1999). His reputation, not only within the Green Party but also within the Left in Germany, led to a fundamental change in attitude towards military intervention. Pacifism however, was not dead. In May 1999, at a special party conference, Joschka Fischer, making probably 'the speech of his political career', had a hard time in convincing the delegates not to call for a ceasefire in order to maintain pressure upon the Milošević regime (*Financial Times*, 14 May 1999).

The CDU instead favoured an enhanced role for the *Bundeswehr* within NATO, and thus had no reservations concerning military operations ranging from peacekeeping to peace-enforcement. The last defence minister of the Kohl government, Volker Rühe, systematically tried to widen the scope of action for out-of-area operations. The Free Democratic Party (FDP) looked favourably upon the idea of adjusting the scope of the *Bundeswehr* military operations to the realities of the post-Cold War environment but had doubts about its constitutional aspects. In 1994, the party requested the Constitutional court to clarify the legality of the *Bundeswehr* activities in Bosnia. The only strictly anti-war political force was the post-communist Party of Democratic Socialism (PDS) which, driven by anti-NATO and anti-American sentiments, denounced what it called the imperialist attitude of the Western powers in Kosovo.

A key issue in the public debate was of course whether a military intervention without UN authorisation could be considered legal. As shown also in Abiew's chapter in this book, among legal scholars this point was highly controversial, as it was embedded in a discussion on the transformation of international law after the end of the Cold War. Most German legal scholars were at best sceptical about the legality of the intervention.[4] Some of them, however, embraced a compromise position according to which the intervention, since it could rely on a humanitarian justification, did not represent a 'mortal sin' against international law.[5] Within the media and public opinion, there was from the start broad consensus on the necessity of the intervention (Maull 2000). Even when, at the end of March, the peace movement organised marches in several German cities, the majority of the population continued to support NATO operations (*Süddeutsche Zeitung*, 29 March 1999). A major shift in public opinion did not come until May 1999, when the approval rate for the intervention slipped from 60 (in April) to 52 per cent while the number of those who opposed the strikes went up from 35 (in April) to 44 per cent. The media, which in the early phase of the conflict had supported the cause of intervention through reports and images hinting at alleged ethnic cleansing, now began to focus on NATO's failures by documenting the destruction of non-military targets in Belgrade.

Kosovo, Germany and transatlantic relations: perspectives and problems

The Kosovo crisis provides a number of lessons useful in a more general assessment of German foreign policy in the late 1990s. The government's desire to be a reliable NATO partner is crucial for understanding the position taken by the Red–Green coalition. German participation in 'Operation Allied Force', however, was also closely linked to a 'moral' debate on military intervention, which served as necessary domestic 'groundwork' for foreign policy decisions. At the same time, Kosovo marked a new plateau for German foreign and security policy since it intensified the discussion about the strategic orientation of the country's foreign policy and enhanced the instruments available for international action.

From a European point of view, one of the most relevant conclusions from Kosovo concerned the emergence of a European Security and Defence Policy (ESDP), prepared by the Franco-British summit in Saint-Malo in December 1998 (Howorth 2001). The weakness of NATO's European members in political as well as military terms during the Kosovo crisis drove the effort to give a greater role in security and defence matters to the EU. Germany regarded such a project as contributing to the establishment of a more balanced transatlantic relationship. Consequently, it actively promoted and pushed ESDP during its EU Presidency in the first semester of 1999, while keeping its Atlantic commitments in place (Regelsberger 2002). Germany, as well as other NATO members, faces a growing gap with the US concerning both military capabilities and levels of interoperability (Lindley-French 2002b). This tension between a continuing modest military role and increasing political ambitions limits the country's foreign policy options and represents also a source of frictions in transatlantic relations. While Germany's basic strategy was, and remains, a multilateral one, it is also true that Germany is trying to find ways to play a more significant role within multilateral institutions in order to exert more influence on their decisions. As a European and Atlantic power, Germany wishes to play the role of 'reliable' but also a 'key' partner. The Kosovo crisis revealed that the issue of military capabilities was a crucial one for living up to these ambitions.

Germany and the Iraq war: fundamental change or casual conflict?

Germany's U-turn: from unconditional solidarity to alienation from the US

Germany's stance during the Iraq crisis has to be analysed in the context of the developments after the terrorist attacks of 9/11. The Chancellor's first reaction was to proclaim 'unconditional solidarity' with the US. Such an attitude was shared by a huge majority of the public and most of the political parties. Hence, the US military intervention in Afghanistan which began in October 2001 was fully supported by the government. It caused, however, intense disputes within the Green Party whose pacifist wing denounced 'Operation Enduring Freedom' as legally and politically unjustifiable. It became clear that the issue of military intervention which had already played a key role during the Yugoslav conflicts, particularly during the Kosovo crisis, would continue to be salient since it represented a fundamental question of faith among Green Party members (*Die Tageszeitung*, 16 October 2001).

Schröder faced serious problems in holding the coalition together as resistance against the US policy gained in strength, and a growing number of Green parliamentarians and regional party leaders began to call for a ceasefire in Afghanistan. Unexpectedly, in November 2001, the Chancellor decided to link the *Bundestag* approval of the deployment of German military forces to Afghanistan, to a motion of confidence, stressing that he saw his political fate intrinsically related to his foreign policy. On 16 November, he won the vote 336 to 326 but four members of the Green parliamentary group and one former member of the Social Democrats voted against him. The Christian Democrats and the Liberals, who in principle backed the foreign policy course, were not willing to lend the Chancellor their support and voted against the motion. Once again, only the post-communist PDS was fundamentally opposed to a German contribution to the US effort in Afghanistan (*Süddeutsche Zeitung*, 24 November 2001). In the end, the vote of confidence served domestic as well as international purposes: the coalition parties were forced to close ranks and the US got the message that Germany was a reliable partner in foreign policy (*Frankfurter Allgemeine Zeitung*, 17 November 2001). Things, however, would soon change.

The breakdown of international solidarity with the US became visible by January 2002 when President Bush announced a wider and more comprehensive international strategy on terrorism focusing on the 'axis of evil'. Foreign Minister Fischer regarded the metaphor as of little use as it lumped together countries (Iraq, Iran and North Korea) that had no real connection (*Neue Zürcher Zeitung*, 13 February 2002). German criticism was not only targeted at the strategy against terrorism but touched also upon other fundamental issues. There was a growing uneasiness about US unilateralism which Germany felt relegated European partners to a second-tier role. Foreign Minister Fischer remarked in a newspaper interview that 'allies are not satellites'. The quip was regarded as a signal sent to Washington that Germany, and Europeans in general, was dissatisfied with such an imbalance in transatlantic relations (*Die Welt*, 12 February 2002). On that same occasion, the Foreign Minister also voiced objections to a possible military strike against Iraq, pleading for a stronger role for the UN and the weapons inspections regime. Growing tensions concerning principles reflected the different conceptualisation of the 9/11 events on the two sides of the Atlantic (Katzenstein 2002). From the German point of view, Iraq was not considered as a legitimate target in the fight against terrorism, and hence there was no legal justification for a military intervention. Germany also feared that the overthrow of the regime in Baghdad would cause more problems in the Middle East than it would solve. As late as July 2002, Chancellor Schröder, following press reports on plans for a military intervention in Iraq, declared that he was not aware of any concrete US plans to attack Iraq (*Westdeutsche Allgemeine Zeitung*, 25 July 2002). Apparently, there was no consultation on the issue and the controversy between Washington and Berlin emerged as a reaction to public discussions and declarations on both sides of the Atlantic and not as a result of personal contacts between the leaders.

The escalation of a controversy: German–US relations at their worst
Still, the German government favoured increasing diplomatic and political pressure on Saddam Hussein. For this purpose, it supported UNSC resolution 1441 of 8 November 2002, which included the threat of 'serious consequences' should the Baghdad regime not comply with it. Its goal was to keep the US working within the UN and discourage it from acting unilaterally. In January 2003, Chancellor Schröder announced that Germany, which had just begun serving as a non-permanent member of the UNSC, would not vote in favour of an armed intervention against Iraq. This premature announcement of the German stance, while the UN inspectors were still working in the country and had yet to present their report, was not particularly helpful to the UN. In late January, however, US Secretary of State Powell announced that the US would take action even without a further UNSC resolution, making it clear that the Bush administration would not make its strategy dependent on other countries or the UN as a whole. To Germany, this meant that it would have no substantial influence on the US policy. Powell's speech on 5 February 2003 presenting alleged proof of violations of the weapons inspections regime by Iraq did not have any significant impact on the German position, nor did the progress report by Chief Arms Inspector Hans Blix in February 2003 reveal any influence in Washington. Chancellor Schröder's statement that he would not send German troops into Iraq even if there was a UNSC resolution authorising the use of force can be considered the culmination of the non-engagement policy pursued by Berlin.

This point represented a potential disagreement also with France, which insisted on the role of the UNSC and had never categorically excluded sending troops into Iraq, if the UNSC were to authorise it. However, this issue never came to the surface as opposition to the US approach was sufficient to keep the Franco-German 'entente' together, and even to reach out for Russia. The German, and more importantly Russian, French and Chinese resistance against a new draft resolution submitted by the US, Spain and Britain on 24 February 2003 was the last act in trying to obtain legitimacy from the UNSC, but was doomed to failure given the predefined positions on all sides. The US, together with Britain, entered Iraq on 12 March 2003, triggering off a number of harsh public protests in Germany and many other European countries.

During the campaign in Iraq, the German government chose to behave rather cautiously, reducing official comments and criticism to a minimum. The government felt that the US attack had been inevitable and hoped for a quick victory that would facilitate the bridging of the transatlantic divide. Even before the attack, there was a barely visible subtext in the German position: Chancellor Schröder announced on 27 November 2002 that the US and other NATO allies would be granted transit, over-flight and access rights in case of a military intervention in Iraq. On 12 December 2002, he also declared that Alliance obligations would be fulfilled although Germany did not intend to take part in an attack.[6] In his TV address on 21 March 2003, immediately after the beginning of US strikes against Iraq, Schröder said: 'A wrong decision was made [...] but this is not the moment of apportioning blame and listing failures ... The differences that exist over a war are clear differences of opinion between governments, not fundamental differences between nations with traditions of friendship. The substance of our relations with the United States of America is not threatened.'[7] There was a subtle distinction in these comments which may have escaped many observers at the time, but which reflected the intention of the government to draw a line between the duties of an ally and the right to disagree on a specific policy. In the end, there was never an attempt to detach German security from NATO or the US, still considered as the main pillars of national defence.

This might not have been clear in Washington and other European capitals at the time, and certainly US hopes for German support were disappointed. After the end of 'Operation Iraqi freedom', however, endeavours by the German and the US governments to mend their relationship drew upon this distinction between fundamental interests as allies and differences in the choice of instruments. Before and during the Iraqi campaign, however, relations with the US were full of mistrust, in particular at the highest political level. Contacts between top officials were kept to a minimum although later, it became apparent that efforts were made by both US and German governments to identify common ground. German support for UNSC resolution 1483 of 22 May 2003, tabled by the US, Britain and Spain, is evidence of such an approach.[8] Germany also stepped up its presence in Afghanistan in support of the International Security Assistance Force (ISAF). When, in August 2003, President Bush publicly recognised the German contribution to the fight against terrorism and acknowledged the country's role in

Afghanistan, this was understood as a message to Berlin that improvement in their bilateral relationship was well under way.

The domestic dimension of the Iraq crisis: the end of a foreign policy consensus?

Domestic politics played an important role during the Iraq crisis, even more than in the case of Kosovo. In early August 2002, the SPD decided, with an eye on the September elections, to place the Iraq issue on the political agenda by signalling a clear rejection of a military solution (*Süddeutsche Zeitung*, 3 August 2002). In a speech in Hanover on 3 August 2002, Schröder declared publicly that unconditional solidarity with the US after 9/11 did not imply participation in 'adventures' (*Frankfurter Allgemeine Sonntagszeitung*, 4 August 2002). From that moment onwards, relations with the US administration steadily deteriorated while in the domestic arena the political debate became increasingly controversial.

The main opposition parties to the Red–Green coalition, the CDU and the FDP, did not agree with the Chancellor's approach of excluding a military option *a priori* since this impaired the strategy of putting pressure on the regime in Baghdad. They also sharply criticised a reference he had made to a 'German way' in foreign policy. They knew, however, that the Chancellor's stance was very popular with the public, and accusations by the Social Democrats that they would lead the country into war placed them in an uncomfortable position during the election campaign. As a result, the conservative candidate Stoiber chose a more cautious campaign strategy, trying to play down the Iraq issue and concentrating on the economic situation of the country. This strategy failed since Iraq had already come to occupy a prominent place in the electoral debate. There is no doubt that Schröder realised that the Iraqi issue could be harnessed to help him win the September elections. In mid-June, the Red–Green coalition was widely regarded as the prospective loser in the elections, but during July and August, its ratings in the polls increased steadily,[9] and a week before the elections the SPD gained a higher share in the polls than the CDU, which it retained on the day of the elections (22 September 2002).[10] It would however be too simplistic to explain the government's position exclusively as an electoral tactic, since there were fundamental disagreements between the Centre-Left coalition and the US concerning the strategy to be used against terrorism and the relationship between the US and its European allies. Had he chosen to align himself on the US position, Schröder would have faced serious difficulties within his own party and his government coalition. Many Social Democrats and even more members of the Green Party would probably not have supported a pro-US policy, which might have seriously destabilised the government.

In general, the coalition had an easier time in dealing with German public opinion than had been the case during the Kosovo crisis. A vast majority of Germans rejected the war against Iraq and were highly critical of US policy.

Even more important, there was widespread support for the course of action chosen by the government. In February 2002, at a rather early stage in the conflict, 80 per cent of Germans according to a poll were already opposed to an intervention in Iraq (*Die Welt*, 20 February 2002). This figure rose to 90 per cent in the following months. The unconditional rejection of military intervention, as spelled out by the Chancellor, even in the case of a UNSC mandate, had the effect of appeasing the pacifist wing of the Green Party as well as the leftist currents within the SPD, which had only unwillingly supported the Kosovo campaign. This choice, however, distanced the Centre-Left coalition from the conservative and liberal opposition, thus driving a wedge into the broad political consensus which had characterised German foreign and security policy since the early post-Cold War period.

Germany, the European Union, and transatlantic relations

The Common Foreign and Security Policy (CFSP) was among the first victims of the Iraqi crisis. As Christopher Hill bluntly puts it: 'Throughout the Iraq crisis the CFSP was almost wholly silent' (Hill 2004: 152). This silence was due to a number of factors. Of key importance was fundamental disagreement, deeply rooted in different visions of 'Atlanticism', among key EU members. This rift within the EU became apparent when eight heads of state produced a statement in support of the US position, which led to political outrage in Paris and Berlin. In a joint statement published in a number of European newspapers in January 2003, the leaders of Spain, Portugal, Italy, the UK, Denmark, the Czech Republic, Hungary and Poland, recalled their bond with the US and called for forced Iraqi disarmament if Saddam Hussein would not comply with resolution 1441 of the UN Security Council. A week earlier, at the celebration of the 40th anniversary of the Franco-German friendship treaty (Elysée treaty), the governments in Paris and Berlin had underlined their determination to do all in their power to prevent a war in Iraq (*BBC News online*, 30 January 2003).

In this phase of deep transatlantic disagreement, the EU aspired to provide itself with a new legal base aimed at unleashing fresh dynamics for integration. The Convention on the Future of Europe, which began its work in February 2002 on the draft Constitutional treaty, was widely regarded as a historical step in this regard. The debates and controversies within the Convention and the subsequent Intergovernmental Conference (IGC) were, although not formally linked, *de facto* interrelated with the foreign and security developments outside the EU. In late April 2003, at the height of the Iraq crisis, a four-nation summit held in Brussels by Germany, France, Belgium and Luxembourg called for increased efforts to build up EU institutional and military capabilities ideally to enable it to act even without recourse to NATO assets. The fact that these four countries belonged to the US-critics camp in the Iraq debate conveyed the impression to London and Washington that they were trying to take steps in order to detach the EU from NATO, and that their position on Iraq was fed by a more general 'Europeanist' ambition.

It was in particular the idea of creating an autonomous EU military headquarters – although the summit declaration did not use this term, speaking instead of a nucleus capacity for planning and conducting EU operations – which led to severe mistrust within the EU. It was here that the transatlantic dimension came into play, as the role of NATO was directly affected. The 'Atlanticist' camp within the EU, led by the British, harshly rejected the plan; so did most of the candidate countries from Central and Eastern Europe. The US reacted with outrage against the proposals and in particular tried to keep the UK on alert (Rees 2004).

Signs of improvement only came after the fall of Saddam Hussein. It was the British government which urged stronger consideration to be given to the UN, when designing a durable political order for Iraq. There were efforts made to define a more coherent EU approach as long as preference given to multilateral solutions was in principle shared by all European partners. The negotiations on a new UNSC resolution involved France, Britain and Germany, bringing them closer together in the UNSC than ever before during the Iraq crisis.

The key to these developments was a rapprochement between the governments in Berlin, Paris and London which launched intense consultations in the second half of 2003 in order to overcome the European and transatlantic disputes of the previous months. A result of these endeavours was the agreement reached on all of the major controversial issues concerning ESDP in late 2003, in particular on structured cooperation, the mutual defence clause and the 'headquarters issue'. The German Chancellor tried to include the British in a dialogue over CFSP and ESDP, in order to overcome the recent disputes and restore 'normal' relations within the EU and with the US. Germany's quest for 'normalisation' met with Blair's efforts to stress his credentials as a 'European', able to take over a leadership role in the Union. For Chirac, it was an opportunity to push a number of issues through the IGC, which would not have been possible without the British. In general, all three leaders seemed to have learned a lesson from the preceding crisis, which was to focus on common European approaches and to overcome the fatal image that the EU has left in the eyes of the public as non-existent in foreign and security policy.

Comparing the cases: changing paradigms of German foreign policy from Belgrade to Baghdad?

Both the Kosovo crisis and the Iraq conflict had a remarkable impact on German foreign policy, symbolising a change in the country's international role and status. In both cases, the question of continuity or change in

Germany's foreign and security policy was the subject of intensive debate. The conclusions however were different. Germany's engagement in Kosovo was considered as a catalyst of an enhanced international responsibility, also in military terms, without redirecting the fundamental course of the country's foreign and security policy. The crucial question was the use of military instruments, in particular military intervention, in pursuing international objectives. In this regard, the Kosovo crisis was the final phase of a process that began after unification. As Hanns Maull comments, 'the evolution of German policies regarding the use of force since 1990 has represented a security-policy reorientation within Germany's traditional post-war foreign policy identity as a civilian power'. This reorientation was rooted in a tension between ideas and principles, without however giving up a fundamentally ethical claim – the defence of humanitarian and democratic values – and still marked by a 'culture of restraint' (Maull 2000: 76).

A few years later the picture has dramatically changed. The Iraq crisis revived the debate on continuity and change in German foreign policy, leading many experts to new conclusions (Maull 2004). The 'continuity thesis' has come under pressure (Hellmann 2004a: 84; Link 2004: 3), giving way to a broader and more controversial discussion about the basic orientation of German foreign and security policy.

The conflict between the Schröder government and the Bush administration was not so much a situational disagreement on how to deal with a country of concern as it was based on different views of how international politics should be organised. Multilateralism versus unilateralism, and multipolarism versus unipolarism became key concepts in the debate. The German government, by refusing to support the Bush administration's Iraq policy, unequivocally rejected US unilateralism, thus adding a strategic dimension to the controversy (Link 2004). While European criticism of US unilateralism was a rather regular theme in the transatlantic debate (Wallace 2000), the rejection of unipolarism went deeper, focusing on the structure of the international system. Within the EU, France has traditionally stressed the need for a multipolar world, opposing a power distribution heavily concentrated upon a single country. During the Iraq crisis, Schröder had publicly sided with this view, coming closer to the French vision of international politics by revealing a preference for a 'cooperative world order' (Link 2004).

Consequently, some authors identify the 'end of the transatlantic era' (Schöllgen 2004) or plead in favour of a stronger orientation of Germany towards Europe (Hellmann 2004b) in order to achieve a better balancing of the transatlantic relationship (Link 2004). Others, in contrast, plead for a renewal of the civilian power concept (Maull 2004), which would still imply tensions with the US (Risse 2004). To date, there is no consensus on the final implications of the Iraq crisis for German foreign policy, but a growing sensation of changing paradigms.

Germany will not change the lodestar of its security and defence policy and hence NATO will remain the main pillar of German security and defence for the foreseeable future. The country's foreign policy, however, is becoming less 'predictable' for Washington. Relations with the US will not wither away, but they most surely will be based less upon common cultural and mental foundations, and become more rational and instrumental in nature. The EU may provide a framework for a coherent German foreign policy in the future, but it will most probably not absorb all ambitions and activities.

Notes

1 See 'Statement on Kosovo issued by the Foreign Ministers of the Contact Group', London, 12 June 1999 available at www.g8.utoronto.ca/foreign/fm980612_2.htm.
2 See the SPSEE website at www.stabilitypact.org/.
3 The data come from the German Ministry of Defence.
4 For this debate in Germany see Pradetto (1998), Tomuschat (1999), Lutz (2000), Ortega (2001), Schirmer (2001).
5 See the interview with one of the leading German scholars of international law, Bruno Simma in the *Süddeutsche Zeitung* (25 March 1999).
6 'Overflight and transit rights for possible military intervention against Iraq' (28 November 2002): www.bundesregierung.de/en/artikel-,10001.451891/Overflight-and-transit-rights-.htm and 'Schröder says alliance obligations will be fulfilled in case of war with Iraq' (12 December 2002): www.bundesregierung.de/en/News-by-subject/International/News-,10990.454395/artikel/Schroeder-says-alliance-obliga.htm.
7 'Speech by Chancellor Schröder after the beginning of the war in Iraq' (21 March 2003): www.bundesregierung.de/en/News-by-subject/International/News-,10990.474180/pressemitteilung/Speech-by-Chancellor-Schroeder.htm.
8 'UN Security Council agrees to Iraq resolution' (23 May 2002): www.bundesregierung.de/en/News-by-subject/International/News-,10990.488645/artikel/UN-Security-Council-agrees-to-.htm.
9 See the data in Forschungsgruppe Wahlen Politbarometer Flash 6/2002, Repräsentative Umfrage KW 24, and Politibarometer Flash 6/2002, Repräsentative Umfrage KW 26.
10 Politbarometer Flash 8/2002 KW 37.

OSVALDO CROCI

11

A tale of two coalitions: Italy faces Kosovo and Iraq

A puzzle to be explained

The role played by the Italian government in 'Operation Allied Force' against Serbia over the Kosovo question might have come as a surprise to those who were familiar with the Italian position on Yugoslavia during the 1990s. During the Bosnian war, for instance, the US and most European countries cast Serbia in the role of 'villain of the Balkans'. Italy instead maintained that stability in the Balkans could not be achieved if one chose to disregard the role, problems, and aspirations of Serbia as the largest state in the region.[1] Italy also insisted that the military operations of NATO in Bosnia had to be legitimised by appropriate United Nations Security Council (UNSC) resolutions. This view had not changed when the Kosovo crisis came to the fore. Foreign Minister Lamberto Dini put it very starkly in July 1998, when he affirmed that 'an intervention by NATO in Kosovo without a UNSC mandate [was] absolutely impossible' (*La Repubblica*, 9 July 1998). Yet, from 23 March to 9 June 1999, Italy played a central role in the logistics of 'Operation Allied Force'.

How can one explain this Italian conversion to a policy of force, especially in view of the fact that the largest member of the governmental coalition, Democratici di Sinistra (DS), was, except in name, the same party that had taken a strongly critical stance against the Gulf war (Donovan 1992)? Its conversion is even more intriguing if one considers that NATO military intervention against Serbia, unlike the Allied one against Iraq in 1991, did not have the explicit authorisation of the UNSC and rested therefore on much shakier legal ground. The first part of this chapter will explain this apparent puzzle while the second will examine Italian government choices during the Iraqi crisis. It will conclude by arguing that the foreign policy choices of the Centre-Left coalition in Kosovo and those of the Centre-Right coalition were remarkably similar and consistent with well-established trends in Italian foreign policy.

Italy and the politics of NATO's intervention in Kosovo

'Operation Allied Force' was the first intervention falling within the new mandate that NATO had given itself to deal with the security challenges and risks perceived to exist in the post-Cold War environment. According to its new 'Strategic Concept', besides meeting its traditional task of repelling an armed attack against the territory of any of its members, NATO had to be ready respond also to new threats, such as 'the uncontrolled movement of large numbers of people, particularly as a consequence of armed conflicts, [that] can ... pose problems for security and stability affecting the alliance'.[2]

The Kosovo case was a perfect example of this kind of threat. The flow of Kosovo Albanian refugees into Macedonia threatened the eruption of a conflict there between the Slav majority and the Albanian minority. Such a conflict could have potentially serious consequences for the Alliance, namely the possibility that both Greece and Turkey might be drawn into it. The flow of refugees also represented a problem for a number of European countries and, given its geographic proximity, for Italy in particular. Hence, the intervention was primarily designed to put an end to the conflict and thus stem the flow of refugees. Italian Prime Minister Massimo D'Alema, for instance, later recalled that NATO stepped up military planning for a possible intervention against Serbia in October 1998 because by that time 'the fear existed that the situation was rapidly degenerating ... Italy felt the emergence more than any other country since it was in the front line of the exodus of refugees' (D'Alema 1999: 11). In early February 1999, he also suggested deploying NATO troops in Albania to assist and provide for Kosovo refugees there.

The problem posed by refugees did not have to result necessarily in the bombing of Serbia. NATO appears to have been inexorably propelled toward this option because of the historical lesson it drew from the war in Bosnia. The lesson that Western leaders, and the American ones in particular, drew from the Bosnian war was that Yugoslav President Slobodan Milošević would yield on Kosovo only if confronted with a clear military threat. In the words of Prime Minister D'Alema (1999: 12, 20): 'NATO logic ... was to show Milošević a loaded gun in order to convince him to negotiate ... We looked to the Bosnian precedent when limited air raids had brought him to the negotiating table. Indeed, in the case of Kosovo initial plans provided only for a couple of raids and nothing else.'

This was the common position that eventually prevailed within the Alliance. The Italian initial position was, however, a bit different, and it can be summarised as follows. Unlike the Americans and some Europeans, who assumed a progressively more marked pro-Albanian attitude and regarded the Serbs as the sole villains, the Italians tended to blame both parties for the degeneration of the situation in Kosovo. They thought that a diplomatic solution was possible if one chose to isolate the extremists of the Kosovo Liberation Army (KLA), support Kosovo Albanian moderate organisations, and offer the Serbs incentives to give back the degree of autonomy that Kosovo had before 1989. Kosovo Albanians, moreover, should be clearly told that the path towards independence was impracticable.[3] When it became clear that diplomatic initiatives were insufficient and NATO began to consider military options, the Italian government suggested the establishment of a kind of *cordon sanitaire* in Albania and Macedonia to stop the flow of personnel, weapons, and supplies to the KLA. This, it argued, would represent an incentive for Serbia to loosen its grip on Kosovo. The Alliance, however, eventually settled on the option, supported in the main by the US, of issuing a threat to Milošević (D'Alema 1999: 49).

The Italians were not fully comfortable with the course of action chosen by the Alliance. Besides doubts about its effectiveness, they were also concerned about the official justification of the so-called 'activation order' (step number four in a series of seven that NATO had to go through before air-strikes could be launched) that was couched primarily in terms of the need to defend human rights in Kosovo.[4] The Italian government was, and remains, sympathetic to the idea that human rights must be protected even if that requires a redefinition of the principle of national sovereignty. Action, however, should be preceded by the development of clear and realistic criteria of intervention. As Foreign Affairs Minister Dini put it at the time, 'The challenge at this point is simply that of being able to identify the ways in which one can, and must, act ... One must uphold values and principles but one must also put their defence into the context of international realities' (Dini 1998). The Italian government thus recognises that in the post-Cold War security environment NATO might have to take responsibility for out-of-area missions, whether humanitarian or not, especially at its periphery. It maintains, however, that such interventions should be launched only with some kind of legitimisation coming from the UNSC or, as put by then Foreign Affairs Undersecretary Umberto Ranieri:

> Italy stresses the necessity of anchoring intervention by NATO, and other regional security organisations, to UN principles and practices. One must work toward a new and more effective complementarity between the UN and regional security organisations based on the development of clear and widely accepted criteria for the authorisation of the use of force. (Ranieri 1999b)[5]

Italian policymakers voiced these doubts, but once the strategy of trying to compel Milošević failed and NATO had to act on its threat, they felt they had to support the intervention. As Dini later stated: 'Italy is part of the Alliance and cannot therefore renege on its responsibilities; fifteen members were in favour of intervention and to disassociate ourselves would have been a pretty dramatic gesture' (*Corriere della Sera*, 8 March 1999).

Italy and 'Operation Allied Force'

The predicament in which the Italian government found itself as NATO launched its attack on Serbia, and the reasons for its decision to support it were best expressed by DS Member of Parliament Michele Salvati in his intervention in the Chamber of Deputies on March 26, 1999:

> Even if I regard NATO's choice as wrong, and the prelude to even bigger problems down the road, I do not think that we face one of those extreme situations in which we are morally compelled to disregard such important issues as that of national interest and loyalty to an Alliance upon which our security and role in Europe depend. Hence, it follows that full and unconditional respect for NATO's decisions is for us an obligation we cannot evade. We can certainly operate within the Alliance and follow its proper procedures in order to have the decisions already taken reconsidered ... But our readiness to assume all the responsibilities that our NATO membership entails must not be a matter of discussion.[6]

There is hardly any doubt that any of the many post-war Italian governments would have made the same decision. D'Alema's government, however, had an additional reason to do so. In assuming power, D'Alema, as well as his DS colleagues, felt that as former Communists they had to prove their reliability as Atlantic partners. In D'Alema's own words: 'My biggest problem [as Prime Minister] was relations with the US, how the Americans would evaluate me' (D'Alema 1999: 3). Supporting the first NATO military intervention in its fifty-year history, out of its area of traditional competence, without a UNSC mandate, and against a regime that still made perfunctory references to socialism, was a good way to provide evidence of reliability.

Military intervention, however, was likely to increase in the short run the flow of refugees, when stopping such a flow was ironically the main reason why NATO's intervention in the Kosovo crisis was deemed necessary. Hence, the first move of the Italian government was to begin planning for this emergency. At the European Council meeting in Berlin on 24 March, D'Alema and Dini requested their European partners 'not to leave Italy alone in the face of a possible humanitarian catastrophe'. Even if 'the refugee emergency' was going to be a problem primarily for Italy, it should be treated as a European problem (*Corriere della Sera*, 23 March 1999).

To pass with flying colours what D'Alema seemed to perceive as a personal as much as a national test, it was also necessary that support be given with conviction and not unwillingly. This would require a difficult balancing act on the part of his government. D'Alema confronted the following difficulties. First, the heterogeneous composition of his Centre-Left coalition government which, besides the DS, included seven other political parties;

within his party (DS), moreover, there was a left wing still sceptical of NATO and susceptible to anti-American rhetoric. Second, the existence of a traditional pacifist movement linked to the Church and Catholic associations. Third, a public opinion that in the end was likely to be negatively influenced by the geographical proximity of the war – some Italians could, after all, literally see and hear the war, since most of the air sorties were taking off from bases in Italy.

The strategy chosen by the government was to present Italy's participation in Operation Allied Force as a result of two imperatives: duty toward NATO and humanitarianism. D'Alema argued that Italy had to show its willingness and ability to fulfil properly the function that the new NATO had assigned to it, namely to 'project stability', in the Mediterranean and the Balkans. This was necessary not only because of an abstract sense of duty but also because the price of evading such a responsibility would be a loss of prestige and, even more importantly, missing an opportunity to become a permanent member of the 'noble circle of Great Powers'. Opting out of the intervention would mean, as D'Alema put it using a soccer metaphor, being 'a second division country' (D'Alema 1999: 21–2, 38, 52–3, 109–10). The government also made great efforts to downplay Italian participation in military operations and emphasise instead the humanitarian ones. Finally, it constantly reminded Italians that its major effort went into trying to put an end to the war by finding ways that could induce Milošević to return to the negotiating table.

On 25 March, at the European Council in Berlin, D'Alema expressed the view that bombing had already achieved its objective and the time was rapidly approaching when the question could be handed over to politics and diplomacy again. He was immediately rebuffed by US National Security Advisor Samuel Berger who pointed out that the Italian Premier obviously had not received a correct military assessment of the situation. D'Alema later explained that he was simply expressing 'hope that the whole question could be solved as soon as possible' (D'Alema 1999: 32). More likely he was trying to strengthen the position of his government in the parliamentary debate on Kosovo scheduled for the following day. The government introduced a motion that took into account the reservations of some members of the coalition but enabled it to fulfil its duties as a NATO member. The motion called for an end to the air raids as soon as possible, engaged the government to pursue diplomatic initiatives, and guaranteed that Italian planes would engage only in defensive missions. As D'Alema later hinted, the approval of this motion (318 votes for and 188 against) signified the signing of an unspoken agreement between the government and its parliamentary majority. The government would fulfil the engagements deriving from the country's membership in NATO, while political parties and individual leaders would be free to voice their criticism of specific aspects of the NATO campaign and Italy's role in it (D'Alema 1999: 34). This compromise did occasionally give the impression of lack of political cohesion but in the end worked out rather well.

After some allies expressed concern about the significance of D'Alema's statement in Berlin, which they feared was a sign of Italy's limited reliability in the war effort (*La Stampa*, 26 March 1999), the Italian government adopted a kind of division of labour within its ranks. D'Alema, whose Atlantic credibility was being tested, devoted himself to justifying and supporting NATO's decisions. The task of uttering reservations and occasional criticism of NATO's actions passed to Foreign Minister Dini, whose Atlantic credentials, unlike those of D'Alema, were impeccable. On 23 April, for instance, Dini criticised the bombing of the Serb television building. D'Alema publicly rebuked Dini and affirmed that while politicians were responsible for establishing the broad parameters of legitimate targets they should not discuss or question 'every single target' (*La Repubblica*, 24 April 1999). At the end of May, Dini suggested that Italy might not take part in a ground invasion unless approved by a UNSC resolution. D'Alema immediately invited him to be more cautious in his public statements. Italy, he then added, would be 'totally loyal' to NATO.

Such a division of labour was not only an artful device designed by the government to cope with parliamentary difficulties but reflected also dilemmas and ambiguities that existed within the executive. The Italian government in fact had to reconcile its duties towards NATO and its role of promoter of political stability in Albania with its policy of supporter of the Yugoslav (Serb-Montenegrin) federation, which it regarded as a necessary bastion against German hegemonic ambitions in the Balkans.[7] Besides geopolitical interests, the Italian government also felt it had to safeguard Italian economic interests in Serbia. These might not have been so significant as to justify a dramatic break with Italy's allies but were important enough to call for a diplomatic effort to put an end to bombing as soon as possible (*La Stampa*, 19 April 1999). Thus, in uttering reservations about some NATO actions, Foreign Minister Dini was not simply playing an assigned role in a carefully crafted representation. He was also acting as the spokesperson of Italian diplomacy whose position on how to deal with Serbia was considerably less hawkish than that taken by the Alliance.

The Italian government did occasionally advance suggestions for diplomatic initiatives, but only after clearing them with the allies. Dini proposed a total embargo to Serbia as an alternative to bombing (*Corriere della Sera*, 4 April 1999), while D'Alema suggested a bombing pause to try to push Russia and China to approve a UNSC resolution (*La Stampa*, 20 May 1999; *Corriere della Sera*, 22 May 1999). The government was also careful to emphasise that its preference for a diplomatic solution did not imply a lack of military resolve. As Dini explained: 'to try to construct an opening to peace does not mean being disloyal to the Alliance' (*La Repubblica*, 21 April 1999).

On the domestic front, the biggest opposition to Italy's participation in

Operation Allied Force came from the party Rifondazione Comunista (RC). Although in the opposition, RC put pressure on the Italian Communists and the Greens, both of which were members of the governmental majority but very critical of NATO's initiative without a UNSC mandate, to withdraw from the majority. Such a withdrawal would not necessarily have led to the passing of a motion of no confidence since the government could have been rescued by the support given to Operation Allied Force by the major parties of the opposition. These however stated that should the government lose a member of its coalition, D'Alema should resign (*La Stampa*, 24 March 1999). Throughout the war, the Italian Communists repeatedly threatened to withdraw their two ministers from the Cabinet or leave the majority altogether. Party leader Armando Cossutta even conducted a personal peace initiative that took him to Moscow and Belgrade (*Corriere della Sera*, 10 April 1999). In the end, however, the two ministers remained in the Cabinet and the party in the majority.

Overall, the government encountered few political difficulties thanks to its effort to present Italian participation in Operation Allied Force as being almost exclusively humanitarian. Thus, on 29 March, it launched the much-touted 'Missione Arcobaleno' (Rainbow Mission), to collect funds for refugees and assist them in camps in Albania and Macedonia. Although plagued by accusations of corruption and ineffectiveness 'Missione Arcobaleno' was a great success with the public and collected over 120 billion lire by the end of the war. The media helped considerably in this attempt to shift attention from the military to the humanitarian aspects of the intervention by devoting more attention to the role of Italian soldiers active in refugee camps than those involved in military operations.[8] Both the press and D'Alema, especially during his highly publicised visit to refugee camps in Albania at Easter, also engaged in graphic and tear-jerking descriptions of supposed Serb atrocities in Kosovo.[9]

At the end of the conflict, the Italian government was in a self-congratulatory mood, arguing that the plan accepted by Milošević incorporated, both in terms of the way it had been developed and of its content, the suggestions it had advanced, namely the active participation of Russia (the plan was developed within the G-8 countries) and UNSC authorisation (resolution 1244 of 10 June 1999) for the deployment of a multinational force in Kosovo. D'Alema, for instance, affirmed: 'It is the peace we have worked for with such unflagging determination and coherence of purpose' (*Corriere della Sera*, 10 June 1999). Defence minister Carlo Scognamiglio argued that 'Italy [had] contributed more than other countries to win the conflict' because 'it [had] carried more than its share of the weight' both in terms of the provision of humanitarian aid and military effort. As a result the Italian government felt that Italy had proved its loyalty and responsibility, and hence acquired more credibility or, as D'Alema put it: 'The Allies now have more respect for us' (*Corriere della Sera* 9 and 13 June 1999; D'Alema 1999: 88–9).

In the conclusion to an essay examining Italy's role in the 1956 Suez crisis published not long before Operation Allied Force, Giampaolo Calchi Novati wrote: 'Whatever her incidental interests might be and wherever her sympathies in any given conflict might lie, Italy could not act against the Alliance which anyway ensured much greater benefits (security, a protected position in the market, a link with the world of 'major politics', etc.) so that, whenever their positions diverged, Italy had no choice but to side with her allies' (Calchi Novati 1997: 43). This assessment applies well to Italy's predicament and behaviour in the Kosovo case. This does not mean, however, that Italy behaved as a 'forced ally', which implies a certain reluctance to act in a common effort and a readiness to exploit any opportunity to escape one's responsibilities. In the Kosovo case, Italy fully supported NATO collective action while at the same time trying, with some success, to maintain a profile of its own. In an article meant to be an *ex-post facto* rationalisation of Italy's behaviour, Foreign Affairs Undersecretary Umberto Ranieri argued that Italy acted on the basis of its national interest as any other 'normal country' would do. Italy's 'national interest' in the Kosovo case, however, 'did not mean the defence of its traditional bilateral interests [with Serbia] but participation in a risky, multilateral enterprise designed to promote security in the region' and which was therefore 'essential for the promotion of Italian security as well' (Ranieri 1999a: 31). Italy's particular, short-term, interests, in other words, might not have coincided with those of any of its allies but Italy's general, long-term, interest required that the government act with the Alliance once the latter had decided on a common course of action.

Torn between two sides: the Italian government and the transatlantic and intra-European rift over Iraq

The military intervention in Iraq by the US – supported militarily by Great Britain and politically by a 'coalition of the willing' which included a number of EU members but not Germany and France – caused a serious split within the Atlantic Alliance and among EU members. The transatlantic rift in particular put Prime Minister Silvio Berlusconi in a bit of a quandary. On the one hand, he considered a close relationship with the US a traditional cornerstone of Italian foreign policy. On a personal level, moreover, he did not wish to displease President George W. Bush of whom he liked to pose as the most loyal friend in Europe. On the other hand, he could not afford to distance himself too much from Italy's traditional partners in Europe, lest he give further ammunition to those who accused him of having abandoned Italy's traditional pro-European stance.[10] On the home front, moreover, it was highly unlikely that he would be able to rely on bipartisan consensus – which had existed both in the case of Kosovo and Afghanistan – since the different components of the opposition (the 'Ulivo' coalition) took position immediately against either military intervention without a UNSC resolution, or against military intervention *tout court*.

There is no doubt that Berlusconi's instinctive inclination, as well as that of some other members of his government, was to side with the US, not because of deference or servility, as charged by the opposition, but because of a substantially similar reading of the issue and choice of strategy. In his speech to the Chamber of Deputies on 25 September 2002, for instance, he described the Iraqi threat in robust terms, much closer to those used in Washington than in other European capitals. He said that his government would work for a solution to come out of the UNSC but pointed out, in what was probably the most sympathetic endorsement of the American position to come out of Europe: 'If the US today emphasises unilateral action and coalitions designed for specific political-military missions, then it means that the system of multi-lateral decision-making has shown unbearable fault lines for a country that has the major responsibility for, as well as a direct national interest in, security in the world.'[11] Much like D'Alema when confronted with the Kosovo issue, however, Berlusconi was obliged to reconcile his own inclination with the traditional guiding principles of Italian foreign policy.

The position taken by his government can be briefly summarised as follows. After the events of 9/11, the international community had to deal with Iraq's reticence to comply with UNSC resolutions asking them to destroy certain types of weapons. Of course, the preferred strategy was to convince Saddam Hussein without resorting to military force. Hence, it was imperative that the US and Europe form a united front to put pressure on Iraq, because the chances of a peaceful outcome would be directly proportional to Saddam's realisation that he could not escape punishment if he failed to comply. A strongly-worded UN resolution that threatened automatic military intervention was preferable to an ambiguous one. Even more important, public disagreement among allies was absolutely to be avoided because it would contribute to compellence failure. The position against a military intervention, taken by Germany and France, had a negative impact on the probabilities – however slim they might have been – that Saddam would comply. If the use of force were to prove necessary, then it was in everyone's interest that it be done with the authorisation of the UNSC, or at least NATO or another multilateral organisation. This position was not – and herein lies one of Berlusconi's weaknesses – reiterated and defended with intellectual rigour, forceful clarity, and charismatic intensity.[12] Berlusconi articulated it in a more fragmentary manner also because he could never pass up a chance to lock horns with his detractors on the left.

After Germany and France defected from this strategy, the Italian government set for itself the task of mediating between the two opposing camps. Berlusconi's objective became that of reconstructing the unity of Europe and of the Atlantic Alliance in order to give a chance to the possibility that the Iraqi question be solved within the UNSC. Such an objective was perfectly consistent with Italy's traditional policy of reinforcing and functionally linking the different multilateral organisations of which the country is a member, particularly the UN, the EU and NATO.

Berlusconi's mediation was not successful for several reasons. First, Europe has rarely managed to find unity on foreign policy issues. Second, the squabble over Iraq was but the manifestation of an underlying and unresolved difference among EU member states over Europe's international role and its relations with the US, especially in the security and defence field. In this respect the Italian government took its traditional stance in favour of a strong Europe within a solid Atlantic Alliance. Third, the transatlantic rift was one of the worst since Suez because it was transformed rather quickly from a debate over assessment of threat and choice of appropriate strategy into a clash about principles, which was far less amenable to a compromise solution. Finally, Berlusconi's inability to articulate and promote the Italian position in a clear, forceful, and convincing manner undermined his role as mediator.

Italian diplomatic efforts over the Iraqi issue began during the summer of 2002, when the government launched a joint initiative designed to have both European and Arab countries (Egypt and Jordan being the major interlocutors) convince Saddam to reopen the door to UN inspectors (*Corriere della Sera*, 8 August 2002). They ended with a suggestion Berlusconi made to President Bush a few days before the beginning of hostilities. He was reported to have told Bush to introduce a second resolution, have it approved by the nine members of the coalition of the willing within the UNSC during the debate preceding the vote, and then withdraw it before it could voted and vetoed by France, Germany and Russia. This would have enabled Bush to make some political capital by claiming to have at least the support of a majority of UNSC members (*La Repubblica*, 15 March 2003). Once the war began, Berlusconi's diplomatic efforts concentrated on Russian President Valadimir Putin, probably because he knew that French President Jacques Chirac and German Chancellor Gerhard Schröder were unlikely to be swayed directly by him but might rethink their position if Putin defected from their camp.

The fact that the government failed to rebuild European unity does not mean that Italian interests would have been better served had Berlusconi aligned himself with Chirac and Schröder, as the opposition indirectly seemed to imply. This could have been understood as acquiescing to French–German directorate in the EU and to Chirac's ambitions of having the EU speak with a French accent on the world scene. All Italian governments, including those formed by the 'Ulivo' coalition, have opposed the formation of a European directorate. Alignment with France and Germany, moreover, would have further isolated Great Britain from its continental partners, widened the rift across the Atlantic, and made any progress towards a European Security and Defence Policy (ESDP) even more difficult.

In the parliamentary debate on 19 March, when US soldiers had already crossed from Kuwait into Iraq, the government argued that although 'at a minimum, the existing resolutions constituted a legitimate basis to act', the government had decided to remain 'non-belligerent' in order to 'respond to the particular sensitivities of Italian public opinion'. It would contribute 'neither personnel nor equipment' but would provide logistical support and would be 'solidly behind the US and Britain' (*La Stampa*, 15 and 18 March 2003). The vote marked the end of a period of bipartisan consensus in Italian foreign policy. Each coalition voted in bloc for its own motion: the government's was approved with 304 votes in favour (246 opposed and 2 abstentions) in the Chamber of Deputies, and 159 in favour (124 against and 1 abstention) in the Senate (*La Repubblica*, 19 March 2003). Although it voted unanimously against the government motion, the 'Ulivo' coalition was split between 'absolute pacifists' whose slogan was 'No to war with no ifs or buts' and 'moderate pacifists' who were ready to consider a military intervention if authorised by the UNSC. The first group included Rifondazione Comunista (RC), the Partito dei Comunisti Italiani (PdCI), the Greens, and Catholics such as former President of the Republic Oscar Luigi Scalfaro, as well as the left wing faction of the DS. The second group included the Socialisti Democratici Italiani (SDI), as well the majority of the Margherita and of the DS.

The divisions within the opposition became even more apparent on the eve of a second protest rally which the so-called 'Fermiamo la guerra' (Let's stop the war) committee had organised in Rome for 12 April. Unfortunately for the organisers, the date came to coincide with the fall of Baghdad and the official end of military operations in Iraq. This event marked a significant shift in public attitude with respect to the beginning of the war. On 11 April, the number of people that approved the intervention had risen to 37 per cent (from 22 per cent on 13 March) while those opposed had declined from 72 to 56 per cent. A change had occurred also in the perception of the role played by various actors. The number of positive perceptions of the role played by the US had increased from 29 to 47 per cent; that of Italy from 41 to 45 per cent, while the number of positive perceptions of the EU had decreased from 45 to 33 per cent, that of the UN from 54 to 42 per cent and that of France and Germany from 56 to 40 and 41 per cent respectively (*Corriere della Sera*, 12 April 2003). Some members of the 'Ulivo' coalition such as the the Gruppo Unione Democratici per l'Europa (UDEUR), and the SDI boycotted the rally arguing that 'the faces of the Iraqis in Baghdad are remindful of those of Italians on 25 April 1945'. The leadership of the DS and the Margherita decided not to participate arguing that one could only rejoice at the fall of Saddam. The bulk of both parties, however, took part marching against 'the unilateralism that led to war' and for the UN's involvement in Iraq's democratic reconstruction. The Greens, the PdCI and RC, instead marched denouncing 'the infinite conflict', that is the wars that they claimed the US was preparing to wage against other countries, from Syria to Iran (*Corriere della Sera*, 11 and 12 April 2003).

No sooner had the war ended, than the government announced that Italy would make an independent contribution to the 'humanitarian stabilisation' of Iraq. The government also hoped that reconstruction would take place under the aegis of the UN (a public opinion poll published in early April showed that 61 per cent of Italians wanted to see a UN-led provisional government in Iraq after the end of the war) but the Italian contribution, the government pointed out, would not depend on UN involvement. Although primarily humanitarian, the contribution would also include, as requested by Bush and Blair, a contingent of 'carabinieri' (a branch of the Italian army acting as police force) with policing tasks. The opposition argued that Italy could not send a single 'carabiniere' to Iraq without a UNSC authorisation, but when Parliament was called to approve the mission on 15 April, only the Greens, RC and the PdCI voted against, while the DS, the Margherita, the SDI, and the UDEUR abstained. The same divisions reappeared after fourteen 'carabinieri' of the Italian contingent based in Nassirya were killed in a suicide attack on 12 November 2003. Those who had voted against the mission now called for the immediate recall of the contingent.

After the war ended, however, the opposition seemed to file the Iraqi issue away. At the end of April 2003, for instance, the daily *La Repubblica* revealed that Italy had, after all, helped in the war effort. About twenty Italian intelligence service agents had gone to Iraq between January and February 2003 with the mission to contact high officials of the army and convince them to desert the Baath regime. Once the war began, because of their excellent contacts, they had also helped in localising military objectives and in the search for Baathist fugitives. *La Repubblica*, usually vitriolic in its comments on the Berlusconi government, this time simply rejoiced with the agents for a job well done, while the opposition passed on the opportunity to attack the government for having lied in its declaration of non-belligerence (*La Repubblica*, 23 April 2003).

Some skirmishes resurfaced in December 2003, after the capture of Saddam, when Berlusconi tried to make some political capital out of it and invited the left to acknowledge that 'Italy was on the right side'. The opposition, however, calmly retorted that the capture of Saddam did not make the war just and advised that the government act 'within a European position', that it call for the UN to play 'a central role' in reconstructing Iraq, and that it work to convince Washington to include France and Germany in the reconstruction process. On these conditions it promised that the bipartisan spirit of the past could be revived (*Corriere della Sera*, 15 and 16 December 2003).

During the months preceding military intervention in Iraq, the Italian government undertook an almost impossible task: to try to rebuild European unity, maintain transatlantic cohesion, and work towards a peaceful resolution of the crisis, or at least solve it within the UNSC. The government moved, in other words, along the traditional path of Italian foreign policy. It did not succeed in its mediating effort not only because of some shortcomings in its tactics and style, but also because European unity, transatlantic solidarity, and multilateral procedures were less important to the US, Germany, and France, than they were to Italy. They all refused to find a policy compromise and chose to defend principles and pursue their own perceived national interests. If Europe ended up divided, the fault – if one can indeed speak in such terms in politics – did not rest with the Italian government but with Schröder's temptation to tie his hands for domestic political reasons, and with Chirac's miscalculation that threatening a veto might persuade the Americans to give the inspectors more time. The Berlusconi government may be faulted for all sorts of things but its handling of the Iraqi crisis does not seem to be one of them. After all, if the Kosovo conflict can be taken as an indication of its behaviour, the 'Ulivo' opposition would have most likely adopted the same course of action as the government had it been in power rather than in opposition. The 'Ulivo' probably considered that since the rifts within the EU and the Atlantic Alliance happened very early, became increasingly radicalised, and involved major powers, they were beyond Italy's capacity to mend given the country's small weight on the international scene, the limited goodwill enjoyed by Berlusconi in Paris and Berlin, and his dubious diplomatic skills. Hence, it might as well concentrate on making some political capital by riding the wave of public pacifism. The Iraqi issue also demonstrates that the 'Ulivo' has yet to find a clear identity (Pasquino 2001 and 2003). It seems that when the making of foreign policy moves beyond the simple enunciation of general principles and calls for taking a clear stance on concrete political problems, the members of the coalition end up being sucked back, as it were, by their own subcultures and become divided and more prone to infighting and internal differentiation than to unitary action.

Conclusions

The foreign policy choices made by the Centre-Left government coalition led by D'Alema over Kosovo and those made by the Centre-Right government coalition led by Berlusconi over Iraq are characterised by continuity more than change. Both of them, in fact, followed the two lodestars of Italian foreign policy since the end of World War II, namely support for the Atlantic Alliance and for European integration, the latter understood as a process firmly entrenched within the former. When these two lodestars have tended to diverge (as in the case of Iraq), Italian governments have tried to bring them back on the same course. If this attempt failed and they were called upon to make a choice between following some – usually French – attempt to establish Europe as a third force, or a counterweight to the US, they always shied away from following such passing chimeras and privileged the transatlantic link. This was the case with all the Christian Democratic coalitions that ruled Italy until the early 1990s (Nuti 2003). It was also the case with the

Centre-Left coalitions of the 1990s. The 'Ulivo' coalition government led by Romano Prodi, for instance, refused to support a French proposal aimed at giving command of Allied Joint Force Command Naples (AFSOUTH) to a French (or European) office because it was not prepared to go along with plans that could be interpreted as loosening transatlantic ties without offering any concrete gains in terms of the defence of Europe (Dassù and Menotti 1997). The behaviour of the Berlusconi government over Iraq has been consistent with this well-established trend in Italian foreign policy.

Notes

1. On the position of the US, Canada, Germany, the UK, France and Russia toward Yugoslavia, see Macleod and Roussel (1996). On the position of Italy, see liMes (1998) and D'Alema (1999: 66, 72 and 85).
2. 'The Alliance's Strategic Concept': www.nato.int/docu/pr/1999/p99–065e.htm.
3. The outlines of the Italian position can be found in the speech Foreign Minister Lamberto Dini gave to the Chamber of Deputies on 17 March 1998.
4. For details on the 'activation order', see 'Steps NATO must take for air-strike approval': www.cnn.com/WORLD/europe/9810/08/kosovo.nato.steps/. For comments on the text of the activation order see *New York Times* (18 October 1998).
5. See also Dini's speech at the UN Assembly in *La Repubblica* (12 October 1999).
6. The report of the debate is at camera.it/_dati/leg13/lavori/stenografici/sed513/s090.htm.
7. On the geopolitical reasons of Italian support of Serbia, see Serpicus (1998).
8. See, for example, *Corriere della Sera* (1 May 1999). At times this effort went to ridiculous extremes as when a newspaper headline claimed: 'Our kitchen dishes out 10 kgs of pasta every 8 minutes; others offer only potatoes' (*Corriere della Sera*, 19 April 1999). The government only had to deal with some protests in mid-April, when it became clear that Italian planes were taking part in the bombing raids on Serbia. D'Alema, however, silenced the critics by arguing through some verbal somersaults that these missions were part of that 'integrated and active defence' duty that Parliament had approved on 26 March (*Corriere della Sera* and *La Stampa*, 15 April 1999).
9. The worst culprit in this process of demonisation of the Serbs was *La Repubblica*. On 21 April, for instance, it published a report entitled 'Rubano sangue ai bambini' ['Serbs steal blood from children']. The only newspaper that raised questions about the reliability of accounts of Serb atrocities based exclusively on KLA information was *Il Manifesto*.
10. For details on the political diatribe concerning the foreign policy of the Berlusconi government, especially towards the EU and the US, see Croci (2005a, 2005b).
11. The text of the intervention can be found at http://testo.camera.it/.
12. The most eloquent and cogent presentation of the position of the Italian government was given by Foreign Minister Franco Frattini in a speech to the French National Assembly on 26 February 2003.

NICHOLAS REES

12

The neutral states and the challenge of ESDP: Kosovo, Iraq and the transatlantic divide

Introduction

This chapter looks at the foreign policy orientations of the four 'neutral' states (Ireland, Austria, Finland and Sweden) in the post-Cold War period.[1] It considers how their foreign policies have been changed since the end of the Cold War and how EU membership has affected their foreign policy outlooks. It questions whether neutrality has any particular relevance in the post-Cold War environment, arguing that it is an artefact of the Cold War, but one that can still influence and shape the role that the neutrals play in responding to international crises. The chapter examines the impact the changes in foreign policy orientations have had on the positions and role the states have played in the EU foreign and security policies. It highlights the difficulty of reconciling domestic public attitudes which remain supportive of neutrality, but which can be inconsistent and contradictory, with a broader political desire amongst the majority of the political and military elite in these states to be involved in European Security and Defence Policy (ESDP). The third section considers the Kosovo and Iraq crises, looking at the EU positions and actions and the response of the neutral states, while the final section looks at the challenges of ESDP for the neutrals and considers the positions they have taken on ESDP issues in the Constitutional Convention and intergovernmental conference (IGC) of 2003–04.

Beyond neutrality: Ireland, Finland, Sweden and Austria inside the EU

What meaning does neutrality have in the post-Cold War climate and in the context of the types of security threats and challenges that exist in the twenty-first century?[2] Are the four states now post-neutrals, given their membership in the EU, although not members of any military alliances, or does neutrality still play a role in their foreign policy outlooks?[3] It may, for the purposes of analysis, be useful to group the four states together and refer to them collectively as the 'neutrals', but it also worth noting that the differences between the four states may be as great as the similarities among them. Grouping the states together as 'neutrals' does serve to highlight that at least in the past these states have had foreign policy orientations that are different from many of the other EU member states.[4] Neutrality may be 'a thing of the past', as High Representative/Secretary-General Javier Solana has claimed (*EUobserver*, 19 January 2001), but it is important to recognise that there remain varying degrees of public attachment to neutrality in these states and they see European and international security issues from different perspectives to those of other EU states.

In comparing how the states' positions have changed in the post-Cold War period, it is worth distinguishing the different origins of neutrality in each instance, as each state's security orientation was a product of very different circumstances. Ireland's claim to neutrality has rested on its non-membership of military alliances, although its wartime history, despite its claims of neutrality, suggests that it did side with the allies, and since the 1950s it has been involved in a range of (West) European organisations (Keatinge 1984, 1996, 1998; McSweeney 1985; Salmon 1989; O'Halpin 1999). Finland's neutrality, a product of the Cold War, was based on political necessity, given the state's geographic proximity to the Soviet Union, and its desire to maintain its independence and sovereignty (Ojanen 2000, 2003; Huldt et al. 2004). Sweden, in contrast to Finland, was geographically secure, did not border the Soviet Union and chose a policy of neutrality in the mid-nineteenth century. Its security policy during the Cold War was focused on preserving peace and maintaining the state's independence (Pesonen and Vesa 1998; Ojanen, Herolf and Lidahl 2000), but as recent evidence suggests, the state secretly cooperated with NATO and had it been attacked the latter would have come to its assistance (Vaahtoranta and Forsberg 2000). Finally, Austria's neutrality was enshrined in the 'State Treaty' of 1955, which re-established the Austrian state. The new government adopted by means of a constitutional act a position of 'permanent neutrality', making it distinctly different from the other three cases (König 1999).

For all of the states the end of the Cold War, and EU membership, has had an impact on their positions as neutrals and their foreign and security policy outlooks. Ireland, which was the first of the four states to join the EC, had little difficulty adjusting to being a member of a political and economic community, despite some initial concerns about the impact of EC membership on neutrality, and only on a small number of occasions did Ireland find itself at odds with the other members in relation to its foreign policy. By the late 1990s, however, Ireland's position of neutrality was no longer politically realistic in light of the changing international security environment and increasingly 'neutrality' was reinterpreted to pragmatically allow Ireland to participate in European security developments (Keatinge 1996, 1998; Tonra 2001). In the course of the 1990s the Irish government produced the first ever White Papers on foreign policy and defence (Government of Ireland 1996, 2000), which elaborated the principles and objectives of Irish foreign and security policies. While restating a commitment to military neutrality, they linked Irish foreign policy with the development of the Common Foreign and Security Policy (CFSP). Arising out of these developments there were sporadic domestic debates on the issue of neutrality, with heated discussions during EU referenda over whether the EU was becoming militarised and whether ESDP was a threat to Irish neutrality (Coakley, Holmes and Rees 1997; Rees 1998, 1999). Successive governments sought to reassure the public that there was no threat to neutrality and that Ireland's objective was to play a positive role in conflict prevention and peacekeeping through participation in the EU, as well as in the Partnership for Peace (PfP) programme, the Organisation for Security and Cooperation in Europe (OSCE) and the UN.

In the other three states, the end of the Cold War, and the prospect of EU membership, had different impacts on their foreign policy outlooks. In Finland, the 1948 'Treaty on Friendship, Cooperation and Mutual Assistance' with the Soviet Union was revoked and the government defined the core of neutrality as being an independent defence and military non-alliance (Government of Finland 1995, 1997, 2004). Neutrality, as previously defined, was no longer relevant in the context of EU membership, and was redefined in a pragmatic way to fit with Finnish security interests. The emphasis was placed on having a credible defence capability, remaining militarily non-allied and participation in international cooperation. In Sweden, the change in foreign policy began in 1990, under the Carlsson government, and continued under the successor Bildt government (1991–4), which adopted a strongly pro-EC stance and redefined neutrality to limit its scope to conflicts occurring in its geographic proximity (Agius 2002). The Bildt government refocused Swedish foreign policy, placing an added emphasis on a security policy within a European identity, while maintaining a policy of military non-alignment. Neutrality was put to one side and the government adopted the term 'military non-alignment' (von Sydow n.d.).

In the Austrian case, with the end of the Cold War much of the rationale for and relevance of Austria's policy of neutrality no longer existed (Luif 1998) and following EU membership the federal constitution was amended (Article 23f) to allow for Austrian participation in the CFSP (Lantis and Queen 1998; Phinnemore 2000). On 12 December 2001 the Austrian Parliament adopted a new resolution on security and defence doctrine which made no mention of permanent neutrality, referring instead to Austria as a non-allied state. The new foreign policy included non-participation in wars, non-alignment with any military alliance and the exclusion of foreign troops from Austrian territory. The core elements of the new security and defence doctrine include the notion of comprehensive security and a commitment the principle of European solidarity (Gustenau 1999).

What these brief examinations suggest is that the four states, to varying degrees, have been adapting their foreign and security policies as part of their integration into the EU (Miles 2000; Rees and Holmes 2002). They have had to reform and reshape their own security policies to be able to play a more active part in ESDP. Equally, the political and military elites have sought to play an active role in the development of the CFSP and, more recently, the ESDP. Most importantly, they have sought to bring their own foreign policy orientations to bear on the development of CFSP/ESDP, placing a particular emphasis on the EU role in conflict prevention and crisis management. It is worth noting that the inclusion of the Petersberg tasks in the Amsterdam treaty was the result of a Swedish–Finnish initiative, which was taken in part to highlight that the two states were not opposed to the use of military force per se.[5] Similarly, the development of the EU 'Northern dimension' has been a product of Finnish thinking and Nordic cooperation. The degree of adaptation and Europeanisation in each state is debatable, but in all cases there is evidence to suggest the neutral states have become more supportive of EU policy and positions and have moved beyond their traditional positions of neutrality.

Nevertheless, public attachment to neutrality in each state, to varying degrees, remains strong and is a potential constraint on those political and military leaders that might wish to place neutrality in the past. In each state there remains some opposition to participating in CFSP and ESDP (as well as opposition to NATO membership), as there is a concern that such participation may compromise 'neutrality' or military non-alignment. Table 12.1 highlights the fact that Swedish and Finnish support for CFSP and ESDP remains below the European average, and at the bottom of the table, although there has been a marked increase of support over the last five years. In contrast in Austria and Ireland public support for CFSP and ESDP has remained constant during this period although it is still lower than the European average.

The neutrals and ESDP

The rapid development of European security policy has challenged the neutral states and led them to consider what role they can play in Europe's evolving security order. On joining the EU, the three new members had to adjust to the requirements of the Maastricht treaty, and more recently, the treaties of Amsterdam and Nice. However, these states were reassured by the fact that Ireland was able to participate in CFSP and the willingness of the other member states to accept Ireland's position. Similarly, at the Cologne European Council in June 1999, the EU members accepted that there were differences among the states with regard to the idea of a collective defence

Table 12.1 Support for CFSP and ESDP in EU member states

Country	1999		2003	
	ESDP	CFSP	ESDP	CFSP
The Netherlands	81	70	78	71
Italy	81	75	86	79
Belgium	80	68	80	73
Luxembourg	79	74	92	84
France	77	67	77	69
Germany	74	68	81	77
Greece	71	70	84	82
Spain	67	62	76	70
Portugal	64	54	75	62
Austria	62	62	62	65
UK	58	43	47	37
Denmark	53	56	57	55
Ireland	50	59	51	61
Sweden	45	46	56	55
Finland	44	49	51	56
EU Average	71	63	74	67

Source: *Standard Eurobarometer* 51 (Spring 1999) and 59 (Spring 2003)

guarantee (Eliasson 2000: 20). The EU has explicitly recognised that certain member states may have difficulties in participating in greater security and defence cooperation. Notably, the acceptance at the European Council in June 2002 of Ireland's national declaration on neutrality (and the Seville declaration on the Nice treaty) reflects such an understanding. More recently, the EU's willingness to accommodate different security outlooks has been reflected in the agreement within the constitutional treaty, which provided for a smaller group of states to engage in enhanced cooperation on defence and security issues if they so desired.

In practice, the neutral states have played an active role in developing the EU's security and defence policy, which has been evident during their presidencies, when they have been eager to ensure that they are included in all ESDP discussions. Finland played a key role in building on the Cologne agreement in the lead-up to the Helsinki European Council in December 1999. Finland was supported by Sweden, with both states eager to emphasise the civilian aspects of crisis management and their willingness to play a role in this area, but cautious about participating in any collective agreement about European defence.[6] Again, this demonstrates how much has changed in the post-Cold War period, but also how the two states continue to adopt a distinctive approach to European security policy. Similarly, the Irish Presidency in the first part of 2004, which was charged with further developing concrete measures to make operational the European security strategy, sought to promote initiatives on EU–UN cooperation in crisis management and the role of civil society in the prevention of armed conflict. The Irish Presidency was also active in moving forward operational initiatives on the battle-groups concept and reaching agreement on a new Headline Goal for 2010, suggesting that it was both willing and able to move the security agenda forward during its presidency.

At an operational level, the neutral states have participated in all of the political and military structures that have been established in Brussels, as well as contributing at an operational military level to the EU's headline goals. They are involved in a range of current peace operations, including most of the EU military and police operations (Missiroli 2003a), as well as in a variety of UN and NATO-led operations (see Table 12.2). It is important, from the perspective of the neutral states, to be at the heart of European decision-making on security, and not to be left out in the cold, as some feel may happen if a group of larger member states moves forward on the basis of enhanced cooperation.

In light of the changing international security environment, and as a result of involvement in EU military structures and the PfP programme, the neutral states have had to rethink their military contributions to European security. In effect, as with other EU member states, the neutrals have had to re-evaluate the role their armed forces might play as part of the European Rapid Reaction Force (ERRF), as well as in relation to the emergence of the battle-groups concept and its role in crisis management. An increasing emphasis in EU policy has been placed on building flexible and interoperable military forces that can rapidly respond to an emerging crisis. Notably, in the case of Austria and Finland, early participation in PfP and EU membership has led to a re-evaluation and re-focusing of defence force strategies. Austria has put greater focus on the creation of a larger number of mobile forces – brigades – focused on crisis management and the adoption of more forceful rules of engagement, whereas Finland has retained a higher level of commitment to territorial defence, although there has been some emphasis on three new readiness brigades. In Sweden there have been significant defence reforms (with defence cuts and base closures) aimed at reducing costs and creating a modern, highly operational force (Wedin 2004). In Ireland there have been some defence cuts and a refocusing of the defence strategy on the creation of a more flexible, mobile, better equipped and interoperable defence force (Government of Ireland 2000). Such changes, however, have been implemented slowly and there remain practical problems in creating the type of capabilities that the EU sees as necessary to undertake crisis management operations.

As the following tables highlight, despite the small size of the military forces and budgetary constraints in these states (see Table 12.3), all of the neutral states have committed military as well as civilian forces to the EU's headline goals (see Table 12.4).

Table 12.2 Participation of neutral states in peacekeeping operations (2004)

UN peacekeeping operations	Austria	Finland	Sweden	Ireland
UNTSO	Y	Y	Y	N
UNMOGIP	Y	Y	Y	N
UNFICYP	Y	Y	Y	Y
UNDOF	Y	N	Y	N
UNIFIL	N	N	Y	Y
UNIKOM	Y	Y	Y	Y
MINURSO	Y	N	Y	Y
UNOMIG	Y	N	Y	N
UNMIK	Y	Y	Y	Y
UNAMSIL	N	N	Y	N
MONUC	N	N	Y	Y
UNMEE	Y	Y	Y	Y
UNMISET	N	N	Y	Y
UNMIL	N	Y	Y	Y
Multi-national tasked and UN authorised				
Multinational Force in Iraq	N	N	N	N
NATO/ NATO- led				
SFOR	Y	Y	Y	Y
KFOR	Y	Y	Y	Y
ISAF	Y	Y	Y	Y
EU operations				
EUMM	Y	Y	Y	Y
EUPM	Y	Y	Y	Y
CONCORDIA	Y	Y	Y	N
ARTEMIS	Y	N	Y	Y
PROXIMA	Y	Y	Y	Y
EUFOR – ALTHEA	Y	Y	Y	Y

Notes:
- For definitions of the operations listed, see www.un.org/dpko.
- The table excludes participation in OSCE operations in which the neutral states have been actively involved in a variety of roles.
- Operations Concordia (Macedonia) and Artemis concluded in 2003.
- A further number of small EU operations have been approved including EUJUST THEMIS in Georgia (2004, concluded 2005), EUPOL Kinshasa (2005+), EUSEC RD Congo (2005+) and EUJUST Lex in Iraq (2005+).

Source: SIPRI Yearbook (2004) and Europa website www.europa.eu.int

Table 12.3 Military expenditure as a percentage of GDP in the neutral states

State/Year	1995	1996	1997	1998	1999	2000	2001	2002
Ireland	1.0	1.0	0.9	0.8	0.8	0.7	0.7	0.7
Finland	1.5	1.7	1.5	1.5	1.2	1.3	1.2	1.2
Sweden	2.3	1.5	2.0	2.1	2.0	2.0	1.9	1.8
Austria	0.9	0.9	0.9	0.9	0.8	0.8	0.8	0.8

Source: SIPRI Yearbook (2004)

Table 12.4 Military commitments of neutral states to the Headline Goals, 2003

State	Ireland	Finland	Sweden	Austria
Military Forces	1 light infantry battalion; special forces group	1 mechanised infantry battalion (POK); 1 transport co.; 1 CIMIC co. (2000 personnel)	2 corvetts; 1 support ship; 1 mechanised infantry battalion; 1 engineering unit; 1 MP unit; 1 marine unit; 4 AJS 37 a/c (to be 8 JAF 30 in 2004); 4–C-130	1 mechanised infantry battalion; light infantry battalion; 1 NBC unit; 1 helicopter transport squadron, 1 transport company

Source: Adapted from Missiroli (2003b)

The reality remains that while these states will contribute to the operational aspects of the ESDP, including EU civilian and military operations, the major contributions are likely to come from Britain and France, as well as Germany, and to a lesser extent Italy, Spain and Poland (Everts et al. 2004). Nevertheless, Sweden and Finland have announced that they intend to create a joint EU battle group, as a part of their contribution to an EU rapid reaction force. In contrast, Ireland, while not opposed in principle to contributing to such a military group, has indicated that it may be not practical in the context of the Irish requirement that Irish forces cannot be deployed without a prior UN mandate, as well as requiring the assent of the Dáil (one of the Houses of the Irish Parliament) and government.

Past foreign policy and security orientations continue to assert an influence over and shape the response of the neutral states to European and international security matters. There can be little doubt that in organisations, such as the UN, they are closely aligned with other EU states. However, in relation to international crises, as the following examination of Kosovo and Iraq illustrate, they are reluctant to take sides, prefer to work within the UN framework, and are cautious and sometimes critical of major security actors, such as the US and Britain.

The neutrals' response to the Kosovo and Iraq crises

The Kosovo crisis highlighted the dilemmas that the neutral states faced, both as members of the EU, as well as more broadly as members of the international community. As the Kosovo crisis unfolded, it provided an early test of how such states, as members of the EU and committed to supporting CFSP, would react to the use of NATO military force, and reconcile their national viewpoints with those of the other EU member states, who were NATO members. The EU was not a central actor in the Kosovo crisis and showed limited leadership in addressing the security issues. The EU role was largely limited to a mix of declarations, sanctions, and refugee relief, as well as developing a long-term perspective on the region. The European Council did not endorse NATO's actions but did justify them in terms of the need to put an end to the humanitarian catastrophe. The crisis and the ensuing NATO military action, 'Operation Allied Force', did not cause divisions within the EU. A number of EU member states played leading roles in the diplomatic effort: Germany, France, Italy and the UK were all part of the International Contact Group, while Germany and then Finland, which held the EU Presidency in 1999, were at the centre of the diplomatic efforts. Similarly, many of the EU's NATO members were involved in the NATO operation. There were concerns among some EU states, especially the neutrals, about the basis for this military action and whether it could be justified in terms of international law and without a United Nations Security Council (UNSC) mandate.

In contrast the war in Iraq, which began with the American-led coalition attack on 20 March 2003 and concluded early in May, drove a wedge between Europe and the US and divided EU member states into at least three groups. The first, which supported US action, included the UK, Spain, Denmark, Italy and a number of the accession states including Poland. The second, which included France and Germany, was highly critical of US intervention and vocally opposed it in the UNSC. A third group, which included the neutrals and the Greek (EU) Presidency, did not support intervention but avoided direct criticism of the US. It also expressed frustration at Iraq's defiant stance. The Greek Presidency was faced with the impossible task of reconciling the differing viewpoints and interests of the EU member states (Hill 2004). Following the outbreak of war, the issue of Iraq took precedence over the planned summit agenda for the European Council meeting on 20–21 March, at which the divisions between France/Germany and UK/Spain prevented the adoption of a common EU position. Mid-way through the conflict, the EU leaders held an informal European Council in Athens, which was joined by UN Secretary General Kofi Annan, and at which the Presidency attempted to heal the rift among its divided members, leading the EU to issue a statement stressing the need for the UN to play a significant role in post-war Iraq.

Ireland

The Kosovo crisis and the ethnic violence in the country visibly shocked the Irish public, but NATO's intervention deeply divided the populace over what should be done. An MRBI poll published by the *Irish Times* (1 June 1999) found that 46 per cent of the public supported NATO's actions, while 42 per cent were opposed, with the rest undecided. NATO's actions also prompted a number of public protests, and the creation of the 'No to War Campaign'. The government's reaction mirrored the public's concerns and fears, with feelings of frustration at the failure of diplomatic negotiations but mixed emotions about NATO's initiative. The matter was debated in the Dáil on 24 March 1999. Speaking on behalf of the government, Michael Smith, the Minister of Defence, stated: 'There are matters that are totally outside our control. We work within the UN and we have sought to get agreement.' Opposition TDs (Members of Parliament), however, were more critical of the government, and Gay Mitchell (Fine Gael) accused the government of being like an 'ostrich with its head in the sand ... we pretend these things do not happen and we do not contribute to their solution' (quoted in Rees 2000).

Following the EU Council meeting in Berlin, the Minister for Foreign Affairs, David Andrews, stated: 'We are preserving in a principled way our neutral position. Our position is that we would have preferred a United Nations mandate' (*Irish Times*, 26 March 1999). Ireland, like the other neutral states, neither condemned nor supported NATO's intervention, thereby avoiding a potential split among the EU's NATO and non-NATO members. Taoiseach (Prime Minister) Bertie Ahern, speaking on 29 March, suggested: 'We have a role to play and if the international community asks us to play a role, whether it be aid or some other means, we will play that role' (*Irish Times*, 30 March 1999). By April, however, it became more difficult for the government to sit on the fence. EU foreign ministers, at their meeting in Luxembourg, agreed that NATO bombing had been 'necessary and warranted'. The original draft statement said that it was 'justified', but Minister Andrews and his colleagues from the other neutral states opposed this term, as it implied there was a legal basis for the intervention.

Following the informal European Council meeting on 14 April, the Taoiseach stated that Ireland strongly supported the continuation of the bombings, noting that 'these things have to happen' (*Irish Times*, 15 April 1999) while an *Irish Times* editorial (14 April 1999) declared: 'Ireland has stepped off the neutrality fence'. This marked a considerable change in the government's initial position and possibly reflected a desire to maintain EU solidarity. In the face of UN impotence, the government did move beyond neutrality in supporting NATO's intervention as a part of the EU, highlighting once again the growing importance of an emerging EU security policy and Ireland's willingness to play a part in it.

Ireland's position on Iraq was very similar to that of its response to Kosovo in that it did not condemn the coalition's actions, but was unwilling to condone military action. Yet it provided access to Shannon airport and was considered a friendly state by the US (Rees 1998, 1999). On the surface, Ireland had few connections with Iraq, and a potential American incursion only seemed to have indirect implications for Ireland. In practice, American actions had considerable effects. The use of Shannon airport as a transit zone for American troops to the Middle East provoked peace protests and rallies, a debate in the media about Ireland's neutral status, and questions in the Dáil. It raised the questions of whether the Irish government supported the US intervention and what position it should take within the EU.

The government, as a non-permanent member of the Security Council during 2001–02, supported UNSC resolution 1441. It condemned the Iraqi government for failing to comply with it, but argued that it was the responsibility of the UNSC to determine if the resolution had been breached. The Minister for Foreign Affairs, speaking in the Dáil on 29 January, stated that resolution 1441 did not require a second resolution to authorise the use of force. However, on 11 February, again in the Dáil, he argued that a second resolution was a political necessity, and the Taoiseach called it 'a political imperative' and ruled out any Irish participation without such authorisation (*Irish Times*, 2 February 2003).

The legality of the war raised considerable concerns, both at a political and public level, with the smaller political parties, such as the Greens, the Socialist Party, Sinn Féin and Labour disputing the legitimacy of the war. Fine Gael also opposed US over-flights and the use of Shannon airport because it undermined neutrality and undercut the legitimacy of the UN. On the outbreak of the conflict, the Minister for Foreign Affairs was careful to avoid criticism of the US, but stated in the Dáil that, 'it is a matter of the greater regret to Ireland that the Iraqi crisis has reached a point where military conflict has begun'[7]. The government was cautious in its statements, being neither supportive nor critical of the US intervention. While supportive of the UN position, in fact, it was unwilling to criticise a close ally, aware of the US past support for the Northern Ireland peace process and of American investment in Ireland.

Finland

Finland's position and response to the two crises was relatively consistent, with the government opposed to and critical of military action. In relation to Kosovo, it would have preferred to see NATO operating under a UNSC mandate but recognised that the UNSC was unlikely to be able to reach such agreement. The former President, Mauno Kovisto, argued that NATO had violated international law and undermined its own rationale for existence

(Vaahtoranta and Forsberg 2000). Finland's political leaders acted in a more cautious manner, with the Director-General for Political Affairs in the Foreign Ministry suggesting, 'nobody in Finland applauds the use of force; international crises should be resolved by other means. Unfortunately, in this case NATO chose force because other alternatives did not exist' (Forsberg 2000: 42). In practice, however, while the government did not want to support the air attacks, it had to accept that human rights abuses had occurred. Following the air attacks, the Finnish President Martti Ahtisaari accused Milošević of committing atrocities and noted his country's willingness to help in the reconstruction process. The government, if reluctantly, endorsed the EU statement that the NATO attack was 'necessary and warranted'. At the Euro-Atlantic Partnership Meeting in Washington on 25 April, President Ahtisaari strongly supported the notion of the international community intervening in states where violations of human rights were occurring.

Finland played a constructive role during the Kosovo crisis, helping both in bringing it to a conclusion and in the reconstruction process. President Ahtisaari was appointed as the EU representative in the peace negotiations with Milošević, which gave Finland a prominent role in the process. At the same time, Finland as part of the EU Presidency troika was involved in the EU diplomatic efforts and in monitoring the application of sanctions. Finland also actively participated in the post-war reconstruction contributing 800 troops to the KFOR peacekeeping operation and, as holder of the EU Presidency, chairing the July reconstruction summit in Sarajevo.

In terms of public opinion, there was a narrow majority of 54 per cent in favour of NATO's action, with 36 per cent opposed, although there was little support for any involvement by Finland in the war (*Turun Sanomat*, 3 April 1999; *Helsingin Sanomat*, 1 May 1999). The Finns were willing to participate in peacekeeping operations, and there was strong support for participation in KFOR, but not in military enforcement actions. There was, however, public condemnation of the human rights violations and an acceptance that something had to be done. The issue did not polarise the country on a simple left–right dimension, although many on the left did oppose the war, while others supported the need for intervention. The Kosovo crisis served to intensify the debate over NATO in Finland, with competing views as to whether Finland should join NATO and whether this offered the best option in terms of being able to assert influence in the security arena. Vaahtoranta and Forsberg (2000) suggest that in Finland, NATO's air attacks reinforced the view that NATO was a key actor in European security, and while Finland should not join it, it was in everyone's interest to cooperate with it. The published polls showed that support for the Alliance dropped during the Kosovo war from 30 per cent to 15–20 per cent (Forsberg 2000). Hence, as Forsberg concludes, the Kosovo crisis seems to have strengthened both Finland's Europeanist tendency and its neutral tradition.

Finland deemed the war in Iraq to be in breach of international law. The Finnish government's position prior to the US-led attack was that the crisis should be solved through the UN and it suggested that 'any use of military force w[ould] require authorisation from the UN Security Council'.[8] The Finnish government did not support the US-coalition or its EU critics – the French and Germans. Finland, like the other neutral states, was concerned about the rift in the EU and the failure to agree on a common position. In advance of the extraordinary European Council meeting on 17 February, the government highlighted the importance of a unified EU position and reiterated its support for the Greek Presidency's approach to the growing crisis. However, by 7 March the Finnish government, while continuing to support a peaceful resolution of the dispute, suggested that inspections could not continue for ever and, if Iraq did not cooperate, the use of military force could not be ruled out. The use of force would require however UNSC authorisation. On 20 March, the Cabinet Committee on Foreign and Security Policy discussed the issue and lamented the fact that the US and its allies had begun military action without UNSC authorisation. At this juncture, it was more critical of the US and declared that it would not participate in any military action. The President, Tarja Halonen, in an address to the Parliament on the situation in Iraq on 26 March, regretted the attack on Iraq and reaffirmed Finland's support for a return to the UN. Public opinion in Finland was opposed to the US-led attack and this hardened opposition to NATO. There was general opposition in the media, comments on the failure of the EU to adopt a united front, and fears that this would undermine the work of the Constitutional Convention.

Sweden

In relation to Kosovo, Sweden shared Finland and Ireland's concern about the lack of a UNSC mandate, did not endorse NATO's intervention and was strongly supportive of the UN's efforts to end the conflict. However, despite its concerns the government supported the EU position and regarded NATO's intervention into Kosovo as inevitable since little else could be done. The Social Democrats and Moderates were divided, with the latter being more inclined to support NATO. Among the Social Democrats, former Prime Minister Ingvar Carlsson and another former minister were openly critical of the air attacks, while others criticised the government for not being more critical. The smaller Folkpartiet supported NATO's intervention, whereas the Greens and the Left Party strongly opposed it.

As in Finland, a small majority of the public supported NATO's actions (*Dagens Nyheter*, 29 April 1999), although overall Swedish support for possible NATO membership declined during the period of the conflict (Vaahtoranta and Forsberg 2000). Many Swedes felt military intervention was necessary and supported Swedish participation in the follow-up KFOR peace operation. Moreover, the UN Secretary-General, in appointing two special representatives for the Kosovo crisis, included the former prime minister, Carl Bildt, thereby giving Sweden a prominent role. Thus, in some respects the Swedish response mirrored its traditional view that a more active foreign policy was necessary to meet challenges in the international security arena, especially in an instance where a humanitarian catastrophe appeared to be occurring.

The Swedish position on Iraq mirrored the Finnish government's stance, as the government fully supported the UNSC resolution and was opposed to any military action unless authorised by the UN.[9] The Prime Minister, Göran Persson, suggested that the attacks were a 'contravention of international law' and that any such action should only be undertaken in the framework of the UN.[10] There was no expectation that the EU should play any direct part in the US-led military intervention in Iraq. The government believed that the UN arms inspectors (headed by Swedish national Hans Blix) needed to be given time to complete their work. Like its neighbour, however, the government did not rule out the use of force. The government was also critical of the US, but its approach was low-key and there were few public statements. The issue of Iraq was debated by the Parliament in a special debate on 20 March. Following the attack, a special group of state secretaries was created to coordinate the efforts of government departments.

Prime Mnister Persson was critical of the EU's inability to adopt a common view on the crisis and the EU was generally seen as failing to respond to the crisis. Notably, the Swedish Foreign Minister and her Greek counterpart published a joint article 'No more Iraqs' in April, aimed at developing proposals for strengthening the Non-Proliferation Treaty, disarmament on tactical nuclear weapons, and measures to stop the spread of weapons of mass destruction and long-range missiles.

Austria
Of all the neutral states, Austria was most likely to be tested by the Kosovo crisis, given its proximity to the region, and its desire to play a significant political role in the development of South-eastern Europe. In the latter part of 1998, Austria also held its first EU Presidency and was, therefore, at the centre of the EU diplomatic efforts to avert the crisis. At the Vienna European Council in December 1999, the Presidency authorised the Council to develop a common strategy on the Western Balkans. Austria was also involved in the negotiations before the NATO attack. Wolfgang Petrisch, the Austrian Ambassador to Belgrade, was appointed as the EU's Special Envoy for Kosovo, and was one of the three negotiators at the Rambouilett talks. Thus, for Austria, Kosovo was to prove a particular challenge, as the state had to balance its own standing as a neutral state with the EU's tough stance on Kosovo.

Nevertheless, Austria's position was similar to that of the other neutrals, despite the apparent sea change in its security outlook during the 1990s, which might have prompted a more active approach to a problem occurring closer to home. It retained its position as a neutral state and, as a non-NATO member, was not involved in Operation Allied Force. The Austrian government was opposed to participation because no UN mandate existed and refused to grant permission for NATO over-flight of its territory.[11] It was, however, party to the Berlin European Council declaration, which condemned President Milošević and which supported NATO's intervention on humanitarian grounds. Chancellor Viktor Klima stated: 'We have great understanding for the necessity of this operation' (quoted in Donfried 1999: 8). Austria defended its position by referring to constitutional restrictions, which it was argued did not permit it to assist a military force intervening without a UNSC mandate in the affairs of another state. However, the ambiguity of Austria's position was highlighted by the EU's implied consent and endorsement of the operation.

At a societal level, a majority of the public thought the air attacks were useful, some 52 per cent, with 35 per cent suggesting they were 'not useful'. However, 74 per cent opposed Austrian participation and only 19 per cent favoured it (Donfried 1999: 8). NATO's actions further undermined support for the Alliance within Austria. There were also significant Serb protests against the war, in Vienna on 28 March.

In relation to the coalition attack on Iraq, the Austrian Foreign Minister, Benita Ferrero-Waldner, acknowledged that the use of arms had 'unfortunately become bitter reality' and that while Austria and other states had sought to resolve the crisis peacefully through the UN weapons inspection, these efforts had failed.[12] The government was of the view that any use of force against Iraq required UN approval. It supported the EU position that the UNSC should seek to implement all relevant resolutions, including 1441. It also stated that it was exclusively the right of the UNSC to determine whether Iraq had complied with this resolution and to interpret what the term 'serious consequences' meant.

As in the case of Kosovo, the Austrian government's position was that neutrality did not permit it to participate in the US-led coalition and that it could not allow over-flight of Austrian territory or permit the transportation of material and troops through its territory. The Ministry of Foreign Affairs did note that if the UNSC passed a new resolution authorising force, then the Austrian government would reconsider its position. Amongst the public the war was not popular – a majority of Austrians were strongly opposed to it – and anti-war protests were held.

Conclusions

These two case studies suggest that there are considerable similarities in the ways in which the neutral states responded to the crises and that they adopted similar positions that were consistent with their past foreign policy orientations. All of them were strong defenders of the UN, wary of actions that were not UNSC authorised and careful about being seen to side with any party to the conflict. Nevertheless, as members of the EU, they supported EU positions, and in the case of Kosovo, they supported the EU's endorsement of NATO's operation, despite the lack of a UNSC mandate. In contrast, in the Iraq case, the lack of an agreed common EU position, linked with concerns about the basis for the US-led coalition's military action, led some of the states to be more critical of US action. There was acknowledgement that Iraq's failure to comply with UNSC resolution 1441 necessitated a response, although the states favoured this being a UN one. Iraq was a problematic issue for these countries testing their standing as neutral states, as well as their own relations with the other EU states, the US and Canada. Ireland was unwilling to criticise the US for its actions and was considered by the US as a supporter. In contrast, the two Nordic states were more critical of the military intervention, but were also concerned about the future of transatlantic relations.

The challenge for the neutral or post-neutral states is one of managing their security policies and commitments inside the EU, ensuring that they have the relevant civilian and military capabilities to participate in ESDP activities, while balancing domestic political concerns about 'neutrality' and ESDP developments. The neutrals' foreign policy orientations have changed, and they have all increasingly adopted European positions on CFSP/ESDP issues. They all share, to varying degrees, a common interest in developing the EU as a security actor, but they have different views as to how this can and should be achieved. The military capabilities at their disposal mean that their chances of participating in military operations are likely to be limited, unless they work with others. The two Nordic states and Ireland have a particularly strong commitment to developing the civilian aspects of crisis management and conflict prevention. Finland, Sweden, Ireland and Austria are likely to involve themselves in areas where they have their own particular strengths and where they feel most able to contribute and can match EU needs with their capabilities.

The neutrals do share a number of common concerns about how ESDP develops and have coordinated their positions on these matters in the Constitutional Convention and IGC. In particular, Finland has played a coordinating role, and as a group they have been supportive of many of the ESDP proposals, sometimes joining together to support or oppose proposals made by the other member states. They have supported the idea of including a solidarity clause in the constitutional treaty, but were opposed the idea of mutual defence. In so doing, they were largely concerned to retain the right to make such decisions on a case-by-case basis. The possibility of structured cooperation, whereby a group of states might move forward on defence cooperation, also raised fears that they might be left out of such cooperation. The neutrals argue that such cooperation could be detrimental to the interests and development of the EU. The neutral states want to move ahead with other member states in developing the ESDP, but want to do so on their own terms and in ways that fit with their own orientations and values.

Notes

1 The chapter focuses on those neutral states that were members of the EU during the two crises and not on Malta and Cyprus, who joined the EU in 2004.
2 On the concept of neutrality, see Goetschel (1999) and Karsh (1988).
3 For analysis on each of the member states' foreign policy positions see the Foreign Policy network briefs at www.fornet.info/.
4 In this instance, EU refers to the EU of 15, prior to the 2004 enlargements which made it an EU of 25 states.
5 There has been considerable cooperation between Sweden and Finland and the two states have been working since 1996 on creating a multi-national Nordic crisis management brigade under NORDCAPS (Nordic Coordinated Arrangement for Military Peace Support).
6 Both states were also heavily involved during the 1990s in trying to ensure that non-NATO troop contributors could participate in crisis management and played active parts in PfP and the Euro-Atlantic Partnership Council.
7 See Dáil debates, vol. 563, 20 March 2003: http://historical-debates.oireachtas.ie/D/0563/D.0563.200303200004.html
8 Press Release 325/2002, Ministry of Foreign Affairs (4 December 2002) http://formin.finland.fi/english/.
9 Statement of Government Policy in the Parliamentary Debate on Foreign Affairs, 12 February 2003.
10 Press Release, Ministry of Foreign Affairs, 20 March 2003: www.sweden.gov.se/sb/d/911/a/8693
11 Austrian policy on this matter seems to be contradictory, as it did grant over-flight and transit rights during the Gulf War in 1991. It did so by amending a law on the shipment of war material from Austria and by putting UN resolutions above Austrian neutrality (Mistleberger 1992).
12 Press Release, 'Ferrero-Walder on the initiation of the military action against Iraq', Ministry of Foreign Affairs (20 March 2003): www.bmaa.gv.at/view.php3?f_id=744&LNG=en&version=.

BILL MCGRATH[1]

13

A change of road: Canadian foreign policy from Kosovo to Iraq

Introduction

Canada travelled the roads to Kosovo and Kabul in partnership with the US and Great Britain but the Canadian government decided not to continue this journey to Baghdad. This chapter examines Canada's policy responses to proposals to use armed force against the Federal Republic of Yugoslavia in 1999, Afghanistan in 2001, and Iraq in 2003. The Canadian government provided military help and political support to the US in the first two instances but did not give help in the form desired in the third case. In an attempt to soften this refusal, the Canadian government hedged its policy responses with compensatory adjustments and avoided direct opposition to its superpower neighbour.

'Human security', humanitarian intervention and Kosovo

Coercive intervention in the affairs of individual states by one or more states generally should not occur, according to international law. This non-intervention principle, of course, is not always upheld. Indeed, military intervention is an important phenomenon in world politics. Its justification on humanitarian grounds became a notable trend during the 1990s. Military intervention for ostensibly humanitarian purposes remains, however, a controversial issue (Holzgrefe 2003). The Canadian government has been a noteworthy contributor to the debate on this matter (International Commission on Intervention and State Sovereignty 2001) and has ultimately adopted the view that military intervention is legitimate in certain extreme circumstances. This conclusion is regarded as congruent with the government's supposed commitment to a 'human security' agenda.

'Human security' rhetoric began to figure prominently in Canadian foreign policy discourse during the 1990s (Irwin 2001; Hampson et al. 2002). The government proclaimed its commitment to human security as a foreign policy objective with particularly striking enthusiasm during the tenure of Lloyd Axworthy as Canada's foreign minister from 1996 to 2001.[2] Both Lloyd Axworthy and 'human security' represent controversial subjects within the community of scholars, journalists and publicists who study Canadian foreign policy. Axworthy has many admirers who believe his performance as Canadian Foreign Minister was first-rate but he also has more than a few detractors who question his judgement concerning policy priorities and his rhetoric related to accomplishments and Canada's role in the world. He certainly had a propensity to emphasise the importance of Canadians' values in the making and conduct of governmental policy. So much so in the eyes of some observers that he lost sight of important interests in Canadian foreign policy and most especially failed to realise the significance of the requirement for positive relations with Washington.[3] Axworthy was both a nationalist and an internationalist. He strongly wished that Canada would be seen as a 'fighter who punched above his weight' scoring diplomatic victories that contributed to the alleviation of global problems. The times were far from propitious for the achievement of such ambitions. Deficit elimination and debt reduction were the order of the day in Canada's government during Axworthy's tenure as Foreign Minister. The impact of budgetary cutbacks on Axworthy's department and its programmes was severe. Furthermore, the role of the Prime Minister and his advisors in the Prime Minister's Office and the Privy Council offices were such that the Foreign Minister had little say in relation to various important policy files. The Prime Minister's staff closely monitored, in particular, the Canadian–American bilateral relationship. Perhaps these circumstances contributed to Axworthy's receptivity to the theme of 'human security'. One way to promote the priorities of his Ministry during a period of budgetary restraint was to emphasise their connection to security. Promoting the security of people abroad, Axworthy argued, contributed to the security of Canadians at home. Even if such arguments failed to loosen the Finance Minister's purse strings he might be deterred from authorising still further cutbacks. The idea of 'human security' won support in Canada's foreign ministry not just for instrumental reasons. A heightened awareness of the salience of globalisation spread through the department during the 1990s. This prompted questions concerning the adequacy of the traditional understanding of national security. Many became persuaded that a shift in attention from the security of the state to the security of people was required in an age that witnessed the emergence of international human rights treaties that are virtually global in scope. The Human Development Reports of the United Nations Development Programme (UNDP) in 1993 and 1994 provided important statements of this outlook.[4] Various officials in the Canadian government found such views persuasive and they began, during the tenure of Lloyd Axworthy's predecessor, André Ouellet, to emphasise the points that security, international development, and human rights protection go hand in hand.[5] According to Axworthy's own account of how the Department came to embrace the concept:

> The concept of human security emerged as the lens through which to view the international scene. The security risk to individuals was our focal point and around that we developed a strategy for working towards new standards of international behaviour, using soft-power tools of communication and persuasion. While simple in concept, in some ways it was revolutionary since it set the notion of human rights against deeply held precepts of national rights. (Axworthy 2003: 5–6)

The government, he insisted, could not be satisfied with the achievement of national security defined in military terms but must also seek to protect individual human life, both at home and abroad, from diverse security threats, including those imposed by tyrannical governments on their own citizens. This last circumstance, the government would argue, contributed to the Kosovo 'human security' crisis of the late 1990s. President Milošević and his supporters were criticised strongly for the implementation of a repressive policy in Kosovo. Once the Clinton administration became committed to coercive diplomacy directed against President Milošević, and in so doing put NATO's credibility on the line, the Canadian government was ready to lend its support. Later, when coercive diplomacy failed to produce the desired results, it agreed to take the next step and support military intervention

Canada's military contribution to this endeavour was limited. Eighteen CF-18 fighter-bombers were deployed together with pilots, ground crew and airborne tankers for refuelling.[6] Canadian pilots flew 678 combat sorties. Canadian military professionals contend that Canada's force 'performed magnificently' but note as well that its personnel and equipment were both 'stretched to the limit' (Bashow et al. 2000: 56). Sean Maloney (2004: 21) underlines this point, noting a 'cannibalisation' of equipment and personnel necessary for the very deployment of the force. Canadian fighter-bombers were interoperable with US Air Force counterparts, but just barely so with the result that diverse difficulties were experienced during the period of attacks (Middlemiss and Stairs 2002).

Some concerned Canadians debated the legality and the legitimacy of the Kosovo air war and critical questions were raised about the conduct and effectiveness of the bombing campaign. The government, however, was not tested very seriously in Parliament.[7] The majority party's domination of Parliament and its timetable provide limited scope for opposition members to prepare for debate and to present either well-considered criticism or alternatives.[8] Parliamentary committees did hear from such notable critics of NATO and Canadian government policy as James Bissett, Michael Bliss, General Lewis

Mackenzie and Michael Mandel but their challenging views were not reflected in the parliamentarians' own debate.⁹ Generally speaking the press and public opinion seemed satisfied with Prime Minister Chrétien's statement:

> Our values as Canadians, our national interest in a stable and secure Europe and our obligations as a founding member of NATO ... led Canada to take arms with its NATO partners. And it is because of our values, our national interest and our obligations that we must see this job through.¹⁰

The distinguishing feature of the Canadian government's justification for its participation in the Kosovo air campaign was its emphasis on the theme of 'human security'. NATO's use of armed force was cited as an illustration of the 'human security' dynamic at work.

> This war against Serbia was a war of values, a war for human security. Despite some strained efforts in some NATO capitals to marshal classic arguments of national interest to justify action, the fact is that little strategic interest was served in intervening in Kosovo. There was no oil, no geographic commanding height nor maritime sea-line, no precious resources, no scientific secrets, no Hitler-in-the-making, no potential conflagration to be nipped in the bud. What there was, was the abuse of an ethnic minority by an atavistic government in a location where the NATO countries had a capacity to act and a time when they had the will to do so. As Vaclav Havel said in his extraordinary House of Commons address in 1999, it was the first war for values, not interests. (Heinbecker 1999: 21)

The lack of a United Nations Security Council (UNSC) resolution to authorise NATO's armed attack provoked some concern both within the Canadian attentive public and the government but NATO obligations were deemed paramount in this instance.

Axworthy's subordinates credit him with an important role in the diplomacy that ended the Kosovo conflict.

> Minister Axworthy provided the policy leadership, the political sensitivity, and the sense of the moment for Canada to play successfully in the major league of diplomacy. At the first G-8 ministers' meeting in May, he prevented the process from derailing and coined the key compromise on the crucial issue of international security presence. At the ministerial meeting in June, he played a central role in drafting the UN Security Council resolution ensuring that the KFOR (Kosovo Force) would cooperate with the ICTY [International Criminal Tribunal for the former Yugoslavia] on war crimes. (Heinbecker and McRae 2001: 130)

Canada's involvement in Kosovo continued in the post-intervention period through participation in the UN-sanctioned KFOR mission. A task force, tanks, anti-tank and combat engineering resources were committed, facilitating a limited Canadian role in the attempted restoration of order in Kosovo (Sokolsky 2000). The cost of this commitment and its ambiguous results raise questions concerning the organisation of future 'humanitarian interventions' (Nelles 2002).

9/11 and the war in Afghanistan

The terrorist attacks of 9/11 startled the world. Americans particularly came to regard this event as an epochal moment. This impression was reinforced when US President, George W. Bush declared a 'war on terrorism'. NATO quickly responded with an expression of support for the US. The North Atlantic Council met at the prompting of NATO Secretary-General, Lord Robertson, and agreed to invoke the collective defence provision in the Alliance's treaty. The Bush administration welcomed the political support of its transatlantic partners and particularly their acceptance of the American government's report that Osama bin Laden and the al Qaeda Islamist terrorist network were responsible for the attacks. The conclusion that the terrorists were able to organise these attacks because of a close alliance with Afghanistan's Taliban rulers was also accepted (Lansford 2002). The stage soon was set for an American-led armed attack on Afghanistan directed at al Qaeda and the Taliban. UNSC resolutions did not explicitly mandate a military campaign but resolutions 1368, 1378 and 1383 generally manifested support for the US. The Bush administration, though, had no wish to conduct this campaign under UN or NATO auspices. It favoured the formation of a 'coalition of the willing'. The Canadian government was ready to sign up.

Earlier, the immediate Canadian military response to 9/11 had taken place in keeping with North American Aerospace Defence Command (NORAD) commitments. Canadian aircraft had taken to the air to guard against possible further attacks. Now the government took further steps.[11] A six-ship task force deployed to the Arabian Sea was charged with the responsibility to interdict terrorist lines of communication. Forty Joint Task Force 2 (hereafter JTF2) commandos were authorised to fight alongside American Special Forces. Three Hercules aircraft were deployed in order to ferry supplies and personnel from the Persian Gulf to Afghanistan. Two Aurora maritime patrol aircraft were also assigned to the theatre. The decision to make these commitments was generally well received by the news media. The approval expressed by a *Globe and Mail*'s editorial (10 October 2001) that 'this is not an American fight: it is ours' is representative of this response.

On 14 November 2001, the government announced its decision to send ground troops to Afghanistan. The Princess Patricia's Canadian Light Infantry based in Edmonton was placed on 48–hour readiness alert. The deployment of these troops, however, was delayed more than two months due to a lack of transport capability. During this period, the fighting in Afghanistan turned strongly in favour of the US and its allies. This created an opportunity to begin discussions on a post-Taliban government for Afghanistan. A cooperative effort involving representatives of the UN Secretary-General, Afghan leaders, American officials and representatives of governments neighbouring Afghanistan began (Maloney 2003). A conference was held in Bonn, Germany late in November 2001. This culminated in an agreement that included provisions for the organisation of an international force with a UNSC mandate to assist in the maintenance of security for the capital city, Kabul and the surrounding area. The delay in the deployment of Canada's ground forces gave rise to the possibility that they might be attached to the newly agreed upon international force (ISAF) to be organised under British leadership. Canadian interest in this possibility was strong but negotiations to this end were unsuccessful. The British government evinced scant interest in the ground troops Canada had to offer and made a request for specialised support troops. The Canadian government for its part particularly wished to deploy infantry (Granatstein 2004). Yves Fortier, Canada's former Ambassador to the UN, succinctly explains that the government had 'a desire to play, and to be seen to be playing, a more important and direct role' than acceding to a British request for engineers would have allowed (Fortier 2002: 3). Eventually the Canadian and American governments agreed on the deployment of Canadian troops to work with an American-led stabilisation force based in Kandahar. The Korean War provided a precedent for the assignment of Canadian troops to American command during combat, but the Afghanistan deployment was a bilateral agreement organised outside the framework of the multilateral organisations Canada typically favoured.

A controversy flared up in Canada during the period just prior to the deployment when it was learned that JTF2 commandoes transferred Taliban prisoners to American control. American treatment of prisoners captured in the 'war on terrorism' has been a subject of international concern. All four Canadian opposition parties objected to the Canadian government's apparent failure to ensure that the prisoners in question were treated in accordance with the Geneva Convention (*Globe and Mail*, 30 January 2002). Another eruption of public concern was sparked when four Canadian soldiers were killed in a 'friendly fire' mishap that took place when the crew of a US Air Force jet mistakenly interpreted a Canadian military exercise as an operation by hostile forces and bombed it. Despite these problems, the Kandahar mission was sustained for six months. An extension was deemed imprudent in light of the stressed condition of Canada's military forces. Nonetheless, in the government's view, a political purpose was served. The government had put its forces in harm's way in just sufficient numbers that its representatives could say that Canadians had stood 'shoulder to shoulder' with their American neighbours in the first armed struggle following the 9/11 attacks. Later the Chrétien government decided to reassign troops to Afghanistan for participation in the previously mentioned ISAF mission based in Kabul. The significance of this decision will be explored further below.

Once again, the government's domination of Parliament meant that little meaningful debate or discussion took place in the House of Commons (Rempel 2002: 31). Some intellectuals (e.g. Michael Byers, Michael Mandel) challenged the government in op-ed pieces but the government encountered no substantial public opposition to the first commitment of ground forces to combat since the Korean War.

Canada's new National Security Policy

Following the 9/11 attacks, the Canadian government began working towards the development of a national security policy (Whitaker 2004). The security of Canada's trade with the US was called into question on 12 September 2001 when the imposition of tight US controls at the US–Canadian border caused massive backups of transport trucks laden with goods for the US market. In this instance, one might say, it was the Bush administration that was focused upon human security and the physical safety of its citizens. This concern manifested itself, though, in a traditional manner with emphasis upon territorial control and border security. Tom Ridge, the Bush Administration's first appointee as Homeland Security Director and the official most responsible for border security found a cooperative interlocutor on the Canadian side in the person of Foreign Minister John Manley who, in the aftermath of 9/11, would be appointed to the position of Deputy Prime Minister. Under the supervision of these two officials, the negotiation of a 'Smart Borders' agreement was completed. The pre-screening and clearing of goods facilitated the flow of traffic across the border.

In various other ways, the Canadian government began to harmonise its security measures with those of the US. It had to walk a fine line when taking these steps in the face of opposed views expressed by nationalists and civil libertarians. There was also criticism expressed by those favouring further integration with the US – the so-called 'continentalists' – who argued that the measures taken by the government would be ineffective were another 9/11 type of event to occur. Security, intelligence, and law enforcement agencies received new powers and increased budgetary allocations. Special attention focussed on the Canadian–American border and the enhancement of its security. Protection of Canada and Canadians from terrorist attack, no doubt, figured in the government's concerns when adopting these measures but this does not explain the government's decisions. Canada, after all, is not at the very top of the international terrorists' target list. Investments in the promotion of North American security were now required to reduce American worries that terrorists might hit at the US through Canada and to forestall possible Bush administration security initiatives that might transgress Canadian sovereignty. The Chrétien government was concerned above all to guarantee the easy flow of trade and to sustain American interest in all forms of economic partnership (Croci and Verdun 2004).

The Iraq war, the Chrétien government's hedging, and the Canadian compromise

American and British demands for change in Iraq made it necessary for their allies to consider whether they would support the use of military force to secure such a result. The diplomatic crisis that developed within the UN framework during 2002–3 over this issue would test Canada's statesmen severely. Lawrence Martin contends that 'no modern Canadian prime minister had been subjected to so much pressure as Jean Chrétien was on the war against Iraq' (Martin 2003: 409). The claim is debatable, particularly for those with memories of John Diefenbaker's troubles with the Kennedy Administration over the possible acquisition by the Canadian armed forces of American-supplied nuclear weapons, but it is apparent that Prime Minister Chrétien and his Cabinet were confronted with tough decision-making challenges.

In this instance, the Canadian government decided ultimately that it would not directly participate in and support the Anglo-American military intervention in Iraq. The Prime Minister's brief statement announcing the decision cited the lack of an enabling UNSC resolution to provide authority for such a use of force. Canadians were not fully certain what decision would be made until the moment of its announcement. They did know that the government had welcomed the Bush administration's decision to turn to the UN in a seeming attempt to gain support for the ends and means set out in UNSC resolution 1441. Canada's government supported the view that it was legitimate to demand proof of Iraq's disarmament to be verified by a UN inspection team. Canada's attentive public also knew that their Prime Minister was emphatic when addressing the Chicago-based membership of the Council of Foreign Relations in upholding the importance of the UN to a successful outcome in Iraq. 'War must always be the last resort,' the Prime Minister stated 'but if it must come to war, I argue that the world should act through the United Nations. This is the best way to give legitimacy to the use of force in these circumstances' (cited in Martin 2003: 412). He did not at the same time, however, provide any helpful hints on the best means the Americans might use to gain the full support of the UNSC and the melting in that body, particularly, of French opposition to a use of force. A statement such as the one the Prime Minister made in Chicago seems to lead logically to the decision announced in the House of Commons on 17 March. However, other statements were made to indicate the government's determination to leave its options open in the event that the UN inspection process did not lead to a positive result. When questioned in the House of Commons as to whether a second UNSC resolution would be required to authorise the use of force against Iraq, the Canadian Prime Minister replied that this was 'desirable but not legally necessary'.[12]

In March, at a moment when a breakdown seemed imminent in UN discussions on just such a resolution, the Canadian government presented a compromise proposal. Paul Heinbecker, then serving as Canada's ambassador to the UN, tried to secure support for an agreement providing more time for the UN inspectors to complete their work. The deployment of US forces to the Persian Gulf had made the threat of war seem immediate. The compromise solution suggested by Canada provided for a series of tests of Iraqi cooperation on a pass-or-fail basis as well as a limited time frame within which to assess the results.[13] Decades earlier, Canadian diplomacy contributed to the successful resolution by the UN of a Middle East crisis. This did not happen in this case. During the Suez crisis Lester B. Pearson dealt with parties who felt pressure to settle the conflict. Paul Heinbecker had no such luck. The US position was already set on war. Arguably, this was the case long before the seeming attempt to secure UN support for its policy. President Bush's television address on 17 March, presenting Saddam Hussein with an ultimatum demanding that he give up power within 48 hours or face an invasion, effectively pushed the UN and its diplomacy to the sidelines. On that same date, as previously mentioned, Prime Minister Chrétien told the House of Commons that Canada would not participate in the pending attack.

The Prime Minister was reticent on this occasion but subsequent interviews revealed his scepticism concerning all the key aspects of the Anglo-American case for war. Lawrence Martin's generally sympathetic biography describes Prime Minister Chrétien as 'word-challenged' (Martin 2003: 431). Certainly, he lacked Tony Blair's fluency or George W. Bush's hard, simple clarity. Nonetheless, he made it apparent that he did not believe that Iraq possessed the weapons of mass destruction that supposedly were in its arsenal. Nor was he persuaded that a connection between Iraq and terrorists, of the kind suggested by the British and the Americans, had been demonstrated. Finally, he did not accept the view that the present-day Iraqi regime's human rights abuses were of such magnitude as to legitimise an international military intervention.[14]

The Prime Minister and his Cabinet though, were not prepared to engage in an open, extended dispute with their British and American counterparts. Disagreement with one's principal allies on a major international issue is an unsettling experience for any Canadian government. The Chrétien government, in particular, already had reasons for concern over strains in its relationship with the Bush administration. These strains were aggravated when various figures associated with the Liberal Party government made critical, less than diplomatic remarks about President George W. Bush and his administration. Foreign criticism of the President generally is not well received in Washington. Prime Minister Chrétien's responses to the various observations of his colleagues did not help in that these must have seemed to be both tardy and complaisant by American reckoning. Thus, when the war began and a heightened American sensitivity to criticism might be expected, the Canadian government sought to soften the blow of its refusal to lend its political support through military participation in the attack on Iraq. One form of this hedging was anticipatory.

During February 2003 when war clouds loomed darkly over Iraq, the Canadian government decided to contribute forces to the UN-approved ISAF, created to assist in providing security for Kabul in Afghanistan. At Canada's instigation, NATO was persuaded to take command of the mission and Canada contributed troops in an amount constituting 40 per cent of the force (Granatstein 2004: 173). It is very unlikely that the Canadian government decided to authorise this intervention based solely on prevailing circumstances in Afghanistan. The pending Iraq war presumably entered the government's calculations. Indeed the government action 'ultimately had the effect of pre-emptively blocking American pressure to follow through on proposals that evidently had been sent from the Canadian forces senior ranks, which indicated that Canada might accept a limited symbolic role in the Iraqi invasion and occupation' (Ross 2003: 538; Granatstein 2004: 172). In addition to taking on its new mission in Afghanistan, the government also sustained ongoing forms of Canadian-Anglo-American military cooperation with the consequence that Canada played a very limited, unofficial, complementary role in the Iraqi conflict. Canadian officers on exchange with coalition forces remained in place, for example, and the Arabian Sea naval mission continued its operations with some marginal benefits for the Americans and British then preoccupied with the invasion of Iraq (Sokolsky 2004).

Continuing Canadian governmental concern to reduce any tensions generated by the decision on participation in the Iraq war was manifested in various ways. The Prime Minister and Cabinet introduced a motion in the House of Commons during the period of the invasion that expressed the hope that the US-led coalition would complete its mission as quickly as possible. Subsequently, upon the capture of Saddam Hussein, Chrétien would send congratulatory telegrams to President Bush and Prime Minister Blair. The government walked a fine line during this period. It did not wish to indicate any doubts about the correctness of its own decision on direct involvement in the attack on Iraq but it also had no wish to antagonise the British, and especially the Americans. Indeed, it was quick to make minor, mollifying gestures to express continued good will towards the American and British political leaders.

Canadian policy choices in analytical perspective

The following brief overview of the factors shaping Canadian policy in response to the cases considered here is, of necessity, highly selective. Jean Chrétien served as Prime Minister during the crises considered in this chapter. Within the government's circle of last-say decision-makers, he clearly was the individual with the final word on major policy decisions.

Two aspects of the Prime Minister's personal style of leadership stand out in the cases at hand. Jean Chrétien's reputation for political canniness is now clouded due to a domestic political scandal that emerged upon his retirement, but it must be acknowledged that his international security policy choices in relation to the Kosovo, Afghanistan and Iraq conflicts were ones that resonated with a majority of Canadians. When discussing the specific matter of the decision on Iraq, Lawrence Martin suggests that the Prime Minster's ear was 'reflexively cocked to average Canadians and it was average Canadians who had triggered his decision on the war' (Martin 2003: 418). However uninspiring he might have seemed as the nation's principal spokesman, he knew when to be decisive and had a strong instinct for the decisions most Canadians would favour. Though ready to be decisive when necessary, Chrétien also is remembered for cautiousness and the avoidance of boldness that might prove divisive within Canada. He was not a leader who was naturally inclined to favour radical policy innovations. Incremental change represented a more reasonable path in Chrétien's estimation. This outlook did not incline him to respond positively to President Bush's arguments on the need for the use of force against Iraq. The waging of preventive war to achieve regime change represented too great a departure from the generally accepted practices of international politics for Chrétien. The contrary responses of the provincial premiers of Ontario, Alberta and British Columbia suggest that given the opportunity other individuals might have committed Canada to direct engagement in Iraq.

Due consideration, however, must also be given to the factors and forces operative in Canada's international, domestic and governmental environments. The international security environment throughout the relevant period was characterised by the primacy of American military power. During the early phase of the post-Cold War period, American policy in international security affairs was hesitant and uncertain in response to various specific crises but the Kosovo case eventually triggered a hard response. The Clinton administration became determined to take this crisis in hand and force a settlement of it. The Chrétien government did not hesitate to provide military support once the American political leadership decided upon the use of force. In this case, the Canadian government was concerned about the absence of a UNSC mandate but had no inclination to oppose its neighbour, particularly in light of American success in winning support from all of NATO's principal powers. A desire to support the world's only superpower and concern for alliance solidarity factored into the government's readiness to subordinate any qualms felt over the possible illegality of NATO's military action. Clinging uncertainly to middle-power status, the Canadian government's principal hope to exercise influence rested in its NATO and G-8 memberships and a policy of cooperation with its major allies.

The same power politics considerations conditioned Canada's policy responses to the intervention in Afghanistan. In the aftermath of 9/11 and the Bush Administration's declaration of war on terrorism, circumstances demanded a clear, unhesitant Canadian response. The Iraq war produced a different result and in this case the international environment was more complicated. Division in the West altered the transatlantic security framework. The fact that this issue was tackled in the UN meant that Canada's policy towards that institution would figure in the government's calculations. American policy in this forum was presented virtually on a take it or leave it basis. US disinterest in the Canadian compromise resolution was more than apparent. Saying no to war in these circumstances would seem foolhardy to some, as the subsequent responses of the premiers of Alberta, British Columbia and Ontario would indicate, but the Prime Minister and the Cabinet did so decide. They did not believe that power politics dictated the same policy choice made in the case of Kosovo and Afghanistan.

The most significant aspect of the Canadian government environment during the trip from Kosovo to Iraq was executive domination of the foreign policy process. This is a characteristic feature of government based on the Westminster model but the Canadian Parliament during the Chrétien era was particularly ineffectual (Rempel 2002; Bland and Rempel 2004). Elections failed to produce an effective opposition party with representation in all Canada's principal regions. The absence of a government-in-waiting facilitated control of the legislature by the governing party, which was in turn subject to strong Prime Ministerial direction.

Prevailing circumstances in the domestic environment prior to the policy decisions on Kosovo and Afghanistan, viewed from the political executive's perspective, indicated that these generally were permissive in that public opinion on the whole favoured a policy of standing together with the US and other major allies. The House of Commons Standing Committee on Foreign Affairs and International Trade did witness presentations by prominent individuals and representatives of groups opposed to military action, but such criticism failed to stir the mass of the public. The response of the Canadian public to the Iraqi crisis was different. In this instance, reports to the Prime Minister on political debate and opinion in Canada presented a more complicated picture. A division of opinion in the press existed with the greater number of voices expressing views in favour of support for the US. Columnists for the *National Post* were at the forefront of this group. So was the business elite, concerned primarily with sustaining strong economic relations with the US. The *Toronto Star* featured writing in a liberal nationalist vein recommending a stand against war.

This was also the view amongst the public at large. Polls indicated that the majority view of the Canadian public was that peaceful disarmament of Iraq was desirable and feasible. Achievement of this objective through the UN was the strongly favoured position for the Canadian public. Kim Lunman's concise newspaper report on Iraq-related polls (*Globe and Mail*, 16 January

2003) points out that once war began 66 per cent of those surveyed agreed with the Prime Minister's policy decision not to have Canadian forces directly engaged as participants in the attack. Rapid Anglo-American success in the war and an arousal of concern over possible difficulties in Canadian–American economic relations prompted a momentary shift in opinion such that 49 and 48 per cent of respondents in an April 2003 poll expressed support for and opposition to the war. Within a couple of months support for the Canadian government's position was again generally strong. The national representation of opinion suggested that 71 per cent of the public agreed with the Canadian government decision on Iraq. This same poll indicated a majority view in support of the statement that the US knowingly used incorrect or fabricated intelligence to provide justification for attacking Iraq.

Regionalism is one of Canada's most outstanding political features and this has consequences for expressions of public opinion. Analysts who reported to the Prime Minister would have noted in particular the distinctiveness of views expressed in the provinces of Alberta and Quebec. Albertans were more inclined than others to express support for the US, and Quebec's poll respondents were the most strongly opposed to that policy. Robert Bothwell's interpretation of the polling results during 2003 emphasises the point that 'nowhere, even in Conservative Alberta was there a decisive margin in favour of going to war. In Quebec ... there was a very clear majority against it' (Bothwell 2004: 415). The Prime Minister had some reasons to take particular note of the state of public opinion in his home province on the possibility of an Iraq war. The holding of a provincial election during this period prompted all the province's political parties to take a stand on possible war in Iraq and Canadian participation in it. All parties adopted anti-war positions. The election held promise for the governing federal Liberal party that its provincial counterpart would win. Defeat of the Parti Québecois (which seeks Quebec sovereignty) was an outcome that would be attractive to Prime Minister Chrétien under any circumstances but this was especially appealing due to his pending retirement and the inevitable consequent discussion concerning his political legacy. Mention of this point is not meant to express agreement with Mr Chrétien's conservative critics, such as Ted Morton, Senator-elect for Alberta, who complained that the Iraq war policy decision demonstrated that 'Canadian foreign policy is set by public opinion in Quebec' (quoted in Granatstein, 2004: 194). A majority of Quebec's poll respondents expressed opposition to the use of force against Iraq even if the UNSC approved it (Parkin 2003: 5–7). It is likely that the Prime Minister would have been prepared to risk the disfavour of those who held this view if events had unfolded to result in UNSC authorisation of the use of force. He necessarily had to pay attention to public opinion in Quebec but it is improbable that he ever felt captive to it.

Ted Morton's point of criticism raises a more general matter of assessment: how prudent was the Canadian government, especially its leader, in responding to the issues discussed above? The Canadian policy choices made in response to the decisions of allies to use military force in Kosovo, Afghanistan and Iraq were canny ones insofar as domestic politics was concerned. While crediting the Chrétien government on this aspect of its performance, a teacher of international politics cannot resist comment on missed opportunities. The government made its decisions and went about its business without engaging the public strongly in discussions that might have broadened and deepened Canadians' understanding of global security and Canada's place within the global system. The soundness of the government's decisions considered in the framework of that system is harder to judge. A longer-term outcome of events in Kosovo, Afghanistan and Iraq must be awaited before conclusive judgements can be made concerning the statesmanship of the Canadian and other Western governments. For the moment, though, any sentence that linked the names Blair, Bush, Chrétien and Iraq together with the noun 'judgement' in a comparative assessment could not be uncomplimentary to the Canadian prime minister.

Conclusion

The cases considered above highlight the extraordinarily dynamic development of international politics at the turn of the century. This chapter will conclude with a brief consideration of key aspects of this subject viewed from a Canadian perspective. First, the phenomenon of humanitarian intervention calls for attention. This controversial matter came to the fore during the 1990s while states were trying to come to terms with the end of the Cold War. The Canadian government engaged strongly with this issue and decided to support coercive international intervention in the internal affairs of various states for human protection purposes. Taking the road to Kosovo forced the government to devote especially strong attention to the theory and practice of humanitarian intervention. Soon the issue would be overshadowed by the attacks of 9/11 and the Bush Administration's announcement of a war on terrorism, but it did not go away. One of the most notable aspects of the Canadian government's response to it took the form of sponsorship and subsequent championing of the 2001 International Commission on Intervention and State Sovereignty report, *The Responsibility to Protect*. In keeping with this report, Canada is committed in principle to support uses of armed force for the sake of human protection in certain exceptional cases. In practice, the exhausted condition of Canada's armed forces constrains possible Canadian involvement in such endeavours. For the immediate future, Canada is likely to rest in the ranks of the 'in-humanitarian non-interveners' during inevitable instances of internal violence and mass suffering in the zones of the world where peace, order, and good government can only be dreamed about (Chesterman 2003; Boulden 2004).

International military interventionism metamorphosed during the early twenty-first century. Paul Heinbecker, while serving as Canada's Ambassador to the UN, tried to capture the nature of the change with his suggestion that Kosovo concerned the protection of a vulnerable 'other' whereas Afghanistan and Iraq were based on protection of 'self' (quoted in Welsh 2005). The Bush Administration's war on terror and its initiation of military action based on a pre-emptive strategy forced allies to make hard choices. The respective decisions made towards the launching of an attack on Iraq by the American, British, French, German and Canadian governments resulted in both a transatlantic and North American divide. Potential for permanent, irreparable harm exists, particularly in the event of further US decisions to initiate pre-emptive wars, but the nature of the American experience in Iraq has fostered new appreciation for cooperation. In the short term at least, NATO states should be able to avoid a new Iraq-like crisis and begin to forget about the antagonism generated over the second Persian Gulf War.

The circumstances of the present 'age of terror' have forced the Canadian government's hand insofar as security affairs are concerned. The Chrétien Cabinet's disagreement with the Bush administration over policy towards Saddam Hussein's Iraq complicated Canadian–American relations, but their ongoing development has strongly emphasised continental security cooperation. Such efforts expanded vastly in the aftermath of the 9/11 attacks and they continue to evolve. Though the principal motivations of the two governments differ, each is committed to sustained wide-ranging cooperation. The overriding importance of continentalism in Canadian policy is undeniable.

During this same period, Europe experienced significant changes. The broadening and deepening of EU integration has altered Europe with consequences for the world. In Canada's case, this means that 'the idea, once popular in Ottawa, that Europe and NATO could be a counterweight to US power in North America is as dead as the dodo' (Stairs et al. 2003: 6). Nonetheless, a certain limited scope for expanded Canadian–European cooperation in security affairs remains. It is unlikely that the Canadian government will view this possibility indifferently. A full withdrawal into 'fortress North America' is not likely to appeal to any foreseeable Canadian government (Long 2003; Pentland 2003–4). It is also logical to assume a continued Canadian interest in the general promotion of comity in the transatlantic community of states. The implications of strengthened regionalism differ for Canada contingent upon the strength of discord or harmony within the West. Shared transatlantic interests and values might be less emphasised than formerly was the case but these still should figure in the making and conduct of Canadian foreign policy.

Notes

1 The author wishes to acknowledge the research assistance provided by Gregory P. Harris and Daniel Mussel.
2 See Axworthy (2003) for the Minister's own reflections on this issue.
3 See, for example, the trenchant remarks of former Canadian Ambassador to Washington, Allan Gotlieb (2005).
4 UNDP's Human Development Reports can be consulted at http://hdr.undp.org/reports/.
5 'Human security' is, of course, a contested concept. Its meaning and possible feasibility are the subject of debate, hardly an exceptional circumstance, when the proponents of an idea proclaim the introduction of a new paradigm. For a critical review of the concept and its policy applicability, see Paris (2001).
6 Accounts of Canadian participation in NATO's military intervention are in Dashwood (2000), Heinbecker and McRae (2001), and Nossal and Roussel (2001).
7 Canada, *House of Commons Debates* 135 (134), 36th Parliament, 7 October 1998, pp. 921–7; 135 (205A), 12 April 1999, pp. 13613–17 and 135 (216), 27, April 1999, pp. 14360–72.
8 Roy Rempel, at the time the defence policy researcher for the Reform Party, provides an interesting account of his frustrating experience in trying to raise important questions about the Kosovo conflict in a book chapter he titles 'Sleepwalking to war: Parliament and the Kosovo crisis' (Rempel 2002: 140–72).
9 See the Proceedings of the House of Commons Standing Committee on Foreign Affairs and International Trade, 12 May 1999 and 15 and 22 February 2000.
10 Special House of Commons Debate, 12 April 1999.
11 This review of the Canadian response to the Afghanistan war draws upon Geddes et al. (2001), Cohen (2003: 55–8), Dawson (2003) and Granatstein (2004: 120–36).
12 House of Commons, Hansard, 051 (3 February 2003).
13 See Heinbecker's recollections and assessment of events in the *Globe and Mail* (30 March 2004).
14 See, for instance, 'Chrétien restates opposition to war in Iraq': www.cbc.ca/stories/2003/03/18/chretieniraq030318.

OSVALDO CROCI AND AMY VERDUN

Conclusion

This book examines a turbulent period in the history of the Atlantic Alliance, namely that between the military intervention against Serbia by NATO in March 1999 and the one in Iraq by the US and a 'coalition of the willing' four years later. Is the malaise currently affecting the Alliance more acute than previous ones and if so why? David Long argues that the divisions among the allies, even if they have manifested themselves most clearly during the Iraqi crisis, are more long-term and fundamental. They are due to the decline of 'Atlanticism' which he defines as a feeling of solidarity based on the existence of a community of values and the notion of a shared fate. Although members of the Alliance still have 'shared interests' and NATO still provides 'utility' to its members ('interest' and 'utility' being the key variables that realists and institutionalists use to explain the fact that NATO has not disappeared with the end of the Cold War), Long argues that one should expect the difficulties of the Alliance to continue because NATO is no longer perceived as necessary but merely as useful. The bond provided by 'Atlanticism' is loosening because allies increasingly differ in their assessment of how to provide order and stability in the international system, the role the US and the EU should play in such an endeavour, and in the evaluation of threats and how to respond to them. Divisions among allies over Iraq did indeed quickly shift from a debate on the substance of the issue (i.e. how to deal with a dictatorial regime that had defied UNSC resolutions for over a decade) to one on the role of the US and the Alliance in the provision of security in a unipolar world. NATO might not disappear but it will no longer occupy centre stage as it did during the Cold War. It will more likely become simply one instrument among many for the US or the Europeans to use.

According to Sonia Lucarelli 'Atlanticism' is declining because the US and the EU are increasingly interpreting their shared political values and principles in a different manner, which in turn leads them to promote common values through increasingly differing political actions. Particularly relevant to understanding current transatlantic difficulties are, for instance, the EU translation of the universal value 'peace' into the principle of conduct 'international law promotion' and its preference for acting in the promotion of the value 'peace' through 'structural prevention' (i.e. trying to address the cause rather than the symptoms of a problem) and 'multilateralism'. As Lucarelli points out, however, the translation of values and principles into action encounters several limits, the most important of which is 'inconsistency' understood both as the EU dealing differently with similar cases and the EU and some of its member states approaching the same case differently.

Applying Lucarelli's analysis of interpretation of values and their translation into actions to EU member states would undoubtedly help explain intra-European divisions, which in the case of Iraq have been as marked as those dividing the US from the countries Defence Secretary Donald Rumsfeld called 'Old Europe'. Divisions among member states – France and the UK in particular, as Macleod points out – certainly continue to exist especially concerning the relationship between the European Security and Defence Policy (ESPD) and NATO and notwithstanding the great leaps forward, as Menon shows, ESDP has made in the wake of recent transatlantic crises and the Iraqi one in particular. Differences over the role and significance of ESPD are in turn a reflection of the French and British differences concerning relations with the US. The British work under the assumption that once the US administration has decided on a course of action the best way to retain some influence over outcomes is to travel with it. The French instead often give in to the temptation to reassert France's traditional Gaullist ambition to shape the external role of the EU in a way that would constrain the actions of the remaining superpower. It is interesting to note in this context – as Facon discusses – that Russia has faced the same dilemma in its attempt to retain influence in world affairs. In the end, Russia seems to have decided to privilege its direct relationship with Washington instead of attempting to build with some European partners a counterweight to the US. It should also be noted that 'inconsistencies' in the way Europeans interpret core values and translate them into action apply also to the way they relate to each other both within the EU and the Alliance. German Chancellor Gerhard Schröder, for instance, announced that Germany would not take part in, nor pay for, any 'adventure' in Iraq before the issue could be discussed within a European or Alliance forum. French President Jacques Chirac's un-diplomatic chastising of the countries about to join the EU after they had signed a public declaration supporting the US was a clear indication that France fancies itself playing within the EU the same role it accuses the US of playing within the Alliance. Neither Schröder nor Chirac can be said to have acted on these occasions according to the precepts of 'multilateralism'.

Francis K. Abiew discusses another issue which might cause friction within the Alliance. NATO's intervention against Serbia was justified exclusively on humanitarian grounds. The fact that the US intervention in Iraq put an end to the brutal dictatorship of Saddam Hussein implicitly suggested a humanitarian motivation as well even if the humanitarian argument was not emphasised because the Iraqi government's worst acts of domestic repression had occurred more than ten years earlier, in 1989 and 1991. Alliance members agree that the practice of humanitarian interventions can easily be reconciled with that of sovereignty. In line with its promotion of the concept of 'human security', the Canadian government, as both Abiew and McGrath point out, has taken the lead in this effort by convening a so-called 'International Commission on Intervention and State Sovereignty' which has produced a set of guidelines (*The responsibility to protect*) that should make it easier to establish when international intervention is required. It is unlikely, however, that future interventions will be decided exclusively or even primarily on the basis of these guidelines. Other considerations, such as the security interests of Alliance members, and the proximity of the place of conflict, as well as the perceived costs of intervention versus non-intervention, are likely to be relevant. Even more complex is the question of who should intervene, especially in a situation in which the United Nations Security Council (UNSC) is deadlocked. The US has not explicitly taken any position which implies that it prefers to judge each case on its own merits and circumstances. The quasi-totality of European members of the Alliance tends instead to regard the Kosovo case as an exception or, as Sloan puts it, 'neither as a new rule nor as the last time NATO might act without a UN mandate'. They are of course concerned that if Kosovo is seen as a new rule other regional organisations might invoke it under perhaps dubious circumstances. At the same time, they do not wish to tie their hands should other cases similar to that of Kosovo happen in their immediate neighbourhood.

Events in the South-eastern Balkan region, as Cohen shows, provide an example of how the US, NATO, the EU and member states can work together, using different instruments and accepting a degree of division of labour, to pacify, stabilise and rebuild an entire region. The questions to ask in this context are: does the South-eastern Balkan region represent an exception, and if so why? Can the degree of cooperation and division of labour exhibited by the allies and their various organisations in this region be replicated in other areas of turmoil? Or does cooperation become more difficult the further away the region to be stabilised is from Europe?

The chapters in the second part of this book – besides discussing specific aspects of the foreign policies of key members of the Alliance as well as those of European 'neutrals' – also suggest something important concerning the future of the Alliance: transatlantic tensions seem to increase, or at least manifest themselves more virulently, when a Republican administration is in power in Washington and social-democratic ones prevail in Europe. This might be because Republicans profess a more orthodox free-market approach to economic issues and a more hawkish approach to foreign policy, both attitudes being at odds with prevailing European values and practices. If true this would not only explain the virulence of the crisis over Iraq but also suggest that tensions will continue to ebb and flow as different administrations succeed each other on both sides of the Atlantic.

These changes apart, however, what is the future of the Alliance? Some academic observers claim that the period from Kosovo to Iraq has been one of the most, if not the most, turbulent in the history of the Alliance and that the very future of the Euro-Atlantic partnership is now in question. As if scared by the implications of their assessment they then hurry to conclude that of course the Alliance has proven resilient in the past and will continue to be so in the future (for example Lindstrom 2003; Gordon and Shapiro 2004; Pond 2004). Such a hope is corroborated by other observers who point to the similarities between the debates within the Alliance today and those during past crises. Their implicit suggestion is that nothing much has changed and that the Alliance will outlive its current crisis as it outlived others in the past (for example Anderson 2005; Armitage 2005).

The writers in this volume do not seem to disagree with this hopeful assessment except that they make one important qualification: recent turbulence has occurred in a different type of international system: one in which the bipolar constraints on the Alliance no longer apply. The Iraqi crisis has played out in a unipolar system. Indeed, it could be defined as a crisis of unilateralism. The assertive policy embraced by the US administration is primarily based on the belief that the power position it occupies in the international system gives the US the duty to act, unilaterally if necessary, to maintain order in the system as a whole. The US preference to act alone, especially when the action required is military, is linked (as both Sloan and Long point out in this volume) in no small degree to the Kosovo crisis during which the political requirements of the Alliance hampered the effective conduct of military operations without adding significant military resources. The systemic glue that kept the Alliance together in the Cold War is no longer present under unipolarity, which means that the continuation of the Alliance will depend primarily on the belief that 'international governance', i.e. predictability and order in the international system, is possible only if the allies continue their partnership, a partnership that other powers could join but could not weaken or challenge. For the Alliance to endure, the US has to make sure that its 'assertive leadership', which is needed, does not degenerate or even appear to degenerate into 'arrogant unilateralism'. The US, in other words, has to make sure that its hegemonic position in the international system and in the Alliance does not translate into dominance. Dominance inevitably invites the formation of countervailing forces, which in a unipolar system can only mean turbulence and conflict.

The crisis of unilateralism is not only a US problem however. The Europeans, understood here primarily as the EU, have to accept the fact that not all problems can be solved through 'structural prevention'. Sometimes dealing with the symptoms has to precede tackling the causes. The Europeans must also accept the fact that the further the problems are from their immediate neighbourhood and the more threatening they appear to be to the US, the less significant their political voice and ability to influence outcomes will be – at least as long as their security horizon remains primarily regional and their capabilities limited. Iran's nuclear ambition is likely to be the problem that will either show that the members of the Alliance have learned from the Iraqi crisis or lead to a new rift. They all should know however that the consequences of a new rift might be more serious than those caused by the rift over Iraq. Occasional disagreements might spice up a relationship, but recurring and predictable divisions will tear it apart. Post-Iraq transatlantic relations allow us to conclude on a positive note: the allies seem to have learnt from recent difficulties and seem keen on renewing their solidarity vows so that the Alliance can continue under unipolarity.

BIBLIOGRAPHY

Abiew, Francis K. (1999) *The evolution of the doctrine and practice of humanitarian intervention*, The Hague: Kluwer Law International.
Adler Emanuel and Barnett Michael (eds) (1998) *Security communities*, Cambridge: Cambridge University Press.
Agius, Christine (2002) 'Swedish security policy in the 21st century: from neutrality to non-alignment', Paper presented at the University Association for Contemporary European Studies Conference, Belfast, UK (2–4 September).
Albright, Madeleine (1993) 'Use of force in a post-Cold War world', Address at the National War College, National Defense University, Fort McNair, Washington, DC, 23 September, *US Department of State Dispatch*, 4 (39): http://dosfan.lib.uic.edu/ERC/briefing/dispatch/1993/html/Dispatchv4no39.html.
Anderson, Stephanie B. (2005) 'Understanding the failure of the European Defence Community: Lessons for the ESDP?', Paper presented at the European Union Studies Association (EUSA) Conference, Austin, Texas, 30 March–2 April.
Annan, Kofi (1999) *Protecting civilians in armed conflict: towards a climate of compliance*, New York: United Nations Press.
Arbatov, Alexei G. (2000) 'The transformation of Russian military doctrine: lessons learned from Kosovo and Chechnya', George C. Marshall Centre Paper, Garmisch-Partenkirchen: George C. Marshall European Centre for Security Studies, July.
Armitage, David T. Jr. (2005) 'Echoes for today: lessons from US policy toward the European Defence Community', Paper presented at the European Union Studies Association (EUSA) Conference, Austin, Texas, 30 March-2 April.
Arnison, Nancy (1993) 'International law and non-intervention: when do humanitarian concerns supersede sovereignty?', *Fletcher Forum of World Affairs*, 17 (2), 198–211.
Ashdown, Paddy (2003) 'Speech by the High Representative Paddy Ashdown to the BiH Parliamentary Assembly' (10 September): www.esiweb.org/pdf/esi_europeanraj_reactions_id_23.pdf.
Asmus, Ronald (2002) *Opening NATO's door: how the Alliance remade itself for a new era*, New York: Columbia University Press.
Axworthy, Lloyd (2003) *Navigating a new world. Canada's global future*, Toronto: Alfred A. Knopf Canada.
Ayoob, Mohammed (1995) 'The new-old disorder in the third world', *Global Governance*, 1 (1), 59–78.
Badie, Bertrand (1999) *Un monde sans souveraineté. Les états entre ruse et responsabilité*, Paris: Fayard.
Baker, Susan and McCormick, John (2003) 'Sustainable development: comparative understandings and responses' in Vig and Faure (eds), pp. 277–302.
Bashow, Lieutenant-Colonel David, et al. (2000) 'Mission ready: Canada's role in the Kosovo air campaign', *Canadian Military Journal*, 1 (1), 55–61.
Baylis, John (1993) *The diplomacy of pragmatism: Britain and the formation of NATO, 1942–1949*, Kent: Kent State University Press.
Bettati, Mario (1992) 'The right of humanitarian intervention or the right of free access to victims?', *The Review: International Commission of Jurists*, 49 (1), 1–11.

Biscop, Sven (1999) 'The UK's change of course: a new chance for the ESDI', *European Foreign Affairs Review*, 4 (2), 253–68.
Bland, Douglas L. and Rempel, Roy (2004) 'A vigilant Parliament: building competence for effective parliamentary oversight of national defence and the Canadian armed forces', Montreal: IRPP Paper series 'Policy Matters', 5 (1): www.irpp.org/pm/archive/pmvol5no1.pdf.
Blechman, Barry (1996) 'Emerging from the intervention dilemma' in C. A. Crocker, F. O. Hampson, and P. Aall (eds), *Managing global chaos: sources of and responses to international conflict*, Washington, DC: United States Institute of Peace Press, pp. 287–95.
Blumenthal, Sidney (2003) *The Clinton wars*, New York: Farrar, Strauss and Giroux.
Boniface, Pascal (2003) 'European security and transatlanticism in the twenty-first century' in Moens, Cohen and Sens (eds), pp. 55–66.
Booth, Ken (1995) 'Human wrongs and international relations', *International Affairs*, 71 (1), 103–26.
Bothwell, Robert (2004) 'Back to the future: Canada and empires', *International Journal*, 59 (2), 407–18.
Boulden, Jane (2004) 'Paul Heinbecker', *International Journal*, 59 (2), 419–28.
Boutros-Ghali, Boutros (1992) *An agenda for peace: preventive diplomacy, peace-making and peace-keeping*, New York: United Nations.
Bowring, Bill (1995) 'The "droit et devoir d'ingerence": a timely new remedy for Africa?', *African Journal of International and Comparative Law*, 7 (3), 493–510.
Calchi Novati, Giampaolo (1997) 'Italy and Suez 1956: how to be committed and equidistant', *Il Politico*, 62 (1), 19–46.
Cameron, Fraser vs. Moravcsik, Andrew (2004) 'Should the European Union be able to do everything that NATO can?' in *For and against: debating Euro-Atlantic security options*, Brussels: NATO Public Diplomacy Division, pp. 15–22: www.nato.int/docu/debate/debate-eng.pdf.
Caney, Simon (1997) 'Human rights and the rights of states: Terry Nardin on non-intervention', *International Political Science Review*, 18 (1), 27–37.
Carrère d'Encausse, Hélène (2003) 'Le duo Moscou/Washington à l'heure irakienne', *Politique internationale*, 100, 273–87: www.politiqueinternationale.com/PI_PSO/fram_pi.htm.
Cerutti, Furio (2003) 'A political identity of the Europeans?' *Thesis Eleven*, 72 (1), 26–45.
Cerutti, Furio (2001) 'Towards the political identity of the Europeans: an introduction' in Cerutti and Rudolph (eds), pp. 1–32.
Cerutti, Furio and Rudolph, Enno (eds) *A soul for Europe*, Volume 1, *On the political and cultural identity of the Europeans. A reader*, Leuven: Peeters.
Checkel, Jeffrey T. (2001) 'Why comply? Social learning and European identity change', *International Organisation*, 55 (3), 553–88.
Chesterman, Simon (2003) 'Hard cases make bad law: law, ethics, and politics in humanitarian intervention' in A. F. Lang Jr (ed.), *Just intervention*, Washington, DC: Georgetown University Press, pp. 46–61.
Cimbalo, Jeffrey L. (2004) 'Saving NATO from Europe', *Foreign Affairs*, 83 (6), 111–20.
Clark, Wesley K. (2001a) *Waging modern war: Bosnia, Kosovo, and the future of combat*, New York: Public Affairs.
Clark, Wesley K. (2001b) 'Civil Military Affairs and U.S. Diplomacy: The Changing Roles of the Regional Commanders-In-Chief (CINCs)' Washington, DC (30 May): http://wesleyclark.h1.ru/military_reform.htm.
Coakley, John, Holmes, Michael and Rees, Nicholas (1997) 'The Irish response to European integration: explaining the persistence of opposition' in A. W. Cafruny and C. Lankowski (eds), *Europe's ambiguous unity: conflict and consensus in the post-Maastricht era*, Boulder: Lynne Rienner, pp. 209–38.

Cohen, Andrew (2003) *While Canada slept: how we lost our place in the world*, Toronto: McClelland and Stewart.
Commission on Global Governance (1995) *Our global neighbourhood*, Oxford: Oxford University Press.
Cordesman, Anthony H. (2001) 'The Quadriennial Defence Review and force transformation: notes for a cautionary analysis', Washington DC: Center for Strategic and International Studies: www.csis.org/burke/hd/reports/qdr.pdf.
Cornish, Paul and Edwards, Geoffrey (2001) 'Beyond the EU/NATO dichotomy: the beginning of a European strategic culture', *International Affairs*, 77 (3), 587–603.
Crane, Conrad C. and Terrill, W. Andrew (2003) 'Reconstructing Iraq: insights, challenges, and missions for military forces in a post-conflict scenario', US Army War College, Strategic Studies Institute (February): www.carlisle.army.mil/ssi/pubs/2003/reconirq/reconirq.pdf.
Croci, Osvaldo (2005a) 'The "Americanization" of Italian foreign policy?', *Journal of Modern Italian Studies*, 10 (1), 10–26.
Croci, Osvaldo (2005b) 'Much ado about little: the foreign policy of the second Berlusconi government', *Modern Italy*, 10 (1), 59–74.
Croci, Osvaldo (2003) 'A closer look at the changing transatlantic relationship', *European Foreign Affairs Review*, 8 (4), 469–91.
Croci, Osvaldo and Verdun Amy (2004) 'Security threats and institutional response: the case of Canada', Paper presented at the 5th Pan-European International Relations Conference, The Hague, Netherlands, 9–11 September.
Crowe, Brian (2003) 'A common European foreign policy after Iraq?', *International Affairs*, 79 (3), 533–46.
Daalder, Ivo H. (2000) *Getting to Dayton: the making of America's Bosnia Policy*, Washington, DC: The Brookings Institution.
Daalder, Ivo H. (1996) 'The United States and military intervention in internal conflict' in M. E. Brown (ed.), *The international dimensions of internal conflict*, Cambridge, Mass: MIT Press, pp. 461–88.
Daalder, Ivo H. and O'Hanlon, Michael E. (2000) *Winning ugly: NATO's war to save Kosovo*, Washington, DC: The Brookings Institution.
D'Alema, Massimo (1999) *Kosovo. Gli Italiani e la guerra. Intervista di Federico Rampini*, Milano: Mondadori.
Dallmeyer, Dorinda G. (1995) 'National perspectives on international intervention: from the outside looking in' in D. C. F. Daniel and B. C. Hayes (eds), *Beyond traditional peacekeeping*, New York: St. Martin's Press, pp. 20–39.
Damro, Chad (2004) 'To multilateralize or not: the EU's role in international competition policy', Paper presented at the ECPR Joint Sessions, Workshop 7, Uppsala, 13–18 April.
Damrosch, Lori F. (1993a) 'Concluding reflections' in L. F. Damrosch (ed.), *Enforcing restraint: collective intervention in internal conflicts*, New York: Council on Foreign Relations Press, pp. 348–67.
Damrosch, Lori F. (1993b) 'Changing conceptions of intervention in international law' in L. W. Reed and C. Kaysen (eds), *Emerging norms of justified intervention*, Cambridge, MA: American Academy of Arts and Sciences, pp. 91–110.
Dashwood, Hevina (2000) 'Canadian participation in the NATO-led intervention in Kosovo', in M. Appel Molot and F. O. Hampson (eds), *Canada among nations 2000: vanishing borders*, Don Mills: Oxford University Press, pp. 275–302.
Dassù, Marta and Menotti, Roberto (1997) 'The ratification of NATO enlargement: the case of Italy': www.nato.int/acad/conf/enlarg97/dassmeno.htm.
Dawson, Grant (2003) 'A special case: Canada, Operation Apollo and multilateralism' in D. Carment, Fen O. Hampson and N. Hilmer (eds), *Canada among nations 2003: coping with the American colossus*, Don Mills: Oxford University Press, pp. 180–99.

Deng, Francis (1995) 'Reconciling sovereignty with responsibility: a basis for international humanitarian action' in J. Harbeson and D. Rothchild (eds), *Africa in world politics: post-Cold War challenges*, Boulder: Westview Press, pp. 295–310.

Department of Foreign Affairs and International Trade and the Department of National Defence (1995), *Towards a rapid reaction capability for the United Nations: Report of the Government of Canada*, Ottawa: Government of Canada.

Deutsch Karl, et al. (1957) *Political community and the North Atlantic area*, Princeton: Princeton University Press.

Dini, Lamberto (1998) 'Una netta visibilità della nostra politica internazionale', *Vita Italiana* 4 (May): www.esteri.it.

Dobbins, James, et al. (2003) *America's role in nation-building: from Germany to Iraq*, Santa Monica: The Rand Corporation.

Donfried, Karen (1999) 'Kosovo: international reactions to NATO air strikes', Washington DC: CRS Report for Congress (21 April): www.au.af.mil/au/awc/awcgate/crs /rl30114.pdf.

Donnelly, Jack (1993) 'Human rights, humanitarian crisis, and humanitarian intervention', *International Journal*, 48 (4), 607–40.

Donovan, Mark (1992) 'Catholic "pacifism" and the Gulf War: pluralism, cohesion and politics' in S. Hellman and G. Pasquino (eds), *Italian Politics: A Review*, Vol. 7, London: Pinter, pp. 159–73.

Duchêne François (1973) 'The European Community and the uncertainties of interdependence' in M. Kohnstamm and W. Hager (eds), *A nation writ large? Foreign policy problems before the European Community*, London: Macmillan, pp. 1–21.

Egan, Patrick T. (2001) 'The Kosovo intervention and collective self-defence', *International Peacekeeping*, 8 (3), 39–58.

Eliasson, Jan (1995) 'Interview: the U.N. and humanitarian assistance', *Journal of International Affairs*, 48 (2), 491–506.

Eliasson, Johan (2000) 'Neutral countries in a changing European Union: Sweden, the European security and defence initiative and NATO membership', Paper presented at the ECSA-C Conference, Quebec (31 July – 2 August).

European Commission (2003a) *Eurobarometer 60. Public opinion in the European Union*: http://europa.eu.int/comm/public_opinion/archives/eb/eb60/eb60_rapport _standard_en.pdf.

European Commission (2003b) *The European Union and the United Nations: The choice of multilateralism*, Communication from the Commission to the Council and the European Parliament, Brussels, COM (2003) 526.

European Commission (2000a) *The European Community's development policy*, COM (2000) 212.

European Commission (2000b) *Integrating environment and sustainable development into economic and development co-operation policy*, COM (2000) 264.

European Commission (2000c) *Communication on the precautionary principle*, COM (2000), 1.

European Council (2003) *A secure Europe in a better world. European security strategy*: http://ue.eu.int/uedocs/cmsUpload/78367.pdf.

European Council (1999) 'Common Strategy of the European Union of 4 June 1999 on Russia' (1999/414/CFSP): http://europa.eu.int/comm/external_relations/ceeca/com _strat/russia_99.pdf.

EU Presidency (2003) 'European Defence: NATO/EU Consultation, Planning and Operations' (15 December): http://ue.eu.int/ueDocs/cms_Data/docs/pressData /en/misc/78414.pdf.

Everts, Steven, et al. (2004) *A European way of war*, London: Centre for European Reform.

Falk, Richard (1996) 'The complexities of humanitarian intervention: a new world order

challenge', *Michigan Journal of International Law*, 17 (2), 491–513.
Fallows, James (2004) 'Frontline interview with James Fallows': www.pbs.org/wgbh/pages/frontline/shows/invasion/interviews/fallows.html.
Finnemore, Martha and Sikkink, Kathryn (1998) 'International norm dynamics and political change', *International Organization*, 52 (4), 887–917.
Flockhart, Trine (ed.) (2005) *Socializing democratic norms: the role of international organizations for the construction of Europe*, Basingstoke: Macmillan.
Florini, Ann (1996) 'The evolution of international norms', *International Studies Quarterly*, 40 (3), 363–89.
Fonteyne, Jean-Pierre L. (1974) 'The customary international law doctrine of humanitarian intervention: its current validity under the U.N. Charter', *California Western International Law Journal*, 4, 203–70.
Forsberg, Tuomas (2000) 'Finland and the Kosovo crisis: at the crossroads of Europeanism and neutrality', *Northern Dimensions Yearbook*, Helsinki: Finnish Institute of International Affairs, pp. 41–9.
Fortier, Yves (2002) 'The mature exercise of sovereignty', *Canadian Military Journal*, 3 (1), 3–10: www.journal.forces.gc.ca/engraph/Vol3/no1/pdf/3–10_e.pdf.
Frédet, Jean-Gabriel (1999) 'Alain Richard: ce que le Kosovo m'a appris', *Le Nouvel Observateur*, 15–21 July, p. 32.
Gaer, Felice (2000) 'Effective indignation? Building global awareness, NGOs, and the enforcement of norms' in Schnabel and Thakur (eds), pp. 385–402.
Garigue, Philippe (1993) 'Intervention-sanction and "droit d'ingerence" in international humanitarian law', *International Journal*, 48 (4), 668–86.
Geddes, J. et al. (2001) 'Canada goes to war' *Maclean's* 114 (43), 26–31.
Giddens Anthony (1979) *Central problems in social theory: action, structure and contradictions in social analysis*, Berkeley: University of California Press.
Gillies, David (1993) 'Human rights or state sovereignty? An agenda for principled intervention' in M. Charlton and E. Riddel-Dixon (eds), *Crosscurrents: international relations in the post-Cold War era*, Scarborough: Nelson, pp. 455–70.
Gnesotto, Nicole (2003) 'EU, US: visions of the world, visions of the other' in G. Lindstrom (ed.), *Shift or rift: assessing US–EU relations after Iraq*, Paris: European Union Institute for Security Studies, pp. 21–42: www.iss-eu.org/chaillot/bk2003.pdf.
Goetschel Laurent (1999) 'Neutrality: a really dead concept', *Cooperation and Conflict*, 34 (2), 115–39.
Gordon, Philip H. (1997/98) 'Europe's uncommon foreign policy', *International Security*, 22 (3), 74–100.
Gordon, Philip H. and Shapiro, Jeremy (2004) *Allies at war: America, Europe, and the crisis over Iraq*, Washington DC: Brookings Institution.
Gotlieb, Allan (2005) 'Romanticism and realism in Canada's foreign policy', *Policy Options*, 26 (2), 16–27.
Government of Finland (2004) *Finnish security and defence policy*, Government report 6, Prime Minister's Office: www.defmin.fi/chapter_images/2574_2160_English_White_paper_2004[1].pdf.
Government of Finland (1997) *The European security development and Finnish defence*, Report by the Council of State to Parliament (17 March).
Government of Finland (1995) *Security in a changing world: guidelines for Finland's security policy*, Report by the Council of State to Parliament (6 June): virtual.finland.fi/finf'Иракский кризис и борьба за новое мироустройство
Government of Ireland (2000) *White Paper on defence*, Dublin: Department of Defence: http://merln.ndu.edu/whitepapers/Ireland-2000.pdf.
Government of Ireland (1996) *Challenges and opportunities abroad. The White Paper on foreign policy*, Dublin: Department of Foreign Affairs: www.foreignaffairs.gov.ie

/information/publications/whitepaper/default.asp.
Graff, James and Crumley, Bruce (2003) 'France is not a pacifist country' *Time* (24 February): www.time.com/time/archive/preview/0,10987,1004280,00.html.
Granatstein, J. L. (2004) *Who killed the Canadian military?*, Toronto: Harper Flamingo.
Greenwood, Christopher (1993) 'Is there a right of humanitarian intervention?', *The World Today*, 49 (3), 34–40.
Guillot, Philippe (1994) 'France, peacekeeping, and humanitarian intervention', *International Peacekeeping*, 19 (1), 30–43.
Gustenau, Gustav (1999) 'Towards a Common European Policy on Security and Defence: an Austrian view of challenges for the "post-neutrals"', Occasional Paper 9, Paris: Institute for Security Studies, Western European Union: www.iss-eu.org/.
Haarscher, Guy (2001) 'Europe's soul: freedom and rights', in Cerutti and Rudolph (eds), pp. 91–107.
Habermas, Jürgen (1998) *Die postnationale Konstellation. Politische Essays*, Frankfurt am Mein: Suhrkamp.
Haglund, David G. and Sens, Allen (2000) 'Kosovo and the case of the (not so) free riders: Portugal, Belgium, Canada, and Spain' in Schnabel and Thakur (eds), pp. 181–200.
Haine, Jean-Yves (2003) 'European strategy – first steps', *EU-ISS Newsletter*, 7 (July): www.iss-eu.org/new/analysis/analy058e.html.
Halberstam, David (2001) *War in a time of peace: Bush, Clinton, and the Generals*, New York: Scribner.
Hampson, Fen O. et al. (2002) *Madness in the multitude. Human security and world disorder*, Don Mills: Oxford University Press.
Havel, Vaclav (2002) 'Prague Predictions', *NATO Review*, 1, 2–3: www.nato.int/docu/review/pdf/i1_en_review.pdf.
Healey, Denis (1957) 'Beyond power politics' in T. E. M. McKitterick and K. Younger (eds), *Fabian international essays*, London: Hogarth Press, pp. 195–219.
Heinbecker, Paul (1999) 'Human Security', *Canadian Foreign Policy*, 7 (1), 19–25.
Heinbecker, Paul and McRae, Rob (2001) 'The Kosovo air campaign' in R. McRae and D. Hubert (eds), *Human security and the new diplomacy: protecting people, promoting trade*, Montreal: McGill-Queen's University Press, pp. 122–33.
Hellmann, Gunther (2004a) 'Wider die machtpolitische Resozialisierung der deutschen Außenpolitik, Ein Plädoyer für offensiven Idealismus', *Welttrends*, 12 (42), 79–88.
Hellmann, Gunther (2004b) 'Von Gipfelstürmern und Gratwanderern, "Deutsche Wege" in der Außenpolitik', *Aus Politik und Zeitgeschichte*, B11, 32–9.
Hermet, Guy (1995) 'Rwanda: why Médecins sans Frontières made a call for arms' in F. Jean (ed.), *Populations in Danger 1995*, London: Médecins sans Frontières, pp. 91–6.
Hersh, Seymour M. (2003) 'Offense and defense. The battle between Donald Rumsfeld and the Pentagon', *The New Yorker* (7 April): www.newyorker.com/fact/content/articles/030407fa_fact1.
Hill, Christopher (2004) 'Renationalizing or regrouping? EU foreign policy since 11 September 2001', *Journal of Common Market Studies*, 42 (1), 143–63.
Hindell, Keith (1996) 'An interventionist manifesto', *International Relations*, 13 (2), 23–35.
Hodge, Carl C. (2004) *Atlanticism for a new century: the rise, triumph, and decline of NATO*, Upper Saddle River: Pearson/Prentice Hall.
Hoffmann, Stanley (2003) 'The crisis in transatlantic relations' in G. Lindstrom (ed.), *Shift or rift: assessing US–EU relations after Iraq*, Paris, European Union Institute for Security Studies, pp. 15–20: www.iss-eu.org/chaillot/bk2003.pdf.
Hoffmann, Stanley (1995/6) 'The politics and ethics of military intervention', *Survival*, 37 (4), 29–51.
Hogg, David R. (2002) 'Rapid Decisive Operations: the search for the Holy Grail of joint

warfighting' in W. Murray (ed.), *Transformation concepts for national security in the 21st century*, Carlisle: Strategic Studies Institute, US Army War College, pp. 375–404: www.carlisle.army.mil/ssi/pubs/2002/transcon/transcon.pdf.

Holzgrefe, J. L. (2003) 'The humanitarian intervention debate', in J. L. Holzgrefe and R. Keohane (eds), *Humanitarian intervention: ethical, legal and political dilemmas*, Cambridge: Cambridge University Press, pp. 15–52.

Hosmer, Stephen T. (2001) 'The conflict over Kosovo: why Milošević decided to settle when he did', The Rand Corporation, MR-1351-AF: www.rand.org/publications/MR/MR1351.

Howorth, Jolyon (2003a) 'Ideas and discourse in the construction of a European Security and Defence Policy' in Moens, Cohen and Sens (eds), pp. 37–54.

Howorth, Jolyon (2003b) 'Saint-Malo plus five: an interim assessment of ESDP', Policy Paper 7, Paris: Groupement d'Études et de Recherches Notre Europe: www.notre-europe.asso.fr/IMG/pdf/Policypaper7.pdf.

Howorth, Jolyon (2003c) 'France, Britain and the Euro-Atlantic crisis', *Survival*, 45 (4), 173–91.

Howorth, Jolyon (2001) 'European defence and the changing politics of the European Union: hanging together or hanging separately?', *Journal of Common Market Studies*, 39 (4), 765–89.

Howorth, Jolyon (2000a) 'Britain, NATO, and CESDP: fixed strategy, changing tactics', *European Foreign Affairs Review*, 5 (3), 377–96.

Howorth, Jolyon (2000b) 'European integration and defence: the ultimate challenge?' Chaillot Papers 43, Paris: Institute for Security Studies, Western European Union: www.iss-eu.org/chaillot/chai43e.pdf.

Howorth, Jolyon and Keeler, John T. S. (eds), (2003) *Defending Europe: the EU, NATO and the quest for European autonomy*, New York: Palgrave.

Huldt, Bo, et al. (eds) (2004) *The new Northern security agenda: perspectives from Sweden and Finland*, Stockholm: Swedish National Defence College.

Hulsman, John C. (2003) 'Cherry-picking as the future of the transatlantic alliance: the re-emergence of European Gaullism' in S. A.-M. Auger (ed.), *The transatlantic relationship: problems and prospects*, Washington DC: Woodrow Wilson International Center for Scholars, pp. 59–66.

Hyde-Price, Adrian (2001) 'Germany and the Kosovo war: still a civilian power?', *German Politics*, 10 (1), 19–34.

Ikenberry, John G. (1996) 'The myth of post-Cold War chaos', *Foreign Affairs*, 75 (3), 79–91.

Independent Commission on International Humanitarian Issues (1988) *Modern wars: the humanitarian challenge*, London: Zed Books.

International Commission on Intervention and State Sovereignty (2001) *The responsibility to protect*, Ottawa: International Development Research Centre: www.iciss.ca/pdf/Commission-Report.pdf.

International Federation of Red Cross and Red Crescent Societies (1996) *World disasters report 1996*, Oxford: Oxford University Press.

Irwin, Rosalind (ed.) (2001) *Ethics and security in Canadian foreign policy*, Vancouver: University of British Columbia Press.

Ivanov, Igor S. (2002) *The new Russian diplomacy*, Washington DC: The Brookings Institution.

Ivanov, Igor S. (2003) (The Iraq crisis and the struggle for a new world pattern)', *2003 Diplomatic Yearbook of the Russian Ministry of Foreign Affairs Diplomatic Academy*: www.ln.mid.ru/brp_4.nsf/sps/CA86999961A0DB25C3256E200048309E.

Jonah, James (1993) 'Humanitarian intervention' in T. G. Weiss and L. Minear (eds),

Humanitarianism across borders: sustaining civilians in times of war, Boulder: Lynne Rienner, pp. 69–84.

Kagan Robert (2003) *Of paradise and power: America and Europe in the new world order*, New York: Knopf.

Kant, Immanuel ([1795]1991) 'Perpetual peace. A philosophical sketch', in Hans Reiss (ed.), *Kant political writings*, 2nd edition, Cambridge: Cambridge University Press, pp. 93–130.

Kaplan, Lawrence (2004) *NATO divided, NATO united: the evolution of an alliance*, Westport: Praeger.

Kaplan, Robert D. (2005) 'How we would fight China', *Atlantic Monthly*, 295 (5), 49–64.

Karsh, Efraim (1988) *Neutrality and small states*, London: Routledge.

Katzenstein, Peter (2002) 'Sonderbare Sonderwege: Germany and 9/11', Washington DC: AICGS German–American Dialogue Working Paper Series: www.aicgs.org /Publications/PDF/katzenstein.pdf.

Keating Tom and Gammer, Nicholas (1993) 'The new look in Canada's foreign policy', *International Journal*, 48 (4), 720–48.

Keatinge, Patrick (1998) 'Ireland and European security: continuity and change', *Irish Studies in International Affairs*, 9, 31–8.

Keatinge, Patrick (1996) *European security: Ireland's choices*, Dublin: Institute of European Affairs.

Keatinge, Patrick (1984) *A singular stance: Irish neutrality in the 1980s*, Dublin: Institute of Public Administration.

Keohane, Robert O. and Lisa L. Martin (1995) 'The promise of institutional theory', *International Security*, 20 (1), 39–51.

Keukeleire Stephan (2002) 'Re-conceptualising European foreign policy: structural foreign policy', Paper presented at the 1st pan-European Conference on European Union Politics, Bordeaux 26–28 September.

König, Ernest (ed.) (1999) *Framework for the development of a military doctrine*, Vienna: National Defence Academy.

Kononenko, Vadim (2003) 'From Yugoslavia to Iraq: Russia's foreign policy and the effects of multipolarity', UPI Working Papers 42, Helsinki: Finnish Institute of International Affairs.

Krause, Joachim (2000) 'Deutschland und die Kosovo-Krise', in J. Reuter and C. Clewing (eds), *Der Kosovo Konflikt, Ursachen, Verlauf, Perspektiven*, Klagenfurt: Wieser Verlag, pp. 395–416.

Kupchan, Charles (2002) 'The end of the West', *Atlantic Monthly*, 290 (4), 42–4: www.theatlantic.com/doc/prem/200211/kupchan.

Kupchan, Charles (2000) 'In defence of European defence: an American perspective', *Survival*, 42 (2), 16–32.

Lantis, Jeffrey S. (2004) 'American perspectives on the transatlantic security agenda', *European Security*, 13 (4), 361–80.

Lantis, Jeffrey S. and Queen, Matthew F. (1998) 'Negotiating neutrality: the double-edged diplomacy of Austrian accession to the European Union', *Cooperation and Conflict*, 33 (2), 152–82.

Lansford, Tom (2002) *All for one: terrorism, NATO and the United States*, Burlington: Ashgate.

Letter to President Clinton on Iraq (1998): www.newamericancentury.org /iraqclintonletter.htm.

Lillich, Richard (1967) 'Forcible self-help by states to protect human rights', *Iowa Law Review*, 53, 325–51.

liMes (1998) *Italy and the Balkans*, Washington DC: Center for Strategic and International Studies.

Lindley-French, Julian (2002a) 'Combined and joint? The development of a security and operational doctrine for the European Union' in E. Reiter, R. Rummel and P. Schmidt (eds), *Europas ferne Streitmacht, Chancen und Schwierigkeiten der Europäischen Union beim Aufbau der ESVP*, Hamburg: Forschungen zur Sicherheitspolitik, 6, pp. 86–118.

Lindley-French, Julian (2002b) 'Terms of engagement: the paradox of American power and the transatlantic dilemma post-11 September', Chaillot Papers 52, Paris: Institute for Security Studies, European Union: www.iss-eu.org/chaillot/chai52e.pdf.

Lindstrom, Gustaf (ed.) (2003) *Shift or rift? Assessing EU–US relations after Iraq*, Transatlantic Books, Paris: Institute for Security Studies, European Union: www.iss-eu.org/chaillot/bk2003.pdf.

Link, Werner (2004) 'Grundlinien der außenpolitischen Orientierung Deutschlands', *Aus Politik und Zeitgeschichte*, B11, 3–8: www.das-parlament.de/2004/11/Beilage/001.html.

Lo, Bobo (2004) 'Principles and contradictions. The foreign policy of Vladimir Putin' in T. de Wilde d'Estmael and L. Spetschinsky (eds), *La politique étrangère de la Russie et l'Europe. Enjeux d'une proximité*, Bruxelles: Peter Lang, pp. 45–71.

Long, David (2003) 'Transatlantic relations and Canadian foreign policy', *International Journal*, 58 (4), 591–614.

Luban, David (2004) 'Preventive war', *Philosophy and Public Affairs*, 32 (3), 207–48.

Lucarelli, Sonia (2002a) 'Peace and democracy: the rediscovered link. The EU, NATO, and the European system of liberal-democratic security communities', NATO–EACP Final Research Report: www.nato.int/acad/fellow/00–02/Lucarelli%27s.pdf.

Lucarelli, Sonia (2002b) 'Unione Europea, NATO e la costruzione di comunità di sicurezza democratiche in Europa Centro-orientale', *Teoria Politica*, 2, 87–120.

Luif, Paul (1998) 'Austria: adaptation through anticipation' in K. Hanf and B. Soetendorp (eds), *Adapting to European integration: small states and the European Union*, London: Longman, pp. 116–30.

Lutz, Dieter S. (ed.) (2000) *Der Kosovo-Krieg, Rechtliche und rechtsethische Aspekte*, Baden-Baden: Nomos.

Lynch, Dov (1999) '"Walking the tightrope": the Kosovo conflict and Russia in European security, 1998–August 1999', *European Security*, 8 (4), 57–83.

Macleod, Alex and Roussel, Stéphane (eds) (1996) *Intérêt national et responsabilités internationales: six états face au conflit en ex-Yougoslavie (1991–1995)*, Montréal: Guérin.

Maloney, Sean M. (2004) 'Force structure or forced structure? The 1994 White Paper on defence and the Canadian Forces in the 1990s', *Choices* (Institute for Research on Public Policy, Montreal), 10 (5), 2–26: www.irpp.org/choices/archive/vol10no5.pdf.

Maloney, Sean M. (2003) 'The International Security Assistance Forces: the origins of a stabilization force', *Canadian Military Journal*, 4 (2), 3–11: www.journal.forces.gc.ca/engraph/Vol4/no2/operations_e.asp.

Manners Ian (2002) 'Normative power Europe: a contradiction in terms?', *Journal of Common Market Studies*, 40 (2), 235–58.

Manners Ian (2001) 'The "difference engine": constructing and representing the international identity of the European Union', Copenhagen: Peace Research Institute Working Paper No. 40.

Manners, Ian and Whitman, Richard G. (eds) (2000) *The foreign policies of European Union member states*, Manchester: Manchester University Press.

Martin, Lawrence (2003) *Iron man. The defiant reign of Jean Chrétien*, Vol. 2, Toronto: Viking.

Maull, Hanns W. (2004) 'Normalisierung oder Auszehrung? Deutsche Außenpolitik im Wandel', *Aus Politik und Zeitgeschichte*, (B-11), 17–23.

Maull, Hanns W. (2000) 'Germany and the use of force: still a "civilian power"?', *Survival*, 42 (2), 56–80.

Maull, Hanns W. (1995–6) 'Germany in the Yugoslav crisis', *Survival*, 37 (4), 99–130.

McCalla, Robert B. (1996) 'NATO's persistence after the Cold War', *International Organization*, 50 (3), 445–75.

McCoubrey, Hilaire (1999) 'Kosovo, NATO, and international law', *International Relations*, 14 (5), 29–46.

McMillan, Joseph (2003) 'US interests and objectives' in R. D. Sokolsky (ed), *The United States and the Persian Gulf. Reshaping security strategy for the post-containment era*, Washington DC: National Defense University Press, pp. 9–35: www.ndu.edu/inss/books/Books_2003/Persian_Gulf/Persian.pdf.

McSweeney, Bill (ed.) (1985) *Ireland and the threat of nuclear war*, Dublin: Dominican Publications.

Mead Walter R. (2001) *Special providence: American foreign policy and how it changed the world*, New York: Alfred A. Knopf.

Mearsheimer, John, J (1990) 'Back to the future: instability in Europe after the Cold War', *International Security*, 15 (1), 5–56.

Medvedev, Sergei (2004) 'Peresmotr natsional'nykh interesov: rossiyskaya vneshnyaya politika v epokhu Putina', George C. Marshall Centre Paper, Garmisch-Partenkirchen: George C. Marshall European Center for Security Studies, August.

Meiers, Franz-Josef (2002) 'Deutschland: der dreifache Spagat' in H.-G. Ehrhart (ed.), *Die Europäische Sicherheits- und Verteidigungspolitik, Positionen, Perzeptionen, Probleme und Perspektiven*, Baden-Baden: Nomos, pp. 35–48.

Menon, Anand (2003) 'Why ESDP is misguided and dangerous for the Alliance' in J. Howorth and J. T. S. Keeler (eds), *Defending Europe: the EU, NATO, and the quest for European autonomy*, New York: Palgrave, pp. 203–18.

Menon, Anand (2002) 'Playing with fire: the EU's defence policy', *Politique Européenne*, 8, 32–45.

Menon, Anand (2000) *France, NATO and the limits of independence: the politics of ambivalence 1981–97*, New York: St. Martin's Press.

Menon, Anand and Lipkin, Jonathan (2003) 'European attitudes towards transatlantic relations 2000–2003: an analytical survey', Survey prepared for the informal meeting of EU Foreign Ministers, Rhodes and Kastellorizo, 2–3 May, Research and European Issue 26, Paris: Groupement d'Études et de Recherches Notre Europe: www.notre-europe.asso.fr/IMG/pdf/Etud26-en.pdf.

Middlemiss, Danferd W. and Stairs, Denis (2002) 'The Canadian Forces and the doctrine of interoperability: the issues', Montreal: IRPP Paper series 'Policy Matters', 3 (7): www.irpp.org/pm/archive/pmvol3no7.pdf.

Miles, Lee (2000) 'Sweden and Finland' in Manners and Whitman (eds), pp. 181–203.

Ministère de la Défense – France (1999) *Les enseignements du Kosovo* (November).

Miskimmon, Alister and Paterson, William E. (2003) 'Foreign and security policy: on the cusp between transformation and accommodation', *Proceedings of the British Academy*, 119, 325–45.

Missiroli, Antonio (2003a) 'The European Union: just a regional peacekeeper?', *European Foreign Affairs Review*, 8 (4), 493–503.

Missiroli, Antonio (2003b) 'Ploughshares into swords? Euros for European defence', *European Foreign Affairs Review*, 8 (1), 5–33.

Mistleberger, Klaus (1992) 'Problems of orientation: Austria and the new European security architecture', Paper presented at the European Consortium for Political Research Conference, Limerick, Ireland (30 March–4 April).

Moens, Alexander, Cohen, Lenard and Sens, Allen (eds) (2003) *NATO and European security: alliance politics from the end of the Cold War to the age of terrorism*, Westport: Praeger.

Møller, Bjørn (2000) 'The Nordic countries: whither the West's conscience?' in Schnabel and Thakur (eds), pp. 151–65.

Nanda, Ved (1992) 'Humanitarian intervention and international law' in E. Ferris (ed.), *The challenge to intervene: a new role for the United Nations?*, Uppsala: Life and Peace Institute, pp. 27–38.

Nafziger, James A. R. (1994) 'Humanitarian intervention in a community of power' (Part II), *Denver Journal of International Law and Policy*, 22 (2/3), 219–34.

Nelles, Wayne (2002) 'Canada's human security agenda in Kosovo and beyond: military intervention versus conflict prevention', *International Journal*, 57 (3), 459–78.

Neumann, Iver B. (1998) 'European identity, EU expansion, and the integration/exclusion nexus' *Alternatives*, 23 (3), 397–426.

Nolte, Georg and Krieger, Heike (2003) 'Military law in Germany' in G. Nolte (ed.), *European military law systems*, Berlin: de Gruyter, pp. 337–426.

Nossal, Kim Richard and Roussel, Stephane (2001) 'Canada and the Kosovo war: the happy follower' in P. Martin and M. R. Brawley (eds), *Alliance politics, Kosovo and NATO'S war: allied force or forced allies*, New York: Palgrave, pp. 181–200.

Nuti, Leopoldo (2003) 'The role of the US in Italy's foreign policy', *The International Spectator*, 38 (1), 91–101.

O'Halpin, Eunan (1999) *Defending Ireland: the Irish state and its enemies since 1922*, Oxford: Oxford University Press.

Ojanen, Hanna (2003) 'Neutrality and non-alignment in Europe today', FIIA Report 6, Helsinki: Finnish Institute of International Affairs.

Ojanen, Hanna (2000) 'Participation and influence: Finland, Sweden and the post-Amsterdam development of the CFSP', Occasional Paper 11, Paris: Institute for Security Studies, Western European Union: www.iss-eu.org/occasion/occ11.pdf.

Ojanen, Hanna, Herolf, Gunilla and Lidahl, Rutger (2000) *Non-alignment and European security: ambiguity at work*, Programme on the Northern Dimension of the CFSP, vol. 6, Helsinki and Bonn: Finnish Institute of International Affairs/Institute for European Politics: www.upi-fiia.fi/northerndimension/cfsp6.pdf.

Olaf, Osica (2004) 'Poland: a new European Atlanticist at a crossroads?' *European Security* 13 (4), 301–22.

Ortega, Martin (2001) 'Military intervention and the European Union', Chaillot Papers 45, Paris: Institute for Security Studies of the Western European Union: www.iss-eu.org/chaillot/chai45e.pdf.

Padoa-Schioppa, Tommaso (2001) *Europa, forza gentile*, Bologna: Il Mulino.

Paris, Roland (2001) 'Human security: paradigm shift or hot air?' *International Security*, 26, 2: 87–102.

Parkin, Andrew (2003) 'Pro-Canadian, anti-American or anti-war? Canadian public opinion on the eve of war', *Policy Options*, 24 (4), 5–7.

Pasquino, Gianfranco (2003) 'The government, the opposition and the President of the Republic under Berlusconi', *Journal of Modern Italian Studies* 8 (4), 485–99.

Pasquino, Gianfranco (2001) *Critica della sinistra italiana*, Bari: Laterza.

Patten, Chris (2004) 'The Western Balkans: The Road to Europe', Speech to German Bundestag, European Affairs Committee, Berlin, 28 April: http://europa.eu.int /rapid/pressReleasesAction.do?reference=SPEECH/04/209&format=HTML&aged=0& language=EN&guiLanguage=en.

Patten, Chris (2000) 'The European Union: contrasting experiences and common hopes – in Britain and Germany', Speech 00/450, Berlin, Institut für Europäische Politik, 22 November: http://europa.eu.int/comm/external_relations/news/patten/speech_00_450 .htm.

Pentland, Charles C. (2003–4) 'Odd man in: Canada and the transatlantic crisis', *International Journal*, 59 (1), 146–66.

Pesonen, Pertti and Vesa, Unto (1998) 'Finland, Sweden and the European Union', Research Report 77, Tampere: Tampere Peace Research Institute.

Peters, Dirk (2001) 'The debate about a new German foreign policy after unification' in V. Rittberger (ed.), *German foreign policy since unification: theories and case studies*, Manchester: Manchester University Press, pp. 11–36.

Peters, John E. et al. (2001) *European contributions to Operation Allied Force: implications for transatlantic cooperation*, Santa Monica: The Rand Corporation.

Phinnemore, David (2000) 'Austria' in Manners and Whitman (eds), pp. 204–23.

Pond, Elizabeth (2004) *Friendly fire: the near-death of the transatlantic alliance*, Pittsburgh-Washington DC: EUSA and Brookings Institution.

Posen, Barry R (2003) 'Command of the commons: the military foundation of US hegemony', *International Security*, 28 (1), 5–46: http://bcsia.ksg.harvard.edu/BCSIA_content/documents/Posen_summer_2003.pdf.

Powell, Colin L. (2004) 'US will retain command of its forces in Iraq, Powell says', Secretary of State Colin L. Powell roundtable with print journalists, 26 May, Washington, DC: www.useu.be/Article.asp?ID=9687AD4A-EAA2-4E7D-919C-99044385DA11.

Pradetto, August (1998) 'NATO-Intervention in Kosovo? Kein Eingreifen ohne UN-Mandat', *Internationale Politik*, 53 (9), 41–6.

Prodi, Romano (2003a) 'Croatia's journey towards EU membership' Speech 03/360, Zagreb, Croatian Parliament, 10 July: http://europa.eu.int/comm/external_relations/news/prodi/sp03_360.htm.

Prodi, Romano (2003b) 'Culture diversity and shared values', Speech 03/517, New York University Law School, 4 November: www.ebu.ch/CMSimages/en/INFOEN_097_tcm6-8335.pdf.

Ranieri, Umberto (1999a), 'Interesse nazionale e multilateralismo: la strategia italiana nei Balcani', *Europa Europe*, 8 (4), 30–3.

Ranieri, Umberto (1999b) 'L'Europa, la NATO e il ricorso all'uso della forza', *Affari Esteri*, 122, 240–5.

Rees, Nicholas (2000) 'The Kosovo crisis, the international response and Ireland', *Irish Studies in International Affairs*, 11, 55–70.

Rees, Nicholas (1999) 'Ireland's foreign relations in 1998', *Irish Studies in International Affairs*, 10, 267–88.

Rees, Nicholas (1998) 'Ireland's foreign relations in 1997', *Irish Studies in International Affairs*, 9, 135–60.

Rees, Nicholas and Holmes, Michael (2002) 'Capacity, perceptions and principles: Ireland's changing place in Europe', *Current Politics and Economics of Europe*, 11 (1), 49–60.

Rees, Wyn (2004) 'More heat than light, US reactions to ESDP', *FORNET CFSP Forum*, 2 (2), 12–14: www.fornet.info/documents/CFSP%20Forum%20vol%202%20no%202.pdf.

Refugee Policy Group (1991) *Human rights protection for internally displaced persons: an international conference*, Washington DC: 24–25 June.

Regelsberger, Elfriede (2002) 'Deutschland und die GASP – ein Mix aus Vision und Pragmatismus' in G. Müller-Brandeck-Bocquet (ed.), *Europäische Außenpolitik, GASP- und ESVP-Konzeptionen ausgewählter EU-Mitgliedstaaten*, Baden-Baden: Nomos, pp. 28–40.

Rempel, Roy (2002) *The chatter box: an insider's account of the irrelevance of Parliament in the making of Canadian foreign and defence policy*, Toronto: Dundurn Press.

Risse, Thomas (2004) 'Kontinuität durch Wandel: Eine "neue" deutsche Außenpolitik?', *Aus Politik und Zeitgeschichte* (B-11), 24–31.

Risse-Kappen, Thomas (1996) 'Collective identity in a democratic community: the case of NATO' in P. J. Katzenstein (ed.), *The culture of national security*, New York: Columbia University Press, pp. 357–99.

Roberts, Adam (1999/2000) 'The so-called right of humanitarian intervention', Trinity

Papers No. 13, Trinity College, the University of Melbourne: www.trinity
.unimelb.edu.au/publications/papers/TP_13.pdf.
Roberts, Adam (1993a) 'Humanitarian war: military intervention and human rights',
International Affairs, 69 (3), 429–449.
Roberts, Adam (1993b) 'The road to hell: a critique of humanitarian intervention',
Harvard International Review, 16 (1), 10–14.
Robertson, Lord George (2003) 'Securing the peace: the NATO vision', NATO Public
Diplomacy Conference, Brussels, 16 October: www.paginedidifesa.it/2003
/natosg_031017.html.
Rodley, Nigel (1992) 'Collective intervention to protect human rights and civilian populations: the legal framework' in N. Rodley (ed.), *To loose the bands of wickedness: international intervention in defence of human rights*, London: Brassey's Press, pp. 14–42.
Ross, Douglas A. (2003) 'Foreign policy challenges for Paul Martin. Canada's international security policy in an era of American hyperpower and continental vulnerability', *International Journal*, 58 (4), 533–69.
Roth, Ken (2004) 'War in Iraq: not a humanitarian intervention', *Human Rights Watch World Report 2004*: http://hrw.org/wr2k4/3.htm.
Rupnik, Jacques (2003) 'The post-war Balkans and the Kosovo question' in J. Rupnick (ed.), *International perspectives on the Balkans*, Clementsport: Canadian Peacekeeping Press, pp. 215–28.
Salmon, Trevor (1989) *Unneutral Ireland: an ambivalent and unique security policy*, Oxford: Clarendon Press.
Sandoz, Yves (1992) '"Droit" or "devoir d'ingerence" and the right to assistance: the isues involved', *The Review: International Commission of Jurists*, 49, 12–22.
Save the Children (1994) *The United Nations and humanitarian assistance: a position paper*, London: Save the Children.
Scheffer, David (1993) 'Toward a modern doctrine of humanitarian intervention', *University of Toledo Law Review*, 23 (2), 253–93.
Schirmer, Georg (2001) 'Menschenrechte und Gewaltverbot im Völkerrecht', Beitrag auf dem Europäischen Friedenskonvent in Berlin am 23 März: www.uni-kassel
.de/fb10/frieden/themen/Interventionen/schirmer.html.
Schöllgen, Gregor (2004) 'Die Zukunft der deutschen Außenpolitik liegt in Europa', *Aus Politik und Zeitgeschichte*, B11, 9–16.
Schnabel, Albrecht and Thakur, Ramesh (eds) (2000), *Kosovo and the challenge of humanitarian intervention: selective indignation, collective action, and international citizenship*, Tokyo: United Nations University Press,
Sens, Allen (2003) 'The widening Atlantic, Part II: transatlanticism, the "new" NATO, and Canada' in Moens, Cohen and Sens (eds), pp. 19–36.
Serpicus (1998) 'Why we help Serbia' in liMes, *Italy and the Balkans*, Washington DC: Center for Strategic and International Studies, pp. 31–9.
Shannon, Vaughn (2000) 'Norms are what states make of them: the political psychology of norm violation', *International Studies Quarterly*, 44 (2), 293–316.
Sherr, James and Main, Steven (1999) 'Russian and Ukrainian perceptions of events in Yugoslavia', Camberley, Surrey: The Conflict Studies Research Centre, May: www.da.mod.uk/CSRC/documents/Russian/F64.
Sicurelli, Daniela (2004) 'Transatlantic relations on food safety international conflict and policy transfer', Paper presented at the ECPR – Standing Group on the European Union, Second Pan-European Conference on EU Politics, 'Implications of A Wider Europe: Politics, Institutions and Diversity', Bologna, 24–26 June: www.jhubc.it
/ecpr-bologna/docs/611.pdf.
SIPRI (2004) *SIPRI Yearbook 2004: Armaments, disarmament and international security*,

Oxford: Oxford University and Stockholm International Peace Research Institute.

Sjursen, Helene (2002) 'Why expand? The question of legitimacy and justification in the EU's enlargement policy', *Journal of Common Market Studies*, 40 (3), 491–513.

Slim, Hugo (1995) 'Military humanitarianism and the new peacekeeping: an agenda for peace?', *Journal of Humanitarian Assistance*: www.jha.ac/articles/a003.htm.

Sloan, Stanley R. (2005) *NATO, the European Union and the Atlantic Community: the transatlantic bargain challenged*, 2nd edition, Lanham, MD: Rowman and Littlefield.

Sloan Stanley R. (2000) 'The United States and European defence', Chaillot Paper 39, Paris: Paris: Institute for Security Studies, Western European Union: www.iss-eu.org/chaillot/chai39e.pdf.

Smith, Mark A (2003) 'The axis of evil: the Russian approach', Camberley, Surrey: Conflict Studies Research Centre: www.da.mod.uk/CSRC/documents/Russian/F83.

Smith, Karen (1998) 'The use of political conditionality in the EU's relations with third countries: how effective?', *European Foreign Affairs Review*, 3 (2), 253–74.

Sokolsky, Joel J. (2004) 'Realism Canadian style: national security policy and the Chrétien legacy', Montreal: IRPP Paper series 'Policy Matters', 5 (2): www.irpp.org/pm/archive/pmvol5no2.pdf.

Sokolsky, Joel J. (2000) 'Over there with Uncle Sam: peacekeeping, the "trans-European bargain" and the Canadian Forces' in D. G. Haglund (ed.), *What NATO for Canada?* Martello Papers 23, Kingston: Queen's University Centre for International Relations, pp. 15–36: www.queensu.ca/cir/pdf/Martello23.pdf.

Solana, Javier (2000) 'Where does the EU stand on Common Foreign and Securitiy Policy?' Speech given in Berlin at the at the Forschungsinstitut der Deutschen Gesellschaft für Auswärtige Politik, 14 November: www.dgap.org/Publikationen/Veranstaltungen/2000/Where%20does%20the%20EU%20stand%20on%20Common%20Foreign%20and%20Securitiy%20Policy%3F.html.

Solana, Javier (1996) 'NATO's role in Bosnia: charting a new course for the Alliance', *NATO Review*, 44 (2), 3–6: www.nato.int/docu/review/1996/9602–1.htm.

Sperling, James (2004) 'Capabilities traps and gaps: symptom or cause of a troubled transatlantic partnership?', *Contemporary Security Policy*, 25 (3), 452–78.

Stairs, Denis et al. (2003) 'In the national interest: Canadian foreign policy in an insecure world', Calgary: Canadian Defence and Foreign Affairs Institute: www.cdfai.org/PDF/In%20The%20National%20Interest%20English.pdf.

Stevenson, Jonathan (2003) 'How Europe and America defend themselves', *Foreign Affairs*, 82 (2), 75–90.

Stothard, Peter (2003) *Thirty days: Tony Blair and the test of history*, London: HarperCollins.

Strausz-Hupé, Robert, Dougherty, James E. and Kintner, William R. (1963) *Building the Atlantic world*, New York: Harper and Row.

Streit, Clarence K. (1939) *Union Now: a proposal of a federal union of the democracies of the North Atlantic*, London: J. Cape.

Taylor, George R. (ed.) (1972) *The Turner thesis; concerning the role of the frontier in American history*, 3rd edition, Lexington: Heath.

Telò Mario (2001) 'Reconsiderations: three scenarios', in M. Telò (ed.) *European Union and new regionalism: regional actors and global governance in a post-hegemonic era*, Aldershot: Ashgate, pp. 247–74

Tesón, Fernando (1996) 'Collective humanitarian intervention', *Michigan Journal of International Law*, 17 (2), 323–71.

Timmins, Graham (2005) 'EU–Russian relations – a member-state perspective. Germany and Russia – a special partnership in the New Europe?' in D. Johnson and P. Robinson (eds), *Perspectives on EU–Russia relations*, London: Routledge, pp. 55–70.

Toje, Asle (2003) 'The first casualty in the war against terror: the fall of NATO and

Europe's coming of age', *European Security*, 12 (2), 63–76.
Tomuschat, Christian (1999) 'Völkerrechtliche Aspekte des Kosovo-Konflikts', *Die Friedens-Warte*, 74 (1/2), 33–7.
Tonra, Ben (2001) *The Europeanisation of national foreign policy: Dutch, Danish and Irish foreign policy in the European Union*, Aldershot: Ashgate.
Torrelli, Maurice. (1992) 'From humanitarian assistance to intervention on humanitarian grounds?', *International Review of the Red Cross*, 288 (May–June), 228–48.
Touraine, Marisol and Sabin, Philip A.G. (1990) 'Society, state and defence' in F. de la Serre et al. (eds), *French and British foreign policies in transition. The challenge of adjustment*, New York: Berg Publishers, pp. 31–63.
Trenin, Dmitri (2003/04) 'Pirouettes and priorities – distilling a Putin doctrine', *The National Interest*, 74, 76–83.
UK House of Commons (2003), European Scrutiny Committee – Minutes of Evidence, 'Examination of Witnesses' (17 December): www.publications.parliament.uk/pa/cm200304/cmselect/cmeuleg/155/3121704.htm.
UK Ministry of Defence (1999), *Defence White Paper 1999*: www.mod.uk/publications/whitepaper1999/index.htm.
Ullman, Harlan K. and Wade, James P. (1996) *Shock and awe: achieving rapid dominance*, Washington DC: National Defense University Press: www.ndu.edu/inss/books/books%20-%201996/Shock%20and%20Awe%20-%20Dec%2096/index.html.
United Nations Security Council (2005) 'Report of the Secretary-General on the United Nations Interior Administration Mission in Kosovo' (4 February), S/2005/88.
United Nations Development Programme (2005) *Early Warning Report – Macedonia* (March): www.undp.org.mk/datacenter/publications/documents/EWR2005MarchEng.pdf.
US Department of Defence (2001) 'Quadrennial Defense Review Report', Washington DC (30 September): www.defenselink.mil/pubs/qdr2001.pdf.
US Department of State (2004) 'US image bruised in Europe – but policies still see benefits by partnership', Washington DC: Department of State, Office of Research Opinion Analysis, M-43-04, 30 March.
US General Accounting Office (2001) *Kosovo air operations: need to maintain Alliance cohesion led to doctrinal departures*, Washington, DC: GAO-01-784, 27 July.
Vaahtoranta, Taapani and Forsberg, Tuomas (2000) 'Post-neutral or pre-allied? Finnish and Swedish policies on the EU and NATO as security organisations', UPI Working Paper 29, Helsinki: Finnish Institute of International Affairs: www.upi-fiia.fi/julkaisut/UPI_WP/wp/WP29.pdf.
Van den Hoven, Adrian (forthcoming) 'European Union regulatory capitalism and multilateral trade negotiations', in S. Lucarelli and I. Manners (eds), *Values and principles in European Union foreign policy*, London: Routledge.
Védrine, Hubert (2003) *Face à l'hyperpuissance américaine. Textes et discours 1995–2003*, Paris: Fayard.
Venice Commission (European Commission for Democracy through Law) (2005) 'Opinion on the constitutional situation in Bosnia and Herzegovina and the powers of the High Representative', 11 March: www.venice.coe.int/docs/2005/CDL-AD(2005)004-e.asp.
Vig, Norman J. and Faure Michael C. (eds) (2003) *Green giants? Environmental policy of the United States and the European Union*, Cambridge, Mass: MIT Press.
von Sydow, Björn (n.d.) *Sweden's security into the 21st century*, Stockholm: Ministry of Defence: www.forsvarsberedningen.gov.se/debattserien/pdf/security.pdf.
Wallace, William (2001) 'Europe, the necessary partner', *Foreign Affairs*, 80 (3), 16–34.
Wallace, William (2000) 'From the Atlantic to the Bug, from the Arctic to the Tigris? The Transformation of the EU and NATO', *International Affairs*, 76 (3), 475–93.

Wallander, Celeste A. (2000) 'Institutional assets and adaptability: NATO after the Cold War', *International Organization*, 54 (4), 705–35.

Waltz, Kenneth (1959) *Man, the state, and war: a theoretical analysis*, New York: Columbia University Press.

Webber, Douglas (2001) 'Introduction: German European and foreign policy before and after unification', *German Politics*, 10 (1): 1–18.

Wedin, Lars (2004) 'Sweden in European security' in Huldt et al. (eds), pp. 319–35.

Weiss, Thomas (1994a) 'Triage: humanitarian interventions in a new era', *World Policy Journal*, 11 (1), 59–68.

Weiss, Thomas (1994b) 'On the brink of a new era? Humanitarian interventions, 1991–1993', *The Brown Journal of World Affairs*, 1 (2), 245–60.

Welsh, Jennifer M. (2005) *Transatlantic identity and international action. Rapporteur's Report*, Quebec City, The Canada–UK Colloquia (18–21 November 2004): www.irpp.org/events/archive/nov04UK/welsh.pdf.

Welsh, Jennifer M. (2004) 'Conclusion: humanitarian intervention after 11 September' in J. M. Welsh (ed.), *Humanitarian intervention and international relations*, Oxford: Oxford University Press, pp. 176–83.

Wheeler, Nicholas (2000a) 'Reflections on the legality and legitimacy of NATO's intervention in Kosovo', *International Journal of Human Rights*, 4 (3/4), 145–63.

Wheeler, Nicholas (2000b) *Saving strangers: humanitarian intervention in international society*, Oxford: Oxford University Press.

Wheeler, Nicholas and Morris, Justin (1996) 'Humanitarian intervention and state practice at the end of the Cold War' in R. Fawn and J. Larkins (eds), *International society after the Cold War: anarchy and order reconsidered*, London: Macmillan, pp. 135–71.

Whitaker, Rey (2004) 'More or less than meets the eye? The new National Security Agenda' in B. Doern (ed.), *How Ottawa spends, 2003–04*, Don Mills: Oxford University Press, pp. 44–58.

White House (2002) *The National Security Strategy of the United States of America*, (September): www.whitehouse.gov/nsc/nss.pdf.

Whitman, Jim (1994) 'A cautionary note on humanitarian intervention', *GeoJournal*, 34 (2), 167–75.

Whitman, Richard G. (2004) 'NATO, the EU and ESDP: an emerging division of labour?' *Contemporary Security Policy*, 25 (3), 430–51

Whitman, Richard G. (1999) 'Amsterdam's unfinished business? The Blair government's initiative and the future of the Western European Union' Occasional paper 7, Paris: Institute for Security Studies, Western European Union: www.iss-eu.org/occasion/occ07.pdf.

Wolfowitz, Paul (2003) 'Deputy Secretary Wolfowitz Interview with Sam Tannenhaus – Vanity Fair' (9 May): www.defenselink.mil/transcripts/2003/tr20030509-depsecdef0223.html.

Woodward, Bob (2004) *Plan of attack*, New York: Simon and Schuster.

Woodward, Bob (2002) *Bush at War*, New York: Simon and Schuster

Yost, David S. (1998) *NATO transformed: the Alliance's new roles in international security*, Washington, DC: United States Institute of Peace Press.

Youngs, Richard (2001) *The European Union and the promotion of democracy*, Oxford: Oxford University Press.

Zhirnov, D.A. (2004) 'Vneshnepoliticheskoe sotrudnichestvo Rossii i Kitaya v kontekste formirovaniya postbipolyarnoy modeli mezhdunarodnykh otnosheniy' in A. D. Voskressenskiy (ed.), *Severo-Vostochnaya i Tsentral'naya Aziya – Dinamika mezhdunarodnykh i mezhregional'nykh vzaimodeystviy*, MGIMO/ROSSMPEN.

Newspapers

Berliner Morgenpost
Christian Science Monitor
Corriere della Sera
Dagens Nyheter
Daily Telegraph
De Standaard
Die Tageszeitung
Die Welt
Economist
Financial Times
Frankfurter Allgemeine Sonntagszeitung
Frankfurter Allgemeine Zeitung
Globe and Mail
Guardian
Helsingin Sanomat
Independent
International Herald Tribune
Irish Times
La Repubblica
La Stampa
Le Figaro
Le Monde
Libération
Los Angeles Times
New York Times
Neue Zürcher Zeitung
Süddeutsche Zeitung
The Times
Turun Sanomat
Wall Street Journal
Washington Post
Westdeutsche Allgemeine Zeitung

News on the web

Balkan Watch www.pilpg.org/areas/poldev/balkanwatch/
BBC Monitoring www.monitor.bbc.co.uk/
BBC News online http://news.bbc.co.uk/
EUobserver www.euobserver.com/
NewsMax.com www.newsmax.com/

Index

Note: n indicates a note number

Albright, Madeleine 124n
Atlanticism 20, 26–7, 30, 32
Austria
   Iraq 187
   Kosovo 186–7
   meaning of neutrality 175–6

Belgium
   humanitarian intervention 69
'Berlin Plus' 24, 52, 56, 57, 83, 87
Berlusconi, Silvio 167
Blair, Tony 129
Bush, George W. 122, 125n

Canada
   Afghanistan 194–6, 199
   domestic public opinion 201–2
   humanitarian intervention 69–70, 75, 190, 203
   human security 191–3
   Iraq 197–9
   Jean Chrétien leadership style 200
   Kosovo 192–3
   National Security Policy 196
CFSP see Common Foreign and Security Policy
Cheney, Dick 121
Chirac, Jacques 14, 112, 113, 131, 132, 133, 134
Clark, Wesley K. 11, 112
Clinton, Bill 68
Common Foreign and Security Policy (CFSP)
   Iraq 45, 155
   Kosovo 45, 88
   limits to 'modes of translation' 45–7

modes of translation 43–5
origins of 79
'structural foreign policy' 43–4, 46
Contact Group 10, 50, 115, 116, 143, 144

D'Alema, Massimo 160, 162, 163, 164, 165
Denmark
   humanitarian intervention 68–9
Dini, Lamberto 159, 161–2, 164

ESDP see European Security and Defence Policy
EUFOR, see European Union Force
EUPM see European Union Police Mission
European identity 32, 38, 44
European Rapid Reaction Force (RRF) 2, 137, 178
European Security and Defence Policy (ESDP) 2, 17, 24, 30
   directorate 61–2
   Iraq 55–6, 59
   origins of 50–1
   tensions in 51–4
'European Security Strategy' 37–8, 44, 45, 60, 77
European Union Force (EUFOR) 87, 90
European Union Police Mission (EUPM) 56, 83

Finland
   Iraq 185
   Kosovo 183–4
   meaning of neutrality 175

Fischer, Joschka 57, 149, 151
France
  9/11 133
  Bosnia 128–9
  concept of leadership 127–8
  ESDP 131–2, 137–9
  humanitarian intervention 68
  Iraq 136
  Kosovo 129–33
  NATO 130–1
  Russia 96–7, 103
  US 134–5

Germany
  Afghanistan 151, 153
  ESDP 150
  humanitarian intervention 69, 149
  Iraq 152–4
  Kosovo 143–8
  public debate on Iraq 154–5
  public debate on Kosovo 148–50
  Russia 96–7, 103, 143, 147
  US 152–4, 155–8

Holbrooke, Richard 50
Humanitarian intervention
  Iraq 73
  legal opinions on 65–7
  opposition to 70
  state sovereignty 64–5, 74, 76n

IGOs *see* International governmental organisation
International governmental organisation (IGO)
  humanitarian intervention 70–1
Ireland
  Iraq 183
  Kosovo 182
  meaning of neutrality 174–5
Italy
  Bosnia 159
  domestic debate on Iraq 169–70
  domestic debate on Kosovo 163–5
  humanitarian intervention 161
  intervention in Albania 88
  Iraq 166, 170
  Kosovo 162, 165–6
  NATO 161, 163
  Serbia 164
  US 171–2

'Letter to President Clinton' 121

MacShane, Denis 138
Michel, Louis 54

National Security Strategy of the United States 14
NATO
  9/11 12–13, 22–3
  Afghanistan 23
  Bosnia 22–3, 111
  ESDP 24, 51–2, 57–9
  FYROM 82
  humanitarian intervention 76
  Iraq 23
  Kosovo 9–11, 14, 23, 71–2, 115
  military assistance to Turkey 15–16, 137
  new Strategic Concept 21, 92, 94, 96, 160
  Partnership for Peace programme 21
  Prague Summit 15, 22
  Washington Summit 9–10
NATO Response Force 22
NATO–Russia Council/NATO–Russia Permanent Joint Council 22, 94, 105n
Netherlands
  humanitarian intervention 69
'neutral' states
  CFSP/ESDP 60, 176–9, 188–9
  Iraq 181
  Kosovo 181
  meaning of neutrality 174, 176
NGOs *see* Nongovernmental organisations
Nongovernmental organisations (NGOs)
  humanitarian intervention 73

Operation Artemis 56–7, 87
Operation Concordia 56, 83, 84, 87

Patten, Chris 81, 89
Poos, Jacques, 49–50
Powell, Dick 122
Putin, Vladimir 97, 98, 99, 100, 102, 103, 104n, 105n

Ranieri, Umberto 161
Rice, Condoleezza 101
RRF *see* European Rapid Reaction Force
Rumsfeld, Donad 122
Russia
  'America-centrism' 98–9, 101, 102
  centrality of the UN 95, 97–8, 102
  humanitarian intervention 94
  Iraq 94–5, 99–101, 102
  Kosovo 94–5, 97, 102, 103
  NATO 96–7, 100, 104n
  nostalgia for the bipolar era 95–6
  'strategic partnership' with the West 92, 96, 100

Salvati, Michele 162
Schröder, Gerhard 146, 151, 152, 153, 154
Scognamiglio, Carlo 165
Solana, Javier 71, 81, 84
SPSEE *see* Stability Pact for South-eastern Europe
Stability Pact for South-eastern Europe 80–1, 147–8
Sweden
  Iraq 186
  Kosovo 185–6

meaning of neutrality 175

UK *see* United Kingdom
UN *see* United Nations
United Kingdom
  9/11 134
  Bosnia 128–9
  concept of leadership 127–8
  ESDP 131, 137–9
  humanitarian intervention 68
  Iraq 136
  Kosovo 129, 133
  NATO 131, 133
  US 135
United Nations
  humanitarian intervention 65
United States
  Bosnia 110–14
  humanitarian intervention 67, 113
  identity 28, 33
  Iraq 116–18, 120–3
  Kosovo 88, 114–16
  NATO 27
  'Presidential Decision Directive 25' (PDD 25) 67
  'preventive self-defence' 3, 28, 114
  'revolution in military affairs' (RMA) 109, 110, 113, 118–19
  Saudi Arabia 119–20
  UN 109
  view of Europe 28–9
  Wilsonian tradition in foreign policy 36–7
US *see* United States

Védrine, Hubert 132